Media Localism

THE HISTORY OF COMMUNICATION

Robert W. McChesney and John C. Nerone, editors

A list of books in the series appears at the end of this book.

Media Localism

The Policies of Place

CHRISTOPHER ALI

UNIVERSITY OF
ILLINOIS PRESS
Urbana, Chicago, and Springfield

© 2017 by the Board of Trustees
of the University of Illinois
All rights reserved
Printed and bound in Great Britain by
Marston Book Services Ltd, Oxfordshire
1 2 3 4 5 C P 5 4 3 2 1
♾ This book is printed on acid-free paper.

Library of Congress Cataloging-in-Publication Data
Names: Ali, Christopher, author.
Title: Media localism : the policies of place / Christopher Ali.
Description: Urbana : University of Illinois Press, [2017] | Series:
    The history of communication | Includes bibliographical
    references and index.
Identifiers: LCCN 2016023024 (print) | LCCN 2016035369 (ebook)
    | ISBN 9780252040726 (hardcover : alk. paper) | ISBN
    9780252082238 (pbk. : alk. paper) | ISBN 9780252099168
    (e-book)
Subjects: LCSH: Mass media policy—United States. | Mass media
    policy—United Kingdom. | Mass media policy—Canada.
    | Mass media—Law and legislation—United States. | Mass
    media—Law and legislation—United Kingdom. | Mass
    media—Law and legislation—Canada
Classification: LCC P95.8 A445 2017 (print) | LCC P95.8 (ebook) |
    DDC 302.23—dc23
LC record available at https://lccn.loc.gov/2016023024

To Tuna,
My four-legged companion
in walking, writing, and worrying

Contents

Acknowledgments   ix

Abbreviations   xiii

PART I: INTRODUCING LOCALISM

Introduction: Where Is Here?   3

1 Mapping the Local   30

PART II: REGULATING LOCALISM

2 The Policies of Localism: Debates, Dilemmas, and Decisions in Local Television Regulation   53

3 The Communities of Localism: Community Television in the Digital Age   82

4 The Ecosystems of Localism: A Holistic Approach to Local News and Information   107

5 The Solutions of Localism: Regulatory Approaches to the Crisis of Local Television   128

PART III: FIXING LOCALISM

6 The Political Economy of Localism: Critical Regionalism and the Policies of Place   167

7   Interventions in Localism: From Public Goods
    to Merit Goods   183

Conclusion: The Right to Be Local?   197

Appendix: An Essay on Method   205

Notes   211

References   217

Index   247

Acknowledgments

I'm not going to lie; I waited a long time to write my acknowledgments because I found this process so intimidating. How can I thank each and every person who has contributed to this project and to my development as a scholar? The polite Canadian in me was vibrating with anxiety! I will start, therefore, with the usual caveat: that so many people have helped bring this project to fruition that I cannot possibly thank everyone. I have tried my best though, and I hope that those of you who are mentioned and those who are not know that you have my deepest gratitude, respect, and love.

This book began at the Annenberg School for Communication at the University of Pennsylvania. There I had the honor and privilege of working with some of the greatest minds and greatest people I have ever met. In the incomparable Marwan Kraidy, joined by Monroe Price and Victor Pickard, I not only found mentors, but great colleagues and great friends. Monroe was instrumental in convincing me to come to Annenberg—possibly the best decision I have made in my thirty-two years. Victor read the entire manuscript and provided important feedback, especially on my merit goods thesis. Marwan remains my rock in the academic world, being the person I turn to for all manner of advice and wisdom. While at Annenberg I also had the great fortune of working with Elihu Katz—a person whose passion for knowledge and life is contagious and from whom I have learned so much. I would also like to thank Dean Michael Delli Carpini, Barbie Zelizer, Joseph Turow, Katherine Sender, and the global community of scholars and policymakers whom I met while I was at Annenberg: Paddy Scannell, Manuel Puppis, Michael Bromley, Des Freedman, Phil Napoli, Ellen Goodman, Jessica Clark, Damian Radcliffe, Tom Glaisyer, Katie Donnelly, Larry Gross, Christian Herzog, Michael Copps, and Todd O'Boyle. Commissioner Copps read the entire manuscript right down to the footnotes and provided greatly valued feedback. I cannot thank him enough for his support. I would also like to thank those who I interviewed for this research in Ottawa, Washington, and London; without them, this research would have been much less compelling.

My amazing friends at Annenberg, Nora Draper and Katherine Wong, kept me sane, fed, and inspired. Nora also took the time to read several chapter drafts and was essential in helping me articulate why critical regionalism is so important to media localism. Her friendship and support mean the world to me. Others at Annenberg deserve mention too for their friendship, encouragement, and willingness to entertain my ramblings over beers or coffees: Piotr Szpunar, Omar Al-Ghazzi, Sara Mourad, David Conrad, Rowan Howard-Williams, and Felicity Duncan. Before Annenberg, there was Concordia University and the University of Alberta and my mentors there: Serra Tinic, Leslie Regan Shade, Matt Soar, Brian Gabrial, and Rae Staseson guided me as I took my first steps into the world of graduate education and the life of an academic.

Moving to Charlottesville and starting at the University of Virginia was both intimidating and inspiring, terrifying and enthralling. I do not think I would have survived the first few years of being a professor without the friendship, encouragement, and support of Andre Cavalcante. Many thanks also go to my wonderful colleagues in the Department of Media Studies, starting with the two chairs I have worked with: Siva Vaidhynathan and Hector Amaya. In addition, Joe Arton, Aniko Bodroghkozy, Andre Cavalcante, Shilpa Dave, Jack Hamilton, Aynne Kokas, William Little, Jennifer Petersen, Andrea Press, Nick Rubin, Francesca Tripodi, and Bruce Williams are the greatest colleagues anyone could ask for. Hector, Siva, Aynne, and Andre were immensely kind and brave to read chapters and even whole drafts of the manuscript, and their feedback greatly shaped the final product. Barbara Gibbons, our fearless department administrator, kept me on track, whether it was in filing forms, baking fig cookies, or making sure that I was taking time for myself. Nick Winter in the Department of Politics was my first-year mentor, and helped my book proposal take shape. I would also like to thank my students at the University of Virginia, most notably those who have taken my Media Policy and Law and Political Economy classes and those whom I have had the honor of working with on *Movable Type*. Major thanks are also owed to Becky Hasselberger, who fearlessly conducted the first full copyedit of *Media Localism* and lived to tell the tale. I would also like to thank my Charlottesville family for their friendship and support: Andre Cavalcante, Stephen Ninneman, Augusta Reel, Lindsay Slater, Ben Blackman, Eli Carter, Tim Lyons, Mike Hill, Jon Kropko, and Cypress Walker.

While working on my manuscript, I had the privilege of presenting chapters on several occasions, and I am grateful for the feedback I received from the brown bag lunch series of the Department of Engineering and Society at the University of Virginia, the Communication Law and Policy Division at the International Communications Association, and the Communication Law and Policy Section of the European Communication Research and Education Association. My time as a visiting scholar at the Department of Media and Communication Research at the University of Fribourg in Switzerland was invaluable in helping me complete a round of edits, and I am grateful for the department's support and for the friends and colleagues I made that summer. Manuel Puppis, my great friend and research partner, needs special acknowledgment, not only for suggesting I apply for a visiting fellowship at Fribourg, but more important for his friendship and support. I would also like to extend my gratitude to Amit Schejter and Krishna Jayakar for inviting me to speak at the "New Media—Old Money" workshop at the Embassy of Switzerland in Washington, D.C, and the scholars at the Information Society Project at Yale University, most notably Valerie Belair-Gagnon. Versions of three chapters of this book also appear in the journals *Communication Theory* (introduction/chapter 6) and the *Journal of Information Policy* (chapter 7), and I thank the editorial teams at both of these journals for working with me to disseminate my research.

Early support for my research was provided by a doctoral award from the Social Sciences and Humanities Research Council of Canada. More recently, I am grateful to the Buckner W. Clay Foundation and the Dean of Arts and Sciences and the Vice President for Research at the University of Virginia for providing support. Danny Nassett and Tad Ringo at the University of Illinois Press also deserve special mention. Danny's encouragement from our first meeting at ICA a few years ago was so important in keeping me motivated during the submission and review process, and Tad has been a terrific project manager. My copyeditor at Illinois, Walt Evans, was essential in polishing up the manuscript for publication.

Last, but certainly not least, it is impossible to understate the importance of my family in Winnipeg. Jeff Thorsteinson and Stephen Capelle have been my best friends for two decades, and though we don't get to see each other nearly enough, I would not be here without them. They are my brothers and members of my family. My parents, Ray and Elaine, are my rocks, confidants, therapists, colleagues, and friends. Our often-daily chats keep me going, and both have read almost every page I've ever written. Their unending supply of love and patience are things that I cannot hope to repay. My mother is one of the strongest people I have ever met, and her career and passion greatly inspired me to work on local media. The way my father sees the world has not only influenced my book in ways that I am still not fully aware of, but has also shaped the person that I am today. My brother Jonathan is not only a great brother but also a great friend, and while I wish we got to spend more time together, I cherish every minute that we do. Auntie Bida and Uncle Rudy keep me going through their equal measures of support and critique and have been so important in helping me realize what is important. Uncle Freddy and I share a love of books and learning, something we inherited from my grandfather. The entire Ali family—the Hot T'Am Ali's—are the greatest family anyone could ask for.

To all in what I call my "front row," thank you again.

Abbreviations

ACD	Alliance for Communications Democracy (US)
ACM	Alliance for Community Media (US)
ACT	American Community Television (US)
BBC	British Broadcasting Corporation (UK)
BCE	Bell Canada Enterprises (Can)
BDU	Broadcasting Distribution Undertaking (Can)
CAB	Canadian Association of Broadcasters (Can)
CACTUS	Canadian Association of Community Television Users and Stations (Can)
CBC	Canadian Broadcasting Corporation (Can)
CDA	Critical Discourse Analysis
CR/R2C	Communication Rights/Right to Communicate
CRS	Congressional Research Service (US)
CRTC	Canadian Radio-television and Telecommunications Commission (Can)
CTF	Canadian Television Fund (Can)
DCMS	Department for Culture, Media and Sport (UK)
DMA	Designated Market Area (US)
DTH	Direct-to-Home (Can)
DTT	Digital Terrestrial Television (UK)
EPG	Electronic Programme Guide (UK)
FCC	Federal Communications Commission (US)
FFC	Fee-For-Carriage (Can)
GI	Geographic Interleaved (UK)

IFNC	Independently Funded News Consortia (UK)
IPTV	Internet Protocol Television
ISP	Internet Service Provider
L-DTPS	Local Digital Television Programme Service (UK)
LFA	Local Franchising Authority (US)
LPIF	Local Programming Improvement Fund (Can)
MuxCo	Multiplex Company (UK)
MVPD	Multivideo Program Distributor (US)
NAB	National Association of Broadcasters (US)
NATOA	National Organization of Telecommunications Officers and Advisors (US)
NOI	Notice of Inquiry (US)
NPR	National Public Radio (US)
NPRM	Notice of Proposed Rulemaking (US)
Ofcom	Office of Communications (UK)
OIC	Order-in-Council (Can)
OTA	Over-the-Air (Can)
PEG	Public, Educational, and Governmental (US)
PSB	Public Service Broadcasting/Broadcaster (UK)
PSP	Public Service Publisher (UK)
RSL	Restrictive Service Licence (UK)
SMLPF	Small Market Local Programming Fund (Can)
UGC	User Generated Content
VFS	Value-for-Signal (Can)

PART I

Introducing Localism

Introduction
Where is Here?

THE CABLE SONG

by Dave Carroll (2009)

> Cable companies out of control
> They're glad to pay for HBO
> And it's going to kill this country's local TV shows
>
> Seems they don't think it's worth a dime
> For stories that are yours and mine
> So come on now CRTC, it's show time
>
> Who's gonna to tell our stories when the storyteller's gone?
> When our hometown local news is hurt and barely hangin' on
> Them cable company cash cows, are taking milk for free
> By refusing to pay the local TV
>
> There's big news from New York to Rome
> But matters that matter at home
> Are getting swept away with cuts and budgets blown
> Our culture's on the highest table, without help it's bound to fall
> And though they're able, cable won't play ball
>
> Meanwhile cable bills are flying higher than a kite
> Soon they'll get 'em high enough to charge us for space flight
> Like others they should pay the cost of doin' business too
> Instead they pass it on to me and you
>
> Who's gonna to tell our stories when the storyteller's gone?
> When our hometown local news is hurt and barely hangin' on
> Them cable company cash cows, are taking milk for free
> By refusing to pay the local TV
>
> 'Cause fair is all we're asking, cable please

Local TV Matters?

In 2008, amid what was being called a crisis in Canadian local broadcasting, a group of television networks—CTV, Global, /A\, V—launched a campaign called "Local TV Matters." The campaign was designed to draw public attention to broadcasters' petition to the Canadian Radio-television and Telecommunications Commission (CRTC) for permission to charge cable and satellite companies for distributing their signals to subscribers (known then as fee-for-carriage). "The Cable Song" was part of a three-minute commercial run by participating broadcasters. It was sung by Dave Carroll, who gained renown in 2008 after releasing a YouTube video chastising United Airlines for breaking his guitar. "The Cable Song's" cheeky lyrics were intended to shore up support for the broadcasters' campaign, and the accompanying music video played up this point by featuring a literal "cash cow." To broadcasters, fee-for-carriage (FFC) meant a second, more reliable source of income. This would compensate for the global recession, which eviscerated advertising revenues, as well as the changing media consumption habits of viewers that saw a shift away from linear, appointment-style television to a "pull" model of content consumption. Broadcasters claimed it was not just local stations that were in jeopardy, but the very foundations of local news—something all parties agreed is vital to Canadian democracy. "Who's gonna to tell our stories when the storyteller's gone?" sings Carroll. To cable and satellite companies, fee-for-carriage amounted to a "TV tax" on their business—a tax that they would pass on to consumers. They contended that Canadian broadcasters had brought this fate upon themselves by paying extravagant fees for American programs and failing to invest in Canadian productions.

By 2013, it was clear that broadcasters had failed to convince the CRTC to enact fee-for-carriage. Nevertheless, for the first time in the history of Canadian broadcasting, local television was at the forefront of a very public debate regarding media regulation. In hindsight, "The Cable Song" lyrics raise much larger questions that now require both regulatory and critical attention—namely, what *is* local TV, anyway? What, exactly, does it mean to be local, and why do we care so much? As an ordinary word, we tend to take the local for granted; it is a word we all use, and one we think we understand. It is rhetorically pleasant and politically safe; who could be against the local? Wilken (2011), quoting Bryson and Mowbray (1981), likens words like "community" (and by extension, "local") to "motherhood" and "democracy," terms that "tend to be accepted as indubitably a good thing" (p. 29). But a lack of critical engagement with the local's foundations and implications has important consequences for the media that are meant to inform us about what Carroll calls "the matters that matter at home."

It is not only Canada that has experienced this regulatory turn in the direction of the local: Regulators in the United States and the United Kingdom have also used the first decade of the twenty-first century to give renewed discursive energies to investigating and promoting the local as a site of media business, democratic participation, and civic engagement. While each country refers to the protection of local markets, voices, stories, and news in a slightly different way, and each country's broadcasting regulations contain certain specific properties, challenges confronting the regulation of local media are similar enough to be comparable. These include audience gravitation to digital and social media platforms, advertiser withdrawal, and the oft-decried "crisis of journalism" that has manifested in the diminishing quality of local news, concerns for the commercial viability of local journalism, and the subsequent closure of local media outlets. Though the local daily newspaper has certainly borne the brunt of these challenges, local television is not far behind. Regulators also share the much larger and epistemological challenge of how to define the local in the digital age. Here, the spatially defined understanding of the local—as a city, town, or village—has been increasingly debated and doubted, leaving regulators to ponder how a locality is defined, what counts as local news, what constitutes a community, if the information needs of communities are being met, and the role of local media in a democracy. Put more concretely, when Carroll sings of the "stories that are yours and mine," to what exactly is he referring?

This book analyzes the complex ideas we hold about the local within media policy and regulation. While localism can be loosely defined as the mandate for broadcasters to be responsive to their communities, localism as a symbolic category means different, often contradictory things to different people at different times. This subjective quality complicates regulatory attempts to study and protect local voices, and has stymied consideration of larger questions about the value of localism. Ideas about the local have been further complicated by the rise of the Internet and the decline of traditional journalism to which it has contributed. By exploring the roots of these different concepts and their implications for the broadcasting industry, this book seeks to clarify the tangled mess that is the current discourse of localism in media regulation and policy. Using the analytical frameworks of critical political economy (Mosco, 2009) and critical regionalism (Frampton, 1983), *Media Localism* points the way forward for a meaningful engagement with the substantive concerns that have motivated the Federal Communications Commission (FCC), the Office of Communications (Ofcom), and the Canadian Radio-television and Telecommunications Commission (CRTC) to come out strongly in support of local media.

In what follows, I offer a working definition of localism, and discuss its manifestation in American, British, and Canadian political economy and broadcast histories. This is followed by an introduction to the conceptual challenges of defining localism in an age of globalization and neoliberalism. I then describe the methods used to assess critically how the local is mobilized in regulatory discourse, and the critical arguments this research has led me to assert, namely the development of a "political economy of localism." I conclude this introduction by returning to "The Cable Song." This song, it turns out, does a great deal of intellectual labor for us as we begin to unpack the complicated discourse of localism in media policy and regulation in three Western democracies.

Localism: A Working Definition

The United States, UK, and Canada are all experiencing a resurgence of "the local" in everything from commerce ("Small Business Saturday"), ecology ("Buy Fresh, Buy Local"), boosterism ("Keep it Local"), and politics ("Big Society"). Not to be left out, media regulators have also been struck by this local agenda. Indeed, the reemergence of the local in society and culture has put questions of local control, local content, and local news squarely on the media regulation agenda. But what exactly does it mean to be local within the confines of media policy and regulation? This is not an easy question to answer, as our relationship with the local and with related concepts such as "community" and "place" are contingent upon individual subjectivities, experiences, histories, politics, cultures, and discourses. Technology, of course, directly mediates how we experience the local. Throughout the history of broadcasting, regulators have attempted to "fix the meaning of places" (Massey, 1992, p. 12) through frequency allocations, but spectrum has never respected political borders. More recently, digital media, or what Wilken (2011) calls "teletechnologies," have further pulled us away from the geographically derived places we call home, forcing us to experience a condition of "no sense of place" (Meyrowitz, 1985; Massey, 1992). The neoliberal reflex within the global political economy has further accelerated a "time-space compression," allowing us to live lives engendering what Castells (1996) calls the "space of flows" of capital, texts, and mobility, rather than the "space of place" to which the human condition for centuries has been tethered (Harvey, 1989, 2005; Casey, 1998). These competing tensions of space and place, global and local, capital and community, or what Tönnies (1957) classically labeled *Gemeinshaft* and *Gesselschaft*, will all be explored at greater length in the following chapters. In the meantime, we need to establish a working definition of the local within media policy to set the framework for the rest of the book.

Regarding the media industries, the local is articulated through a set of policies that we may call "media localism." When we speak of media localism in media policy we are talking primarily about broadcasting, for it is here where regulators have greatest jurisdiction. Media localism can be loosely defined as the belief that broadcasters should be responsive to the local, geographic communities to which they are licensed (the "community of license"). This generally includes the airing of community responsive programming, particularly local news and information programming, and being engaged with the local community. Until recently, "localism" was a term employed exclusively in the American policy milieu. In the last few years, the term has gravitated to the UK, where regulators now speak of localism and "localness." In Canada, the term has yet to gain purchase. For simplicity I use "localism" not as an immediate reference to the American terminology, but rather as a catchall for local media policies and regulations.

Given that broadcasting emerged in each of these countries from the humble beginnings of local radio, localism is seen by many as the "bedrock," "cornerstone," and "building block" of Western broadcasting, particularly in the United States and Canada (Kirkpatrick, 2006; Cole & Murck, 2007; CRTC, 2008a). In the UK, where local television has been limited, its absence has been called "the biggest gap in British broadcasting . . . because, ironically, in an age of globalism, people feel the need for stronger not weaker connections to the communities in which they live" (Hunt, 2010, np). As this quote from the UK's former Culture Minister Jeremy Hunt underscores, localism rests on a belief in the salience of place-based communities, predicated on an understanding that "local communities and nations continue to define their selves and their aspirations within territorial parameters" (Cowling, 2005, p. 354). Local television stations have been thought of as essential to fostering these goals, particularly through the provision of local news. This belief in the ongoing relevance and resonance of place-based localities (or what I will call "communities of place") has manifested in regulations such as local ownership, the location of the station, local programming quotas, and community dialogue. These regulations are enforced by the national communications regulator, in our case, the FCC in America, the CRTC in Canada, and Ofcom in the UK.

Localism also brings with it forceful normative assumptions of democracy and citizen participation whereby local media facilitate dialogue and a deliberative democracy—a "local public sphere," as it were (Habermas, 1989; Friedland, 2001; Aldridge, 2007). It is not for naught that the CRTC should contend that local media "help to shape Canadian's views and to equip them to be active participants in the democratic life of the country" (2008a, par. 57). Localism falls under the larger rubric of the "public interest" and is meant to facilitate the decentralization of information, ensure diversity and pluralism, encourage public participation in the democratic process, bring power and accountability closer to citizens, and foster community identity (Napoli, 2001a; Cowling, 2005; Kirkpatrick, 2006). To this end, many have begun to think of local news and information as what neoclassical economists call a "public good"—a concept that will be revisited throughout my book (Pickard, 2013, 2014).[1]

Though individual regulatory details are always country specific, the basic definition of localism that I have described—the community responsiveness of broadcasters—holds true for the FCC, CRTC, and Ofcom. The following brief review of the history of traditional local media (newspapers and broadcasting) reveals that localism has been an area of contention for policymakers and broadcasters since the origins of broadcasting. As I have already mentioned, the broadcasting systems in each of these countries began at the local level—with individually owned and operated local radio stations. Since then, broadcasting has assumed a unique look and feel with the rise of private, commercial, and networked broadcasting in America, a publically funded and nationally oriented model in the UK, and the mixed media system of Canada, with private local stations affiliated with national networks, complemented by a strong public broadcaster.

UNITED STATES

Localism has a special place within American media policy, tied as it is not only to broadcast regulation but to a distinctly American ethos of decentralized government and local responsibility (Napoli, 2001a). It is a "value . . . deeply embedded in the American legal and political culture" dating back to Thomas Jefferson's "little republics" (Briffault, 1990a, p. 1, 1990b). Localism also has strong ties to the idea of the community as a geographic entity and as the incubator for local values, culture, and tradition (Napoli, 2001a).

The local newspaper was essential in communicating and engendering these values. Interestingly, colonial-era papers preferred to focus their attention on foreign rather than local news because local news could be attained through face-to-face communication (Wallace, 2005). By the mid-1800s and the rise of the penny press, however, the place of local news as the cornerstone of the daily newspaper was indisputable (Wallace, 2005; Kaniss, 1991). Local newspapers—everything from the *Des Moines Register* to the *Emporia Gazette* to the *New York Times*—"promoted the building of America's first postwar suburb; constructed a town where none had existed before; promoted development and new industry; built community awareness, cohesion, and preservation; moved populations from one place to another; participated in campaigns both for and against slum clearance; and carved out communities within communities" (Wallace, 2005, p. 2). For their very survival, local newspapers "needed to produce local identity as much as they produced local news" (Kaniss, 1991, p. 22). For small-town papers, this was accomplished through boosterism and by setting the moral standards of the community (Wallace, 2005). For urban areas, this was done by championing the city as the symbolic center of the entire metropolitan area, particularly during the flight to the suburbs after World War II (Kaniss, 1991).

With localism cemented in American political and quotidian consciousness by the newspaper, the introduction of radio and the 1927 Federal Radio Act saw broadcast licenses awarded on a local rather than national or centralized basis (Napoli, 2001b). This means that localism in the United States has primarily reflected a concern for geographic or place-based communities. Interestingly, the words "localism" and "local" do not actually appear in the 1927 Radio Act, nor its successors, the 1934 Communications Act and the 1996 Telecommunications Act (Cole & Murck, 2007). Nevertheless, localism is understood to be a natural extension of the FCC's legislative mandate to operate in the "public interest, convenience or necessity" (United States, 1934), from which it developed its policy goals of promoting localism, diversity, and competition. When television was introduced in the late 1940s, this tradition continued such that "even the smallest communities received a television license, regardless of their capacity to financially support a television station" (Napoli, 2001b, pp. 374–75).

Many have noted the difficulties the Commission faces when attempting to regulate broadcasting in the name of localism (Cole & Murck, 2007; Braman, 2007; Napoli, 2001a). This is primarily because of the limitations placed on the FCC to enact programming mandates ("behavioral regulations") by the First Amendment and Section 326 of the Communications Act, which prohibits the FCC from censorship. Two additional difficulties have also plagued the history of localism in US media policy. The first is the difficulty of trying to enforce geographic parameters on a natural resource (spectrum) and a technology (broadcasting), neither of which is beholden to geography. As Anderson and Curtin (1999) contend: "Because of its internal contradictions . . . localism has been virtually impossible to enforce in actual cases; it simply cannot account for the diversity of modern societies or for the external forces that integrate local communities into much larger economic and communications networks. In particular, the principle of localism doesn't adequately account for the media's own role in blurring the boundaries of social space" (p. 294). The absence of a consistent and coherent definition for localism at the onset of the broadcasting system also contributed to a lack of understanding of its goals and purposes (Horwitz, 1989). As Horwitz (1989) writes, the localism doctrine never accounted for market forces and rested only on "a vague, progressive, almost Jeffersonian vision of a democratically communicating local community" (p. 186)—of course, the American system can be said to be anything but democratic (Streeter, 1996; McChesney, 1999).

Paralleling this was the political economic challenge of convincing stations to actually serve their communities with local programming, rather than retransmit (arguably more popular) network programming (Horwitz, 1989). It quickly became apparent that any policies regarding actual local programs and even local ownership were inconsistent with the network model that gained prominence in the 1930s and 1940s (Horwitz, 1989; Napoli, 2001b). Kirkpatrick (2006) goes so far as to argue that the entire philosophy behind localism during its formative years in the 1920s was never to privilege local voices but rather a way for urban centers to "modernize" rural communities.

Absent the ability to enact behavioral regulation, the FCC has favored ambiguous recommendations and structural regulation to encourage local program origination and local reflection (Napoli, 2001a). This included early attempts like the 1941 *Report on Chain Broadcasting* and the 1946 *Report on Public Service Responsibilities of Broadcasting Licensees* (the "Blue Book"), both of which lent rhetorical support to the localism principle (Cole & Murck, 2007). Another attempt at structural regulation was the "Main Studio Rule," which required the station to be located within the community of license so as to encourage local participation, community responsiveness, and locally reflective programming (Silverman & Tobenkin, 2001).

The 1970s saw yet another attempt to forge a stronger relationship between the station and the community through the 1971 "ascertainment requirements." This required stations to "undertake extensive, formalized efforts to apprise themselves of the needs and interests of the community" (Cole & Murck, 2007, p. 359). Here, while the FCC was prohibited from mandating programming requirements, it could at least try to force stations to talk to their communities as a condition of license. Another licensing condition at this time was expedited license renewals. This allowed stations that aired a minimum amount of locally produced, non-entertainment programming (8 percent for AM stations; 6 percent for FM stations; 10 percent for TV stations) to undergo expedited license renewal (FCC, 1973). Failure to comply would result in a license review

Table I.1: Local electronic media in the United States (2015)

	Local commercial TV	Local public TV	Local commercial radio (FM)	Local public radio	Low-power TV	Low-power radio	Community TV (cable)	Hyperlocal Web sites
US	1,389	395[a]	6,688[b]	4,090[c]	2,318[d]	1,364	3,000+[e]	1,200[f]

a. Total "educational television stations."
b. Plus 4,692 AM stations.
c. Total "educational radio stations."
d. Low-power UHF, low-power VHF, and Class-A stations.
e. There is no census of public access stations in the United States; however, the Alliance for Community Media represents more than three thousand such organizations (http://www.allcommunitymedia.org/about-us).
f. CPRN, 2012, p. 52 citing a study by Lew Friedland.
Source: FCC, 2015a.

by the entire Commission. In 1976, these requirements were modified such that stations desiring expedited review had to broadcast 5 percent local and informational programming, respectively (FCC, 2004a).

With the coming of the 1980s, deregulatory frenzy struck the FCC, and many local policies were eliminated. The 1984 Television Deregulation Order, for instance, eliminated the ascertainment requirements and the expedited review. This decade also saw the relaxation of where the main studio could be located. The final deregulatory straw was the 1996 Telecommunications Act, which substantially altered the media ownership landscape by permitting vast increases in the number of stations a single entity could own (Aufderheide, 1999). That said, cable operators are still required to carry local stations, or to negotiate with them for compensation to distribute their signal (this is known as "retransmission consent"). Cable operators also have to provide community channels upon request of the municipality. Despite the scattered regulations that remain and the existence of 1,784 local television stations throughout the country (see Table I.1 for a tally of local electronic media in the United States) most agree that localism has experienced a "disappointing career" in the United States (Kirkpatrick, 2006).

CANADA

The association between broadcast localism and political localism is less apparent in Canada, where concerns for nationalism and to a lesser extent regionalism have long taken precedent (Brodie, 1992; Friesen, 2000; Clement, 1983). It is generally agreed that localism has been eclipsed by the nation-building agendas of Canadian governments, particularly in the domain of communication (Tinic, 2005; Laba, 1988). Still, regionalism remains a seminal factor in the Canadian experience (Brodie, 1992; Clement, 1983).

As in the United States, Canadian newspapers played an important role in fostering local identity, particularly given the geographic size and sparse population of the country. Again like its southern neighbor, it was the local paper, rather than the national or regional paper, that was the norm. As Buchannan (2009, 2014) notes, before Toronto's *Globe and Mail* positioned itself nationally, Canada had no national newspaper. The local paper, therefore "literally 'place[d]' readers, and their locality, in the context of the world" (2009, p. 64). In a comprehensive study of two local Canadian newspapers (the *Ottawa Citizen* and the *Toronto Star*) from 1894 to 2005, Buchanan (2009, 2014) charted a stark decline in local coverage after 1970. Buchanan (2014) hypothesizes that the shift to a national orientation echoes "theories that point to the weakening and/or disruption of ties to the local as a feature of modernity." She maintains that "local news binds communities and promotes a sense of attachment to place" but worries about "what will happen if those place attachments, rather than extending to large urban areas, instead fragment onto a jumble of hyper-localities" and is concerned with those communities that may be left out of the melee altogether (pp. 526, 528).

Notwithstanding Buchanan's research on local newspapers, substantive discussions about Canadian local media have been noticeably absent. A dearth of scholarship specifically on Canadian local television further underscores this national malaise vis-à-vis the local (Ali, 2012a). That such a paucity of research exists is both disappointing and frustrating. Compared to the relative bounty of American scholarship on localism, before this present book there had yet to be a single study of "Canadian media localism" (Ali, 2012b).

Canadian communication policy has been marked by protectionism and nationalism, based on the dual threats of American cultural imperialism and the fear of national disintegration by the separatist movements in the French-speaking province of Quebec (Raboy, 1990; Collins, 1990; Barney, 2005; Ali, 2012a). This led O'Regan (1993) to label Canadian communication policy "defensive," and has fostered a policy doctrine of what Charland (1986) calls "technological nationalism"—the use of communication and transportation technologies to foster national identity. This has been abundantly clear since the first comprehensive assessment of broadcasting—the *Aird Report* of 1929—which recommends that the Canadian broadcasting system mimic the nationally oriented public system of the UK and the BBC, rather than the localized and commercial system of the United States. From then on, it was agreed that Canadian broadcasting would be tasked with creating, maintaining, and reifying Canadian national identity (Raboy, 1990; Barney, 2005). In the haunting words of Graham

Spry—a leader in the movement for a sovereign Canadian mediascape—it "is a choice between commercial interests and the people's interests. It is a choice between the State and the United States" (qtd. in Raboy, 1990, p. 40). The Aird report begat the 1932 Broadcasting Act, which created the Canadian Radio Broadcasting Commission (CRBC), later to be replaced in 1936 by a new act, and the stalwart Canadian Broadcasting Corporation (CBC)—Canada's national public-service broadcaster. In establishing the CRBC and CBC, it was believed that a national broadcasting policy, residing within federal jurisdiction and accompanied by a national public broadcaster, would help unify a country heavily divided along regional and linguistic lines (Raboy, 1990; Laba, 1988). At that time, localism had yet to exist in communications policy. The 1936 Broadcasting Act permitted the existence of private (commercial) stations, whose unwritten mission was to serve their local communities (Ali, 2012a). Both private and public elements, however, operated as a "single system" in the "national interests of the Canadian people" (Ali, 2012a, pp. 282–83).

The introduction of television in the 1950s replicated the approach taken for radio: a mixture of private and publicly owned stations, all affiliated with the CBC, and predicated upon national service. To further this goal, Canadian content ("CanCon") quotas were introduced in 1958. Commercial television came to the country in 1960 with the launch of CTV, which, like the CBC, was a national network of local affiliates. As Raboy (1990) observes, "the main distinction made between publicly and privately owned sectors was that the private sector was 'local' while the public sector was 'national'" (p. 97). Even with this general agreement, the Canadian system had yet to formally recognize the contributions of localism. In fact, it would not be until the fifth iteration of the Broadcasting Act in 1991 that the word "community" was added as one of the three pillars of Canadian broadcasting (along with "public" and "private").

Today, Canadian broadcasters are still required to adhere to Canadian content regulations (60 percent from 6 A.M. to midnight, 50 percent from midnight to 6 A.M.). As in the United States, cable providers are also subject to "must carry" regulations, requiring them to carry the signals of all local stations in a local market. Cable companies also provide for community programming through community television channels, although as we will see in chapter 3, these have been on the wane. Currently, there are 117 local television stations in the country (CRTC, 2015, p. 91; see Table I.2 for a tally of all local electronic media in Canada). The introduction of the 1991 Broadcasting Act kicked off a decade of deregulation, particularly

Table I.2: Local electronic media in Canada (2015)

	Local commercial TV	Local public TV	Local commercial radio (FM)	Local public radio	Community radio	Community TV (OTA)	Community TV (cable)	Hyperlocal Web sites
Canada	90	27	590[a]	88	274[b]	13	109[c]	n/a[d]

a. Plus 128 AM stations.
b. Combination of Aboriginal, religious, community, and campus radio stations.
c. From 2013 CRTC Communications Monitoring Report (CRTC, 2013). A census of Canadian community channels have yet to be conducted, however, this number appears quite generous, given other outside assessments (see CACTUS, 2015).
d. An estimate of the number of hyperlocal Web sites in Canada has yet to be produced.
Source: CRTC, 2015.

with regard to corporate consolidation. By the early 2000s, for instance, Bell Canada Enterprises (BCE), the country's largest telecommunications provider (wireless telephony, Internet, and video), owned the CTV network (Canada's largest broadcaster) and the majority of its local affiliates. It also owned the national newspaper of record, the *Globe and Mail*. As Raboy (2006) observes, "Canada tolerates a degree of concentration in media ownership that is unequalled in any country of comparable social, political, and economic standing . . ." (p. 302).

Unlike the FCC, the CRTC has never imposed a national ownership limit for local stations. Its only quantitative restriction is that no company can own more than one television station in a market (with some exceptions). Departing from the FCC in a second way, the CRTC has not been shy about mandating program quotas, as is demonstrated by the CanCon system (see Armstrong, 2010). These quotas, particularly for Canadian dramatic production, are deemed necessary to avoid the complete domination of the media system by less-expensive American imports, to protect domestic production, and to encourage the expression of Canadian culture. Even with these endeavors, advertising revenues derived from the exhibition of popular American programming subsidize the bulk of Canadian television productions (Miller, 2009). The history of the Canadian broadcasting system has thus been waged at the level of the nation-state, and at the expense and obfuscation of regional differences (Ali, 2012a).

UNITED KINGDOM

The UK has historically possessed a highly centralized system of governance, and mirroring this, a highly centralized broadcasting system (Crisell, 1997; North, 2011). As a result, it is only in the past two decades that localism has come to the fore. An impetus for this has been the "Big Society" project—the cornerstone of the Conservative Party's 2010 election campaign (Westwood,

2011; Pattie & Johnston, 2011). The "Big Society" refers to the decentralization of federal programs and a plan for greater community and citizen responsibility (Pattie & Johnston, 2011). While some have rightly critiqued the Big Society as a veiled attempt toward further abandonment of the "social democratic model of the welfare state" (Tam, 2011, p. 31), two interesting consequences have been a focus on local politics through the 2011 Localism Act and on local media through the establishment of a local television service (see chapter 5).[2]

In contrast with the emergent focus on localism in the political sphere, local news has been a feature of British newspapers since the rise of the penny press (Williams, 2010). The UK possesses a unique newspaper sector when compared with Canada and the United States. Its relatively small territory and tightly centralized political and economic system centered in London fostered the rise of national newspapers, complemented by a strong regional and local press (Aldridge, 2007; Williams, 2010). Newspapers with titles like the *Northern Echo* and the *Eastern Daily Press* covered larger English regions, while local papers like the *Evening Post* (Nottingham) and the *Kent Messenger* tended to be city-based (Aldridge, 2007). The shift in the mid-1800s from simply re-reporting the news from London to reporting local news "reflected the way in which provincial newspapers sought to act as 'the notice board for the community covered by their hinterland'" (Williams, 2010, p. 118). Said differently, "the paper was often physically in the centre of town and always at the centre of its life" (Mair, 2013a, p. 21). Like in the United States and Canada, therefore, the local press fostered imagined communities across the UK (Aldridge, 2007).

This model fared well until the 1970s, when British politics became more centralized. This led to both a reduction in local content and to concentrated ownership of papers, following the neoliberal politics of the Thatcher government. Notwithstanding the resilience of free local dailies, Franklin and Murphy (1996) have no qualms about where to lay blame for the decline of the local press since the 1970s: "The dominant tendency which has characterized the three decades of change, not simply in the local press but in the local media ... has been the constant, apparently remorseless advance of the market as the arbiter of the nature, the content, the form, the labour relations and mode of production and the ownership of local media" (p. 22). Shifts in the political economy of the United Kingdom, therefore, substantially altered the role and power of the local press. Until 2013, however, these structural shifts did little to encourage (or discourage) innovation in local broadcasting.

When it comes to the electronic media, the history of British broadcasting is often synonymized with the history of the British Broadcasting Corporation

(BBC), and media policy scholars seldom recall the history of local broadcasting. Most historical work focuses on the establishment of the BBC and the development of public service broadcasting (e.g., Briggs, 1995; Scannell & Cardiff, 1991; Crisell, 1997; Curran & Seaton, 2010). Contrary to this national impulse, radio broadcasting began in the UK with a handful of local stations. During the 1920s these were quickly consolidated first into the British Broadcasting Company and then into the British Broadcasting Corporation in 1927. John Reith, founder of the BBC, pushed hard for the network to articulate a single national voice and agenda, with the effect of eviscerating local radio within five years of its creation (Crisell, 1997). As in Canada, through radio came a national identity, national symbols, and a "knowable community" (Scannell & Cardiff, 1991).

Television was introduced in the 1930s, but only gained traction after the Second World War under the purview of the BBC and funded through a yearly tax on receiver ownership (the license fee). In the 1950s a campaign was mounted to strip the BBC of its monopoly on television. This resulted in the 1954 Television Act, which created a new, advertising-supported television network—ITV—overseen by a new regulator, the Independent Television Authority (ITA). ITV would be a commercial network based on regional franchises, with public service responsibilities including regional news. By 1962, ITV consisted of fourteen regions, with some possessing separate weekday and weekend providers (Johnson & Turnock, 2005). Despite this composition, little was actually regional about ITV. London "remained firmly the economic and talent capital of Britain" (Johnson & Turnock, 2005, p. 20). More important, "the regional structure of the ITV franchises was largely based on the location of transmitters, rather than on the assessment of cultural regions" (p. 20). As with Canada and the United States, the very act of networking also diluted the regional voice of the stations (p. 20).

ITV continued to grow in popularity during the 1960s by offering a more populist and commercial line-up than the BBC. Local broadcasting would not arrive in the UK until 1972 when the Independent Broadcasting Authority (IBA), having replaced the ITA, created a license category called "Independent Local Radio" (ILR). This commercial license was seen as "a bow towards the political fashion for 'localism'; it maximized the broadcasting opportunities for aspiring station operators and advertisers" (Crisell, 1997, p. 186). Later, the conservative political movement of the 1980s and 1990s saw a corresponding push toward light-touch regulation and market fundamentalism in broadcasting. This meant the relaxation of ownership restrictions on ITV franchises through the 1990 Broadcasting Act, which also created a new regulator—the Independent Television Commission (ITC). Further changes in 1994 permitted additional consolidation, allowing "one company to own up to two large franchises (but not both London franchises)" (Johnson & Turnock, 2005, p. 28). Further deregulation ensuing from the 1996 Broadcasting Act ushered in more consolidation among ITV companies. The final legislative hurdles to full consolidation of the ITV network fell with the 2003 Communications Act, which also created the "super-regulator," the Office of Communications (Ofcom).[3] The greatest boon to localized television came in 1996 through a provision in the Broadcasting Act that allowed for a new class of local (over-the-air) television stations called Restrictive Service Licences (RSLs) (Hewson, 2005). In 1998, the ITC awarded RSLs in Leicester and Manchester, and by 2001, nine stations were broadcasting (Blanchard, 2001). Most would prove unsustainable, however, and by 2009 only four RSLs remained operational (Ofcom, 2009a; Ali, 2012c).

With the launch of the fifth terrestrial broadcaster—Channel 5 (now "5")—in 1995, the UK broadcasting sector took on the appearance it has today, with five terrestrial or over-the-air (OTA) broadcasters. This means that they are available without a subscription and with minimal equipment expenditures (a television and antenna is all one needs). There are currently fourteen regions affiliated with ITV, fifteen regions associated with the BBC, and thirty-four local television licensees (see Table I.3 for a tally of local electronic media in the UK). Citizens are assessed a yearly license fee, the proceeds of which go to fund the BBC. The terrestrial networks are: BBC1, BBC2, ITV, Channel 4, and 5. S4C—a dedicated Welsh-language broadcaster launched alongside Channel 4 in 1982—provides additional service to Wales. Taken together, they are referred to as the Public Service Broadcasters (PSB), meaning that

Table I.3: Local electronic media in the United Kingdom (2015)

	Regional public TV (BBC)	Regional commercial TV (ITV)	Local commercial TV (L-DTPS)	Local public radio (FM)	Local commercial radio (FM)	Community radio (FM)	Community TV (cable/Internet)	Hyperlocal Web sites
UK	15	14[a]	34[b]	43[c]	237[d]	221[e]	7[f]	408

a. There are sixteen channel 3 licenses (ITV) serving fourteen geographic regions. The London region has two licenses, and the sixteenth license is for the national breakfast time service.
b. As of December 2015 thirty-four licenses have been awarded and twenty-seven are broadcasting (see chapter 5).
c. Plus thirty-five BBC AM stations.
d. Plus fifty-two AM stations and 402 digital audio broadcasting (DAB) services.
e. Plus six AM community radio stations.
f. An official census of non-broadcast community television has not been conducted. Through an informal search and an e-mail correspondence with the Community Media Association, however, seven cable- and Internet-based community television services were identified: Southwark TV, MonTV, Swindon Viewpoint, Community TV Trust, People's Voice Media, Rural Media Company, Somerset Film.
Source: Ofcom, 2015; Radcliffe, 2015; Community Media Association, personal communication, 03/30/2016.

in exchange for certain privileges, including preferred channel placement and mandatory carriage on cable and satellite systems, they are required to adhere to certain public interest requirements such as news and informational programming.

This brief discussion of politics and broadcasting cannot give justice to the intricacies of localism in the three political economic systems covered. Nonetheless, aligning localism in broadcast policy with political developments illustrates that the local is not only a concern for communication regulators but is also part of an ongoing political and epistemological debate on the nature of democratic governance. Importantly, we can notice similarities within the historical development of local media regulation across the three jurisdictions: a concern for the impact of networking, a concern for local programming, and uncertainty about the role commercial broadcasters should play in the promotion of localism. Each system also lacks a coherent policy framework when it comes to local broadcasting and local media more generally. A final important result of this historical review is that it places my research in historical relief. Indeed, the current regulatory concern for localism is not a unique phenomenon, but rather is cyclical, ebbing and flowing with changes in technology, political ideologies, and social relationships. The timespan of my book (2000–2012) is part of this historical development. Put differently, this book focuses on one specific incident of a recurring trend in the history of Western broadcasting: how to localize the ether.

The Place of Place

Unspoken in the challenges to localism that this brief history section revealed is perhaps the most important question of the book: how are we to define the local? In asking this question, I concur with Dunbar-Hester (2013), who argues that localism derives its discursive strength from its definitional malleability. While I agree that we should not be in a hurry to assign impermeable definitional boundaries, I contend that there is a lack of *any* discussion about localism, and an ensuing lack of alternative considerations. If localism is to survive as a "foundation of communication policy" (Napoli, 2001a), then discussions of localism need to take place among regulators, stakeholders, and the public.

Bookmarking this conversation for a moment, I want to discuss a more concrete policy issue: what is a "local program"? Definitions of local programming can be parsed into "place-based" ("point-of-origin") or "content-based" ("content-oriented") (Napoli, 2001a; Stavitsky, 1994; Smallwood & Moon,

2011). The former requires programming to "be substantially produced and presented within the local community," while the latter just requires that the content be of interest to the community (Smallwood & Moon, 2011, p. 39). Though locally produced programming might be the most obvious source of local content, it is certainly true that non-locally produced programming, such as a news segment on growing interest rates, can be equally relevant to a community. This is where a tension exists for regulators. The FCC, Ofcom, and CRTC tend to rely on the place-based definition of a local program, although broadcasters themselves frequently tout the second definition, and regulators often concede this point. Unfortunately, because of these definitional challenges and the sensitivity around regulatory intervention in our climate of neoliberalism, regulators have been unable to come to a conclusion or even enter into debate regarding what I call the "epistemological question of the local," meaning how we define localism from a social and spatial perspective.

The point-of-origin and content-based iterations of local programming can be labeled the "spatial" and "social" dimensions of localism, respectively (Napoli, 2001a, 2001b; Stavitsky, 1994). Drawing on Hewson's (2005) differentiation between "communities of interest" and "communities of practice," the spatial and social dimensions can also be mapped onto what I call "communities of place" and "communities of interest." As we have learned so far, communities of place—the spatial iteration of localism—have been privileged in regulatory discourse, albeit in ways that rely on taken-for-granted assumptions rather than critical interrogation. Challenging this rather comfortable place-based doctrine, the very idea of "place" and our relationship to it is questioned and doubted in today's "network society" (Castells, 1996). The tensions within media policy with regard to localism and globalism, or between place and placelessness, or place and space, are therefore mirrored in our larger concerns for the "nature of locality in a globalized world" (Appadurai, 1996, p. 56).

In sum, just as regulators in the UK, Canada, and United States have begun to recognize the local as something that deserves consideration, the very definition of the local has come under scrutiny. Though all three communities of regulators continue to rely on a geographically based definition, primary identification with one's territorial community is increasingly disrupted by the proliferation of digital media and global flows of text and capital, which have long violated our taken-for-granted assumptions about geographic places (Dirlik, 1996, 2001; Massy, 1992; Harvey, 1989). Wilken (2011), for instance, writes of the growth of "virtual communities" that have mobilized around social media and digital networks, and which have garnered increased attention as communities of interest and taste (see also Baym, 2010). Some now argue that these communities are more closely aligned with our social existence than physical ones. "Localness is no longer geographical—it is a state of mind," argue Crisell and Starkey (2006, p. 25). In light of these "new global realities" (Massey, 1992, p. 6) it remains increasingly difficult to hold on to the intractable Jeffersonian notions of community and face-to-face communication so beloved by de Tocqueville (1945), Dewey (1927), and Williams (1973). Such articulation compels many to ask whether localism was ever a feasible concept (Anderson & Curtin, 1999; Singleton & Rockwell, 2003), to revisit its historical underpinnings (Horwitz, 1989; Cole & Murck, 2007; Kirkpatrick, 2006), to argue that mediated communication inherently transcends and extends place and space (Anderson & Curtin, 1999; Curtin, 2000; Meyrowitz, 1985), to question whether localism should be permanently divided between the social and spatial (Napoli, 2001a), and to ask whether it is time to do away with the spatial concept altogether (Stavitsky, 1994; Crisell & Starkey, 2006). Stavitsky (1994), for one, believes that "communities ... mobilize in terms of commonality of taste rather than commonality of place of residence" and as a result recommends that we eliminate the spatial aspect of localism (p. 8).

In contrast, others argue that "place still matters" both in theory and in practice (Tinic, 2005; Kirkpatrick, 2006; Escobar, 2003). Castells (1996) calls this the "space of place," while Howley (2010) argues that the "sense of place" "still holds enormous relevance of the human experience" (p. 8). He rightly points to community media to underscore this point, as it can be argued that community broadcasting is the epitome of media localism—the most local of any local media. Westwood (2011) articulates these changes succinctly: "it is clear that the concept of community is changing" given the increased attention to "communities of practice" and increased mobility for jobs and residences (p. 693). Nevertheless, "the geographic, indeed local, element cannot be overlooked" (p. 693).

Recently, some scholars have attempted to walk the line between the two iterations of localism—the spatial and the social. Braman (2007) looks for solutions to what she calls the tensions between "the ideal" and "the real" in localism and recognizes the challenges that arise when "the functions of our daily lives now take place across a number of locales" (p. 277). Napoli (2001a) argues for hybrid localism policies, accepting that the spatial dimension will survive because our social, political, and cultural institutions are tied to geographic localities. But he also acknowledges that "social conceptualizations" need to be included. While these social conceptualizations of localism remain somewhat under-theorized, Napoli's work reminds us that this is not a zero-sum game of spatial versus social. Instead, it reinforces the need for workable solutions.

We are left, then, with definitional, conceptual, and operational challenges with respect to local media policy in the twenty-first century. Taken in isolation, both positions—spatial and social—are incomplete as they seek to reduce the local to something impossibly fundamental and homogenous—an essential culture, language, place, or market. The question is, how can we think through these issues in a productive fashion, instead of simply reducing them to an artificial dichotomy? To start, we need to distance ourselves from the romantic and fetishized impressions we hold of the local as an idyllic and homogenous community, and "overcome the deep skepticism that sees the electronic media as inherently destructive of local identities" (Anderson & Curtin, 1999, p. 302; Joseph, 2007). Bridges need to be built that recognize the importance of both spatial and social localism within media policy, which may in turn lead to a more robust framework for local media in the public interest.

The Policies of Place

Media Localism explains and assesses how regulators and stakeholders define and mobilize "the local" and related terms like "community" and "place." Focusing specifically on the regulation of local television, I ask: How is the local discursively constructed within media policy in the United States, the UK, and Canada? How are regulators defining the local in an era of placeless digital media? How is the discourse of the local mobilized by different actors in the policymaking process? How do findings compare across jurisdictions? And how can these comparisons help us understand the ways in which the local is articulated in the digital age?

I also move beyond the confines of broadcast policy and regulation to reflect on larger philosophical problematics, such as the role of places in our everyday lives. Taken together, I offer a unique understanding of the local in regulatory discourse through the lens of critical theory. This involves mapping the conceptual contours of the local in the fields of critical geography and critical political economy, the results of which are outlined in chapter 1. Interrogating the various interpretations of the local helps frame my analysis of how place, community, and localism are defined in regulatory discourse and the challenges of delineating such terms in an era of placeless digital media. Such an approach also allows me to focus on the theoretical and normative markers of localism, since an in-depth discussion of the social, political, and historical construction of locality within three nation-states would not only be exhausting for the author (and beyond the scope of this book), but tiresome for the reader. A focus on the theoretical, conceptual, and normative aspects of localism helps cut through the clutter of disparate jurisdictions and allows me to investigate the local as a contested experience within the human condition. This approach also demonstrates how critical theory (in the context of this book referring specifically to critical political economy, critical geography, critical regionalism, and critical discourse analysis)[4] can be successfully applied to the analysis of media law, policy, and regulation. Ultimately, I offer a fresh perspective on the enduring question of the local in North Atlantic media systems.

The United States, the UK, and Canada are appropriate choices to conduct a comparative media systems study: They are English-speaking, liberal representative democracies, overseen by a system of common law, and possessing advanced communications systems (see Hitchens, 2006). They are also strongly positioned within the neoliberal framework of the global economy and international trade. The United States and the UK are perhaps more obvious choices for comparison given their historic position as the global templates for media systems (Freedman, 2008; Hitchens, 2006). I contend, however, that Canada is also worthy of comparison. Far too often Canada is lumped together with the United States as exemplifying the "liberal model" of media policy (e.g., Hallin & Mancini, 2004). Instead, I argue that Canada possesses a distinct media system worthy of study in its own right, albeit one that is heavily influenced by both the United States and the UK (Ali, 2012a). Hilmes (2012) agrees, noting how Canada, the United States, and the UK share a history of mutual influence in broadcasting.

My comparative approach draws generally from Hallin and Mancini's (2004) "comparative media systems." As Hallin and Mancini note, "the role of comparative analysis in social theory can be understood in terms of two basic functions: its role in concept formation and clarification and its role in causal inference" (p. 2). Though their approach is vulnerable to critique, what I take from Hallin and Mancini is the ability of comparative media studies to make it "possible to notice things we did not notice and therefore had not conceptualized, and it also forces us to clarify the scope and applicability of the concepts we do employ" (p. 2). Case in point: the local.

Method and Methodology

To investigate the aforementioned research questions, I employed two primary methods.[5] The bulk of the research is based on a critical discourse analysis of more than 18,000 pages of policy and regulatory documents released between 2000 and 2012 from the FCC, Ofcom, CRTC, and federal departments and ministries. This reflects a belief that regulators still have a central role to play in contemporary media systems but also acknowledges that they are one of many actors within the policymaking process (Freedman, 2008; Lunt & Livingstone, 2011). To narrow down potential sources, I relied on Freedman's (2008) apt definitions of policy and regulation, wherein policy represents "the development of goals and norms leading to the creation of instruments that are designed to shape the structure and behaviour of media systems." Media regulation, on the other hand, "focuses on the operation of specific, often legally binding tools that are deployed on the media to achieve established policy goals" (p. 14). With this in mind, and based on similar research by Franklin (2001) and Taylor (2013), I examined government acts and bills, regulatory undertakings and policy decisions, white papers, committee and task force reports, comments filed by interest groups, broadcasters, and the public, hearing testimony, press releases, and news articles.

Document analysis was complemented by in-depth interviews with key stakeholders in London, Ottawa, and Washington, D.C. Interviewees included representatives from Ofcom, DCMS, the BBC (former), the CRTC, and the FCC (former), along with many anonymous sources. These interviews were essential to developing a comprehensive understanding of the place of localism within media policy, and to understanding the priority of localism among regulators. Respondent selection was based on a combination of online directory searches and "snowballing" (see Sender, 2004). Particular attention was paid to interviewees involved in licensing, policy, local television, and those who were current or former commissioners. These methods are consistent with recent innovative studies that sought to combine interviews with document analysis (e.g., Freedman, 2008; Potschka, 2012). It should also be noted that several respondents asked to remain anonymous, and as such are referred to only by nationality (e.g., "American respondent").

CRITICAL DISCOURSE ANALYSIS

To analyze my findings, I relied on a critical approach based on the methodological foundations of critical discourse analysis (CDA) and the analytical frameworks of critical political economy (Mosco, 2009) and critical regionalism (Powell, 2007). These conceptual frameworks share the normative goal of envisioning a more equitable, accessible, and democratic system, in communications and elsewhere through critical interrogation. CDA is a method that is only now gaining traction among policy scholars and requires some unpacking, which I do below. Critical regionalism, which is a central focus of this book, will be further explained in the following chapter. For the moment, it suffices to say that it is an approach that helps us understand our relationship to physical places in an era of advanced capitalism. Critical regionalism reminds us that the local is more than just our feet on the ground. Rather, it is constructed through history, actions, viewpoints, contexts, discourses, and, of course, places.

Commensurate with critical regionalism, critical discourse analysis seeks to understand the structures of power, inequality, and dominance embedded within a text (van Dijk, 1993; Howarth, 2000). Discourse here is defined as "language-in-use [and] specific patterns of interaction via symbolic means" (Streeter, 2013, p. 489). CDA rests on a "hermeneutical tradition of inquiry" (Howarth, 2000, p. 11), an interpretation of meaning, closer to Geertz's (1973) "thick description" rather than to positivism. Given its concerns with power, CDA focuses on the discourses of elites rather than the subordinated (Kraidy, 2005; van Dijk, 1993). It is therefore the appropriate framework for a study geared toward a better understanding of how a discourse of the local is mobilized by powerful actors in the policymaking process. Lentz (2011), for instance, rightly observes that policy documents are themselves discursive constructions and as such contain their own embedded power dynamics that require investigation. Streeter (2013) takes his account of CDA in a direction that aligns it with the normative goals of critical political economy, particularly in the search for alternatives to the status quo of a media system: "looking at policy language in the context of historical and social change helps reveal, not only taken-for-granted assumptions, but also places where those assumptions become unstable and open to challenge" (p. 498). In this spirit, my research sought to be exploratory, descriptive, and explanatory as much as interpretive, critical, and rooted in normative theories of media democracy (Christians et al., 2009).

The Political Economy of Localism

The search for alternatives grounds my central argument: that a system of political and economic pressures work to maintain the status quo and stifle alternative approaches to localism that might resolve the spatial/social duality and challenge our taken-for-granted assumptions. I call this a "political economy of localism." By status quo, I refer to the entrenchment of neoliberalism, market fundamentalism, deregulation, light-touch regulatory oversight, the evacuation of the public interest, and a refusal by regulators to examine critically and systematically what local media are and mean.[6] At its core, this political economy has rendered localism a rhetorically pleasant, but ultimately empty term—an "empty signifier" in the language of poststructuralism (cf. Harvey, 2013).

In the coming chapters, we see examples of what I call "default localism" among regulators that feed into this political economy. Default localism is the process by which regulators skirt the problems of definition and complex conversations by falling back on familiar, uncomplicated, and taken-for-granted assumptions. Three manifestations of default localism appear throughout the book:

1. The local as taken-for-granted: Definitions are based on taken-for-granted assumptions that everyone implicitly knows what constitutes the local. As such it is never adequately defined.
2. The local as geographic: Most often localism is assumed to be strictly geographically based. This myopic perspective tends to reduce the local to a commercial market and obfuscates alternative proposals.
3. The local as tautological: These definitions fall victim to tautological rationalization—defining what is "local" in terms of what is "local."

A critical approach reminds us to keep an eye out for alternatives to the status quo and, in doing so, alternatives to this newly identified default localism. This is particularly salient for critical regionalism, an analytical approach imported from critical architecture that seeks to reconcile the places where we live with the realities of advanced capitalism (Frampton, 1983; Powell, 2007). Critical regionalism forces an interrogation of localism that goes beyond place to include elements of culture, identity, and language. Rather than treating these elements as "add-ons" or "alternatives" to physical dimensions of the local, critical regionalism insists on their inclusion, even when this complicates existing understandings. Critical regionalism is a useful tool for scholars and regulators to build conceptual bridges across the spatial/social duality, and to identify those instances within regulatory discourse where such bridges already exist and can be reintroduced.

This latter task is vital because it demonstrates that there are what I call "moments of critical regionalism": policy windows where the definition of the local is up for interpretation, and where the local is understood not as a static, homogenous, market-based site, but rather as a process constructed through negotiation. The implication here is that there have been periodic moments when regulators have had the opportunity to rethink their concepts and thereby engage in a more complex (and critical) way with the substance of the local, but that they have failed to do so because it might entail challenging a preferred understanding of our media systems.

I want to emphasize that considering the future of localism is not about cementing definitions, nor is it about erasing the connection between locality and place. Static definitions are potentially as damaging as inaction (Dunbar-Hester, 2013). We need to begin instead with spirited, multi-stakeholder discussions. Regulators need to be aware of the many facets comprising a local media ecosystem and the changing nature of the local in order to properly regulate the media under their jurisdiction. If the local is to continue to exist as a framework for media regulation, then the alternative moments that I will describe must enter into popular discussion. To do so, they need to find support. Considerations of the epistemological question of the local, however, have yet to take hold in concrete form either by regulators or reformers. The aforementioned political economic concerns make these conversations substantially more difficult to occur.

"The Cable Song" Revisited

Returning to "The Cable Song" we can see that it performs a hefty amount of discursive work for us, foreshadowing three political economic tensions that I will frequently return to in the forthcoming pages: geography, ideology, and technology.

Tensions of geography are immediately evident in Carroll's reference to local TV. As I have asked before, what is local when we talk about local television? Are we referring simply to commercial markets for advertisers? Or perhaps to communities of place? Or communities of interest? Where is home when Carroll sings of the "matters that matter at home"?

Tensions of ideology are always tricky. As a point of clarification, I use "ideology" in the Gramscian sense, referring to "a conception of the world, any philosophy, which becomes a cultural movement, a 'religion,' a 'faith' that has produced a form of practical activity or will in which a philosophy is contained as an implicit theoretical 'premiss'" (Gramsci qtd. in Hall, 1986, p. 20). In Carroll's song, ideology is represented in two ways, most notably as a tension between regulation and the "free" market: as either a neoliberal belief in market fundamentalism and private accumulation, or the more publicly oriented belief that regulation and regulators are necessary in and for "the public good" and "the public interest"—"come on now CRTC, it's show time," Carroll sings. The second tension of ideology draws on the first and revolves around the idea of local news—"who's gonna to tell our stories when the storyteller's gone?" Local news is taken by most to be a basic requirement for a democracy, one of those "indubitably good things" of which Wilken (2011) speaks. It also represents a "market failure" in the language of neoclassical economics: The market underprovides or fails to provide an adequate quality and quantity of local news (Pickard, 2013)—"our hometown local news is hurt and barely hanging on" because of "cuts and budgets blown." Broadcasters, however, argue that increased regulation will only do it more harm. We need to ask ourselves, how much do we value local news? This should be followed by a second question: Is local news so vital to our democracy that it should represent a "public good" or a "merit good"—something that should be provided through regulation to correct the failures of the market?

The third tension is technology. Broadcasting is a twentieth-century analogue medium struggling to survive in a twenty-first-century digital world. And yet, it remains the most consulted source for local news (Pew, 2011). There are, therefore, technological and economic tensions between broadcasting, cable, and Internet distribution systems. Remember Carroll's line: "'Cause fair is all we're asking, cable please." So, what exactly is the future of local television as a mechanism for the delivery of local news and information? Of course, we cannot expect Dave Carroll to address these tensions, but should we not expect regulators to be at the forefront of these conversations?

Overview

This book is divided into three parts. Part I comprises this introduction and chapter 1. The opening chapter unpacks the theoretical foundations and analytical framework of the local by thematically mapping its various interpretations in critical theory and by introducing the reader to critical regionalism.

Part II comprises four case studies, which can be read either separately or as part of the larger book. Each chapter in this part is divided into sections interrogating the American, Canadian, and British cases, respectively. Chapter 2 assesses the structural regulation of local television, analyzing the FCC's quadrennial ownership reviews, the fee-for-carriage debate in Canada, and Ofcom's reviews of public service broadcasting. Chapter 3 considers a component of domestic media systems that is consistently overlooked by scholars and policymakers: community media. Through an analysis of community television regulation, I argue that it is within discussions of community television that challenges to current definitions of localism arise, and where commentators push the boundaries of what constitutes the local.

One of the many examples of the reemergence of media localism has been an attempt to better understand the "information needs of communities." Chapter 4 is thus comprised of case studies of reports that assess what have become known as "local media ecosystems" or "local media ecologies." Building on this, chapter 5 focuses on regulatory attempts to address contemporary challenges to localism, particularly the decline in local news and the economic sustainability of local television. I analyze three initiatives: the Canadian Local Programming Improvement Fund, the American Broadcast Localism Initiative, and the British Local Digital Television Programme Service. Though the initiatives share a concern with the democratic deficits that occur when local news is reduced in quality and quantity, I demonstrate that these regulatory solutions further extend the status quo of neoliberalism and default localism.

The chapters in part III conclude the book through analysis, intervention, and synthesis. In chapter 6, I analyze my findings through the frameworks of critical regionalism and critical political economy. The chapter is divided in two sections: The first describes how a political economy of localism has come to exist within regulatory discourse. The second reintroduces the moments of critical regionalism as a discursive approach that tempers this political economic system.

Chapter 7 expands on my analysis to offer concrete regulatory interventions. Specifically, I use public finance theory to argue that local news represents not just a public good but also a *merit good* (Musgrave, 1959). While public goods require regulatory intervention only to a point that does not undermine consumer sovereignty, merit goods demand regulatory intervention regardless of consumption habits. Framing local news as a merit good provides nuance to the public good argument and gives economic rationale for increased regulatory and legislative support for local journalism.

I consider the final chapter of my book less of a conclusion and more of an essay on the theme of future research. To that end, I accomplish two things. First, I provide insight into the future policy struggles for media localism, focusing on municipal broadband in the United States and the issues of infrastructure and access more generally. Second, I take a step back from policy and regulation and propose a thought experiment on the nature of the local. Here, I ask: do we have the right to be local?

Where is Here?

Canadian critic and scholar Northrop Frye once said that the Canadian condition is best articulated not by the existential question of "who am I?" but rather by the ontological question of "where is here?" (qtd. in Tinic, 2005, pp. 3–4). This, according to Frye, best reflects the Canadian preoccupation with land, sovereignty, and identity (Tinic, 2005). I suggest that this question is far more universal than Frye had anticipated. It is a seminal question with respect to digital media, but one that has not been considered within media policy. Regulation has not been able to catch up to the multitude of screens, outlets, and platforms available to citizens and consumers, leaving us to ponder: where is here?

It is crucial that we untangle the laws, policies, and regulations that govern electronic media in order to better understand the technologies that mediate our engagements with people, places, and communities. This holds particular importance for local media policy—localism—wherein the very nature of the local is challenged both politically and epistemologically. If the ultimate goal for critical policy scholars is to envision a more democratic media system, then I contend that this begins from the ground up, from the local. Understanding how the local is shifting within policy and within our everyday lives is how we begin to engage with these pressing issues. "Where is here?" encompasses the potential spaces and places for inclusive conversations about what it means to be local, and about those media that enable it to occur.

1

Mapping the Local

> Open-ended though it be, the story of my life
> is always embedded in the story of those
> communities from which I derive my identity—
> whether family or city, tribe or nation, party or cause.
> —Sandel, 1990

What Can Kale Teach Us About Media Policy?

For a book about local television policy, Moscow, Idaho (pop. 24,000) is an odd place to begin. The town does not have a single commercial television station, and its public television station produces little local programming. For a book investigating what it means to be local in the digital age, however, Moscow has much to offer. Moscow is one of the earliest adopters of the "Buy Fresh, Buy Local" campaign, which today boasts more than seventy chapters across the United States (Charney, 2009). As its name suggests, Buy Fresh, Buy Local encourages consumers to purchase locally sourced produce to help support local farmers. Individuals are encouraged to buy locally, while businesses that source locally are encouraged to promote their decision by featuring the Buy Fresh, Buy Local logo in their windows. Embodying ideas of autonomy, self-sufficiency, and civic pride, the Buy Fresh, Buy Local campaign taps into a powerful aspect of American ideology: *localism*. On a larger scale, localism refers to a belief in "greater local power" and autonomy in political and social decision making (Briffault, 1990a, p. 1). As Alkon and Agyeman (2011) conclude, the local food movement "is responding to popular anxieties that modern life is alienating and antisocial, and an American mythology that locates the good life in romanticized small towns" (p. 2). Accordingly, "It is also a vote for small, family-owned farms, as opposed to their large, corporate counterparts, and for creating local communities filled with rich interpersonal interactions" (p. 2). In short, Buy Fresh, Buy Local underscores a romantic attachment to local communities, together with a belief that local communities are best equipped to handle local issues.

But what is the connection between locally grown kale and local media? First, both the local food movement and local media policy rely on the romanticization of the local, with the very word—"local"—conveying notions of morality, values, trust, and quality. Second, both kale and local media are characterized by tension between local content and national policy: Though federal agencies make food policy, produce is grown locally. Similarly, the FCC regulates broadcasting, while (some) content is locally produced. In both cases, we might ask: Do policymakers pay enough attention to the local? Third, questions of class, privilege, and access cut across both the local food movement and local media policy: How can individuals access locally sourced produce without the socioeconomic means to frequent farmers markets or pay the surcharge that often accompanies local food in grocery stores (McEntee, 2011)? Equally, how can individuals access the news and information vital for their day-to-day lives without access to the necessary technologies and infrastructure? Fourth, and perhaps most crucial, there is disagreement on how to define the local. The local food movement is place-bound, defined by a predetermined geographical distance from the point of origin (the farm) to the point of consumption (the table). Local media, on the other hand, do not respect geographical or political boundaries. Thirty years ago, we could perhaps point to the local newspaper or the local television station and what they covered as indicators for what was local (e.g., Kaniss, 1991). Today, we no longer have that luxury. Local newspapers have closed and television has moved away from local production. Meanwhile, social and mobile media possess qualities that are simultaneously hyperlocal (e.g., Facebook's check-in feature) and global (YouTube) (Farman, 2012). Moreover, very few digitally native news sites produce any original local news (Waldman, 2011; Hindman, 2011). What remains of media localism has been fragmented into a variety of media platforms, many of which require us to search them out. In both cases, we are searching for what it means to be local in an age of mobile phones, high-speed broadband, cable television, and yes, even grocery stores.

Acknowledging these similarities, what can the local food movement teach us about local media policy? Two points come to mind. First, the movement serves as a cautionary tale: Policy cannot be made from the nostalgic or romantic ideas we hold about the local. To make policy this way will almost certainly overlook issues of inequality, access, sustainability, and geography. Second, understanding the local food movement helps us better understand the normative values and ideological beliefs that go into filling the signifier of "the local." Before we can understand the local in media policy, we need to understand what the term means in both practice and theory. The goal of this chapter is to probe what it means to be local, to map its boundaries, complexities, challenges, and definitions. If we do not want local media policies to befall the same critiques as the local food movement—of being rhetorically pleasant, but ultimately exclusionary—then understanding the local is a necessary first step.

To understand these dynamics, I situate the local within broader parameters of social thought, drawing heavily from critical geography (Massey, 1992; Entrikin, 1991; Harvey, 1989; Dirlik, 1996; Soja, 1989; Lefebvre, 1991). Here, I enter into discussion with the critical scholar Miranda Joseph (2008) and her ideas on the "romance of the community." Before this, however, I begin with a conversation about the local in practice, where I ask: How can we think about and define the local as an experience of everyday life? I then move on to conceptual and critical understandings of the local, analyzing the themes of "local as place," "local as community," "local as market," "local as resistive," and "local as fetish." Throughout these interrelated discussions, I draw from examples of local media in the United States, the UK, and Canada. While reviewing the academic literature, I encourage the reader to ask: How do we make sense of what it means to be local in the digital age?

I offer three answers to the above question. First, the local cannot be reduced exclusively to geographic place, nor can geography be entirely ignored. Second, the local cannot be divorced from, or be read *against,* the global. Third, we need a critical theory that allows us to think horizontally across these arguments, one which avoids the "either/or approach to questions of place and space" (Dirlik, 1999, p. 179). The ultimate goal of this chapter is to move the reader toward a more holistic understanding of the local, which I identify in the theory of critical regionalism (Frampton, 1983). Drawn from neo-Marxian architectural theory, critical regionalism succeeds where other critical theories fall short by recognizing the local's connections to place while also situating the local within larger geopolitical flows of people, imagery, capital, and ideology. In addition to bridging the gaps in theory and between the competing ideas of communities of place (spatial localism) and communities of interest (social localism) that were discussed in the introduction, critical regionalism helps bridge the gaps in local media policy. It is thus a useful intellectual tool for media policymakers and scholars to identify alternatives to the status quo and craft more robust and sustainable regulations.

Local as Practice

Let us begin with the premise that the local is not a hermetically bound object fixed in space and time. It is not *only* a place on a map; rather, the local is subjective, contextual, material, and mediated, full of contradictions that require a thorough understanding. The local is subjective because it is personal, meaning different things to different people at different times. According to a study by the Office of Communication (Ofcom), the UK's communications regulator, "people have a 'portfolio' approach to identity that draws on a wide range of attachments, activities and environments" (2004b, p. 49). This includes attachments to neighborhoods, cities, communities, and regions. As Ofcom rightly notes, "what counts as 'local' when we buy a pint of milk, go to work or vote for an MP may be three very different things" (p. 2). One may define the local, for instance, by how far one's food has traveled, with the most devoted followers eating only that which has traveled less than twenty-five miles. Similarly, a 2002 UK poll found that "people from a particular area may define their region in different ways and have varying degrees of loyalty to it," which included whether the person was born in the region, their age, if they lived in an urban area, if they had ever resided outside the region, and "their level of engagement with local culture" (ITC, 2002, p. 13). So, it is not just geographic places we take to be local: communities may be local as well. Such were the findings from another UK poll: Local and regional "can mean different things in different contexts, may be restricted to either geographic communities, and may include notion of other forms of community" (Ofcom, 2009a, p. 19). In sum, the local is a place on the map, but it is also an experience that differs from person to person and place to place.

From this, we can add that the local is contextual and contingent upon mobility, class, and life cycle. Where we grew up, for instance, may feel more local to us than where we currently reside. Elsewhere, what is local may be anywhere we use our mobile phones to "check in" on Facebook (Farman, 2012). Mobility is thus another way in which the local is contextual. We move in and out of various spatial locales, sometimes stopping to identify with them, other times just passing through. Larger urban centers, moreover, may contain a multitude of local communities. This leaves Braman (2007) to ask if "it is even possible to think of a city as a single community" because "the functions of our daily lives now take place across a number of locales; we often work within a space served by one local government, live in another, and engage in economic, and recreational and educational activities in yet other jurisdictions" (pp. 240–41).

We may also feel more or less local depending on our stage in life. Young families may be more concerned with schools and housing—staples of the local—than recent college graduates, who may seek greater opportunities for travel and feel less geographically bounded. On the flip side, the elderly may be more rooted to one physical location because of mobility issues or familial commitments (Klinenberg, 2012). Some even suggest that the design of suburban communities themselves "restrict the movement of children and teenagers" along with "the elderly and women" (Schragger, 2001, fn. 153). How and to what degree we identify with these places is therefore as much subjective and context dependent as it is based on our individual material circumstances. Is being local the two-minute walk to the grocery store, what is featured on the local evening news, the office we work from, announcing our location on Instagram, frequenting independently owned stores, or ensuring that the food we eat has traveled less than one hundred miles? It is all of these things and more.

I just hinted at how the local is material, so let us now delve further into this observation. As Marx (1993) reminds us, our material conditions shape our experience of the world (see Harvey, 2010, pp. 195–200). We therefore cannot think about the local without considering class, capital, and labor. Alas, Marx does not give us much to go on with regard to understanding the local through political economy (Soja, 1989).[1] Fortunately, critical geographers have successfully applied Marxism to the study of space, place, and community, providing us with numerous critiques of the intersection of class, capital, and the local (e.g., Soja, 1989; Lefebvre, 1991; Harvey, 1989). As Joseph (2008) writes, "To invoke community is immediately to raise questions of belonging and of power" (p. xxiii). From this perspective, discussions of the local and of community often serve to obfuscate embedded power struggles and a multitude of inequalities and oppressive tactics. Take, for instance, certain recent online news endeavors, which, in attempting to promote hyperlocal news, continue to underserve minority and impoverished areas (Ali, 2010). Not only that, but online local news tends to reproduce existing power structures rather than foster pluralism and diversity (Hindman, 2009).

Our propensity to romanticize communities and localities serves to mask the role advanced capitalism plays in the reproduction of class dominance and inequality (Joseph, 2008). This dominance and inequality works in many different ways. For those enjoying the privileges of what Castells (2000) calls the "space of flows," capital accumulation allows them to experience the local as gated communities and near-unlimited mobility through travel. In contrast, the less well off are confined to their "territorial turfs" and diminishing public spaces (Castells, 2000; Drucker & Gumpert, 2009). Through uneven geographic development, capitalism succeeds at segregating the rich from the poor, the elderly from the young, and various ethnic groups from one another (Lefebvre, 1991; Drucker & Gumpert, 2009; Harvey, 2005). Online local and hyperlocal news are the perfect examples. While many sites have been created to fill the gap in local news left by local newspapers—such as the now defunct *Pits 'n Pots* in England's Stoke-on-Trent or *Seattle P-I,* which formed after the closure of the *Seattle Post-Intelligencer*—the uneven distribution of these sites, coupled with other factors such as a lack of technological access and language barriers, have given rise to what media scholar Michelle Ferrier calls "media deserts"—"a geographic locale without access to fresh news and information" (2014, p. 1).

Lastly, but no less noteworthy, the local is mediated, dependent upon communication. We experience this in everything from face-to-face conversations mediated through language, to local news on television and in newspapers, to digital storytelling enabled through mobile and Web-based geolocation services. While media deserts remind us that local news is on the wane with increased corporate consolidation, the capture of the regulatory process by commercial media ("regulatory capture"), and the abandonment of local investigate journalism, the usage and roles of communication technologies in our everyday lives teaches us a lot about what it means to be local. Local television provides us with an imagined community of where we live, while the static heard when driving away from a radio station's signal reminds us we are leaving one place for another. Mapping the local is more complicated online, but initiatives such as geospatial Web mapping and community wi-fi allow us to reterritorialize the Web through geographically situated "community publics"—groups of individuals brought together through wi-fi access and shared technology (Powell, 2012).

There is general agreement, therefore, that communities are held together by communication, regardless of form or locale (Depew & Peters, 2001). Whether the face-to-face communication of Dewey's Great Community, Putnam's (2000) bowling leagues, the newspaper of Anderson's (1991) imagined community, conversations in cafes and bars (Tarde, 1989), television newscasts (Kaniss, 1991), spiritual communication with a god (Peters, 1999), or checking in on Facebook (Farman, 2012), communities require communication to survive. This idea was integrated into the definition of community developed by Lowrey et al. (2008) after an exhaustive meta-analysis of the scholarly literature on community journalism. The authors determined "that the notion of community is strongly tied to the concepts of negotiated shared meaning *and* geographical location," and define community as being "a process of negotiating shared symbolic meaning" (p. 288). Such a definition respects the salience of the "sharing of social structures, physical spaces, and cultural symbols" while also incorporating virtual spaces and social relations.

Local news, Lowrey et al. agree, is the linchpin connecting community life and communication technologies, and contains normative implications at both the micro and macro levels. From a micro level, local news media are essential to community solidarity, identity, and everyday life (Ewart, 2000; Hutchins, 2004; Cowling, 2005; Kaniss, 1991). The Knight Commission (2009) in the United States, for instance, concluded that not only do community residents require local news to "participate in election and civic affairs [but] people need access to information to better their lives" (p. xiv). Put differently, local news acts as "social glue" for the community (Lowrey et al., 2008, p. 284).

At a macro level, local news assists in the reproduction of citizenship by stimulating deliberation and a local public sphere (Friedland, 2001; Aldridge, 2007; Falomi, 2010). Drawing on Habermas's concepts of the system, lifeworld, and communicative action, Lewis Friedland (2001) calls the public sphere that is facilitated by local media a "communicatively integrated community." Like Habermas (1987), Friedland argues that public talk (Habermas's "communicative action") encourages civic participation and democratic deliberation. He also recognizes that neoliberalism (defined by a focus on deregulation, corporate rights, capital accumulation, and individualism) and communication technologies have shifted our identification with communities and places. Despite this shifting terrain, Friedland maintains that local media covering local issues and reflecting local voices remain the stimuli for democratic conversation. Local media form an information ecosystem, where everything from community television to online news are necessary for a well-informed community. In our era of fragmented identities, citizens and consumers draw on all facets of this local media ecology for their news and information.

Access to the elements of the local media ecosystem remains predicated upon material conditions. Over-the-air television is universally available, but with television stations cutting back on local news, broadband has become a necessity. Yet high-speed Internet, at least in the United States and Canada, remains far from universal, often resulting in a lack of access for minority groups, including the poor, African Americans, Native Americans/First Nations, and the elderly, not to mention the rural (Waldman, 2011; FCC, 2010). This makes over-the-air local broadcasting even more important until universal broadband can be achieved. Access to the local media ecosystem thus defines one's local experience, underscoring the local's subjective, contextual, material, and mediated qualities.

To be familiar with a local media ecosystem, as media policymakers and scholars must, one must address the pressing question of this chapter: What does it mean to be local in the digital age? Inspired by Lowrey et al. (2008), the challenge is to develop an understanding of the local that recognizes its geographic connectedness, its discursive construction, its reliance on social relationships, and its dependence upon communication technologies, as well as the distancing wrought by globalization, mobilization, and digitalization. The remainder of this chapter is therefore devoted to a discussion of the various manifestations of the local in critical theory—from places, to communities, resistances, and fetishes. I argue that in order to successfully understand the local in media policy, we need a theoretical framework to capture and interconnect its changing dynamics and mutable conditions. This can be achieved by employing the theoretical framework of critical regionalism (Frampton, 1983, 1985). However, before we can appreciate what critical regionalism has to offer scholars of media localism and media policy, we must first understand previous theoretical frameworks.

Local as Place

The classic understanding of the local is that it is a place-bound, spatially defined concept (Giddens, 1990). When we think of the local, we tend to think of towns, cities, and neighborhoods. The local is something on a map with political and geographic boundaries—it is the physical "place" in which our everyday lives are performed. In these local places, we go grocery shopping, work, attend school, and vote. This conceptualization of place tends to privilege face-to-face communication, which is the basis of what Dewey (1927) called the "Great Community." On this view, the local is associated with the deliberative politics of the New England town hall—a place of deliberation and debate and out of which emerges democracy, citizenship, and solidarity (de Tocqueville, 1835; Dewey, 1927). Williams (1973) called this the "knowable community" of the country (versus the opaque community of the city). Earlier, Tonnies (1957) separated the tight-knit community from the urban society in his classic distinction of *gemeinschaft* (community) and *gesellschaft* (society). More recently, Castells (2000) labeled it the "space of place," acknowledging that "people tend to construct their life in reference to places, be they their homes, their neighborhoods, their cities, their regions, their countries" (p. 20).

In contrast to the space of place is the "space of flows"—those liminal spaces of global travel and high-speed connections where cosmopolitan elites conduct business (Castells, 1996). This is facilitated by communication technologies or what Wilken (2011) calls "teletechnologies" (e.g., the telephone, the television, the Internet). Teletechnologies enable us to transcend the tyranny of distance, thereby undermining the space of place. Still many, including Wilken, argue that "place still matters" (e.g., Tinic, 2005; Kirkpatrick, 2006; Escobar, 2003). Casey (1998), for one, is quite forceful in his defense of place: "Place is as requisite as the air we breathe, the ground on which we stand, the bodies we have. We are surrounded by places. We walk over and through them. We live in places, relate to others in them, die in them. Nothing we do is unplaced. How could it be otherwise? How could we fail to recognize this primal fact?" (p. ix). According to this camp, the local-as-place continues to be a relevant site of inquiry and experience because it is in and through these geographic places that "the majority of people live, share experiences and construct their identities" (Hutchins, 2004, p. 580). Matei, Ball-Rokeach, and Qui (2001) have noted that local communities "are central in maintaining a viable social fabric . . . where we most sensually experience the conditions of everyday life" (p. 430). For them, storytelling is one of the seminal characteristics of local communities, something that is accomplished through both digital and analogue media (see also Wilkin, Ball-Rokeach, Matsaganis, & Cheong, 2007). This observation is empirically supported by the Future Foundation, a UK-based consumer research group, which reported that the average Briton lives his or her life "within a 14-mile radius of home" (Brown, 2001, p. 1).

Place also remains seminal in our political lives. Western political systems are rooted in geographic localities for governmental representation, censuses, elections, and the delivery of social services (Napoli, 2001a; Briffault, 1990a, 1990b; Anderson, 1988). Moreover, places will continue to remain relevant so long as our many political, cultural, and social institutions remain tied to specific geographic constituencies (Napoli, 2001a). Within the annals of history, the local-as-place is invoked in Thomas Jefferson's vision for "little republics" and feared in Madison and Hamilton's *Federalist Papers*. These classic examples speak volumes to the depths in which localism is rooted in American political consciousness. Today in what Collins (1990) calls the "North Atlantic triangle" (United States, UK, Canada) the relationship between the local and place is most palpable in Britain, where the passing of the 2011 Localism Act allows cities to elect a mayor for the first time and devolves certain federal powers to municipalities (UK, 2011a). Clearly, localism remains entrenched within what Rennie (2006) calls "'quotidian politics'—a politics of the everyday" (p. 189). But this is not an either/or situation, for we are not either "in place" *or* "in space." Such reductive thinking goes against the entire argument of this book. Rather, the current discussion serves to remind us that regardless of the hype of globalization and the digital, the places we call home remain important sites of identity creation, politics, experience, and cultural production. Media policy needs to reflect this reality of experience.

Local as Community

We must also be mindful of the lessons of critical geography: places are social constructs. In other words, there is nothing inherently natural about local places. Nor is the social conception of place exclusively about the geographic. Our relationship to place does not exist *a priori* to our relationships with one another. Local communities are embedded within transnational flows of capital, people, images, and ideologies, and need to be understood as such. This makes it harder to define the local purely within "territorial continuities" because media and capital constantly push us beyond these places (Castells, 1996, 2000). We have already heard Castells refer to this as the "space of flows" while Giddens (1990) calls it the dislocation of "space and place." Massey (1993) goes so far as to completely divorce places from geography, arguing instead for a "progressive politics of place" that privileges social relationships.

There are important challenges to the notion of "local as place": one of the most compelling posits that essentializing the local in a physical place obfuscates the exclusionary qualities of the local (Joseph, 2008; Sreberny-Mohammadi, 1992). Recall the earlier example of the local food movement, where the (largely) white and wealthy may participate while many marginalized communities may not. There are also challenges to the notion of place from a technological perspective, where social relations are "lift[ed] out ... from local contexts of interaction"—first through broadcasting, and now through digital and social media (Giddens, 1990, p. 21). It is worth quoting Kirkpatrick (2006) at length to amplify this point:

> ... "the local" is not primarily a geographical designation, but a social, economic, and even temporal discourse depending on its deployment within a given context. Of course, the local is understood to have a spatial correlate,

but as the literature makes clear, the relationship between physical geography and an idea of a local is ultimately unfixable.... What this indicates, in essence, is the danger of emphasizing the geographical dimensions of locality over the social dimensions: the local—and by extension any notion of a local community—was always socially constructed, not merely an accident of space. (pp. 28–29)

In addition to social organization and technologies of transportation and communication as documented by Kirkpatrick, advanced capitalism further intensifies the disassociation from place (Harvey, 1989, 2005, 2013). By accelerating and intensifying the speed at which business is conducted, messages sent, and distances overcome, advanced capitalism, and more recently neoliberalism, has resulted in a "time-space compression" of our everyday lives (Harvey, 1989). Drawing on the work of Henri Lefebvre (1991), Harvey (1989, 2005, 2013) argues that neoliberalism has unevenly reshaped modern geography by concentrating wealth in geographic enclaves while negatively exploiting other localities. In this view, the local has become an "empty signifier" (a word without inherent meaning), filled primarily with neoliberal ideologies (Harvey, 2013).

Bringing neoliberalism into the discussion of the local provides a useful jumping-off point for Joseph (2008), who contends that romanticizing the notion of community causes us to forget that it too is a site of struggle, exclusion, power, and oppression. More importantly, by "fetishizing community" we suppress its connections to larger structures of capitalism, production, and consumption (p. xvii). Harvey (1993) has a similar critique: "To write of 'the power of place' as if places (localities, regions, neighbourhoods, states, etc.) possess causal powers, is to engage in the grossest of fetishisms" (p. 21). Defining communities through a process of nostalgic romanticism not only obscures their exclusivity (e.g., gated communities) but also erases the "disturbing and violent" experiences that permeate social life (Powell, 2007, p. 13). There is a darker side to the discourses of the local that we should not ignore.

One takeaway from these early discussions is that while place remains an important element of the local, it is weakened by arguments that conceptualize it as more than geography, that point to the disruptive potential of electronic media to spatial boundaries, that invoke the challenges from neoliberal capitalism, that bring to light the fetishization of community, and by arguments reminding us that an overly positive view of the local can mask oppression and struggle. Perhaps, then, rather than "place," it is better to think about the local in terms of the broader notion of "community" so as to avoid the pitfalls I just described. Tonnies (1957) does exactly this when delineating between *gemeinschaft* (community) and *gelleschaft* (society). As we recall from the introduction, "community" is akin to "motherhood" or "democracy." It is something "indubitably" good (Wilken, 2011). The same can be said of the local: Who, I might ask, is against the local, be it in the form of community groups, local farmers, or local businesses? We are hard-pressed to find anyone who is antilocal. "Community" carries the same rhetorical weight. Who is anticommunity?

A community is what we make of it. It can be rooted in place, religion, family, interests and tastes, or, more recently, in the virtual communities of Facebook, Instagram, and e-mail (Wilken, 2011; Turkle, 2011). Raymond Williams (1985) classically defines community as "the quality of holding something in common" (p. 75). As such, it is more flexible and substantially more elusive than the local-as-place. Mobility also places more emphasis on notions of community than of place, allowing us to be "alone together" in the aforementioned cyber*spaces* and spaces of flows (Wilken, 2011; Turkle, 2011; Castells, 1996; Klinenberg, 2012). The flip side is that both "community" and "local" can be mobilized for almost any purpose, from attempts to keep communities ethnically pure to invoking the local to justify human displacement in the name of progress—as with, for example, housing developments and transnational business practices (Soja, 1989; Harvey, 2005, 2013).

Local as Market

Communities are fickle groups, difficult to pin down, and even more difficult to define. I have commented on communities of interest, of taste, and of place, but another community is that of consumers, invoking again the idea of the local as materially experienced. Indeed, returning to the local food movement slogan of "Buy Fresh, Buy Local"—or in the case of one British newspaper, "Buy Local, Live Local, Go Local"—one immediately notices the market as a decisive factor in the construction of the local. We are repeatedly instructed to "buy local" rather than "be local." This local-as-market perspective envisions local communities as markets for goods and services first, and cultural and political communities second. In broadcasting, for example, localities in the United States are defined as "designated market areas" (DMAs) rather than as cultural or political communities. Market segregation also occurs at the global level, where transnational corporations are constantly in search of new (local) markets (Dirlik, 1996). "We are not a multinational, we are a multilocal" says Coca-Cola Inc. (qtd. in Wilson & Dissanayake, 1996, p. 2). It is the local-as-market approach that introduced us to the term "glocalization," which denotes the practice of global businesses localizing their products and services in an effort to attract customers (e.g., McDonald's Chicken Maharajah Mac in India).

In stark contrast to glocalization, Shuman (1998) offers a radical reconceptualization of the local market, arguing for a "new economics of place" that privileges local economies through protectionist intervention. He is concerned with the trend of transnational corporate mobility, which can devastate local economies when companies leave in search of lower operating costs and force localities to compete among themselves for exploitative contracts. Shuman envisions "self-reliant communities" that "encourage local investment in community corporations, and local consumption of goods made or service delivered by them" (p. 49). He calls this "going local." Shuman's approach comes up against a number of different challenges that we have already encountered. Most importantly, he perpetuates Joseph's (2008) romanticization of community by not accounting for how an exclusively local economic model could exacerbate existing class and structural inequalities and modalities of exclusion. While falling short of advocating a walling off from global flows, it is difficult to see how such a dedicated local focus does not turn a blind eye to global flows of capital. Still, Shuman's argument sheds light on the idea of *local ownership,* a common concern for those advocating media policy reform.

Another conceptualization of the local as market approach comes from scholars of global communication who discuss the role of domestic (national) production within global media markets (e.g., Straubhaar, 2008; Curtin, 2007; Kraidy, 2005). Two uses of local are at work here. First is the "localizing" of global genres and business practices. This occurs when a global format such as a reality program or soap opera is localized for a domestic audience (Sreberny-Mohammadi, 1992; Kraidy, 2005). As noted, the neologism "glocal" emerged from this discourse as a way to discuss the localization of global genres, global business practices, and global markets (Robertson, 1996; Kraidy, 2003). More recently, glocalization has been reappropriated to insert an element of agency. The claim here is that the localization of global products is more of a power-laden process of hybridization rather than a strictly speaking imperialist project (Kraidy, 2003). While glocalization gets us closer to understanding the global and the local as mutually constitutive, Carpentier (2008) is correct that it "still tak[es] the global as its starting point for analysis and situate[s] the local in a reactive position" (p. 1). As such, we remain in search of a theory that positions the local in conversation with the global and the market without succumbing to reductionism.

The second way that global communication scholars use local is in relation to "local production." Here, authors often employ "local" to refer to national domestic production. For instance, Weber (2003) refers to China as a local market, and Jin (2007) speaks of local Korean producers. To be sure, these studies are not wrong to do this, but they demonstrate rhetorical slippage when discussing the political economy of media because "local" is often taken to mean "national" when discussing transnational media. As a result, "the 'local' is really the 'national,' while the truly local (subcultural, grassroots, etc. . . .) is ignored" (Sreberny-Mohammadi, 1992, p. 189). For Sreberny-Mohammadi (1992), when the national is mislabeled as "local," inequalities at the *actual* local (subnational) level are obscured. I suggest that part of the job of communication regulators should be to parse these meanings to better evaluate which aspects of localism they mean to address.

Local as Resistive

Any approach that serves to isolate the local by reducing it to a market flattens out inequality and nuance. A second consequence of this reductive tendency is that it contributes to the belief in an "authentic local" that exists and is in need of protection. From this perspective, the local is understood as being resistive to changes that may compromise its authentic nature. Here, the local—be it a community of place or interest—is reduced to a homogeneous culture or tradition, one co-opted by Western capitalism and therefore requiring a resistive response. Consequently we have constructed a lexicon of binaries to characterize the local: traditional vs. progressive, premodern vs. modern, local vs. global, place vs. space, particular vs. universal, small vs. large, urban vs. rural, Main Street vs. Wall Street, values vs. value. The local is presented both as backward and rural, and as moral and safe; either way, we are told we ought to protect this way of life.

Implicitly, efforts of resistance draw on Hall's (1980) "Encoding/Decoding" thesis of polysemous texts. This approach draws on a staunch belief in active audiences and cultural pluralism, and envisions the local as a site of resistive politics, allowing for negotiated and oppositional readings of hegemonic discourse. De Certeau (1984), for instance, argues that everyday practices such as walking down the street and shopping have resistive properties. We see similar discourses of resistance from those who address the emergence of the citizen-consumer, whose consumer choice is equated with democratic choice (Schudson, 2007). As we recall, the local food movement asks participants to "vote with their fork" as a way of resisting food importation and industrial agriculture (Alkon & Agyeman, 2011). To be sure, it can be productive to think of texts, communities, and actions as polysemous while arguing for the democratic potentialities in consumptive practices. That said, these theories have a tendency to overvalue the agency of individuals while undervaluing power dynamics and institutional frameworks (Kraidy, 2005). In an effort to resist the ubiquity of globalization, we overvalue the local, we fetishize it, so much so that we become blind to its inherent inequalities.

Local as Fetish

Resistive practices often lead to what Joseph (2008) calls the fetishization of community or, less jarringly, the "romance of community." Extending this idea while continuing to draw on Marx's notion of the commodity fetish, I suggest we call this perspective local as fetish, whereby the local becomes an object of nostalgic obsession that masks below-the-surface inequality. Jean-Luc Nancy (2006) adds that our uncritical obsession with community brings with it a sense of loss and nostalgia, but a loss that is both artificial and unproductive.

The local as fetish sees the local through the rose-tinted glasses of nostalgia and sentimentality. Robert Putman's (2000) lament in *Bowling Alone* over the demise of community solidarity immediately springs to mind, but it is Ray Oldenburg's (1999) earnest plea for a return of "great good places" that best illustrates the moral panic over the decline of "authentic" communities. Oldenburg points to the erasure of "great good places" as evidence for our declining communal ethos. Gathering spots such as the post office, pub, barbershop, and Main Street represented a time of communal values and civic participation. Their decline signals a decline in "informal public life," which has subsequently put greater pressures on work and family life while rendering everyday life more expensive. According to Oldenburg, we need locally situated "third places" beyond the private life of family and the public life of work in order to accomplish important "collective undertakings."

In contrast with Oldenburg, who seeks to seal off the local from the threat of the global, Kraidy (2005) argues it is more productive to conceptualize the local and the global "as mutually constitutive" (p. 154). This fluid conceptualization does not minimize the distinction of the local, nor does it cater to reductionism or essentialism. In Kraidy's view, the local is part of larger global structures rather than globalization's antithesis. Dirlik (1999), too, has argued that it is more productive to situate the local in conversation with, rather than in opposition to, the global. He suggests thinking about communities as "place-based" rather than "place-bound" in order to distance ourselves from essentialist constructions of the local and recognize an "ecological conception of place" (pp. 21–22). I echo this ecosystem approach (seeing the local as a plurality of elements) in chapter 4 when I write of local media ecologies. Dynamic approaches to the local brought Kraidy (2005) to argue that the local is an inherently hybrid articulation that cannot be reduced to any essential or fundamental characteristic, culture, or ethnicity. Such an understanding forces us to critically interrogate the local and expose many of the erroneous, romanticized, and fetishized elements embedded within its discourses.

Many have proposed alternatives to the debates over place, the local, and community. Massey (1993, 1994), for instance, suggests a "progressive politics of place" that relies on social relationships rather than geography. While valuable in recognizing that places are processes of meaning making, Massey fails to recognize that places are not only created out of "social relations meeting and weaving together at a particular locus" (p. 154) but are also constructed from a combination of geography, social relationships, and a multitude of discourses and actions (Dirlik, 1999)—a "poetic construction," as it were (Powell, 2007, p. 6). What is needed is a theoretical framework that keeps in mind the importance of place but does not reduce it to any single fundamental element—an approach that understands the local as embedded within practices and discourses of the global, the material, the subjective, the contextual, and the mediated, and that does not rest on nostalgia or fetish. I argue that these qualities are found in critical regionalism.

Local as Critical

Critical regionalism is most frequently associated with an influential 1983 article written by neo-Marxist architectural theorist Kenneth Frampton. It is a theory that insists on the inclusion of discourse, history, materiality, experience, and geography in the construction of places. At the heart of Frampton's thesis lies a critique of capitalism and globalization centered on geographic places, including the propensity of advanced capitalism toward uneven geographic development, standardization ("universalization"), and pulling us away from particular places. The growth of capitalism, for instance, is paralleled in the popularity of the International Style of architecture and in the "victory of universal civilization over locally inflected culture" (1985, p. 17). Frampton's response, however, is not to isolate the local as some local-enthusiasts might propose, but to engage in a critical rebuilding of place—a critical regionalism. His theory is dialectic, recognizing the fraught relationship between the global and the local: one cannot exist without the other, yet one is in conflict with the other. For Frampton, critical regionalism is necessary "to mediate the impact of universal civilisation with elements derived indirectly from the peculiarities of a particular place" (p. 21). It blends the universal and the particular, the local and the global.

In media studies, Serra Tinic (2005) sees the usefulness of critical regionalism for the study of local cultural production in Canada. Expanding Tinic's observation beyond Canada, I argue that critical regionalism is useful for any critical scholarship on media localism because it addresses the artificial dichotomy between place and space, or between the local and the global, and suggests that local identity is a construction of multiple discourses (e.g., history, experience, materiality, geography). This is the approach taken by Powell (2007), who extends Frampton's theory to critical cultural studies, and uses it to undergird his research on the discursive construction of the Appalachian region. Powell concentrates on the construction of places and regions but argues that "simply talking about place—or, more specifically, 'the local'—is not enough" (p. 18). Instead, the complexities of a "sense of place" emerge "by looking at those features of a place that seem, at least superficially, to be the permanent stable markers of its identity" (p. 14). There is recognition of the importance of place without catering to reductionism, because places are constructed through history, actions, viewpoints, contexts, and discourses. Powell also tempers Frampton's original framing of critical regionalism as dialectical. Instead, he positions critical regionalism as a dialogue between the local and the global (see also Morley & Robins, 1995)—a position I agree with. Here is Powell on the topic: "Places are not things to be found out there in the world; they are ideas about spaces that are constructed by people, in acts of observation and interpretation, and more durably in writing, in visual arts, in the built environment. Places come to seem like things because over time multiple interpretations and representations begin to coalesce around specific spaces, building on each other in ways both convivial and agonistic" (p. 67).

Two adjacent theories—both called translocalism—help elucidate these ideas for media studies. Carpentier (2008) argues for a translocal approach to community media, contending, "The translocal allows us to think [sic] the ways the local moves beyond locality, without reducing the weight of the local in its definition" (p. 22). This is accomplished by using the local as a point of departure to understand how local media enter into dialogue with other localities. Similarly, Calabrese's (2001) translocalism stresses communication and mobility between localities. His version views translocalism as germane to the evaluation of localism in communications policy, because it moves localism away from its parochial past and into a dialogue within and outside specific geographic locales. Both versions of translocalism treat the local for what it is, rather than immediately comparing or contrasting it with the global. And both versions recognize that communities are not hermetically sealed entities but are instead constantly engaged in a dialogic relationship with other localities and global flows of media and capital. Localities are as much about the social relationships within and between them as they are about the spatial proximities that confine them.

These attributes are subsequently echoed in Dirlik's (1996) push toward "critical localism," which treats the local as a site of experimentation. Dirlik specifically eschews the idea of imposing traditional definitions on the local in favor of open conceptual boundaries. Curtin (2000) agrees with the usefulness of critical localism, noting that it "emphasizes the articulation of progressive forces at the local, national, and transnational levels" (p. 59). For him, "Critical localism encourages one to explore new relationships between people, places, and power" (p. 59). Though Curtin specifically cites its applicability to the study of television history, we can see how theories like critical regionalism, critical localism, and translocalism, which eschew essentialization and polarization, are valuable in thinking through localism in contemporary media policy. Critical regionalism is what bridges the spatial and the social. It "negotiates between these two poles . . . to avoid either the excesses or the limitations of each" (Powell, 2007, p. 20). From this perspective, the local is articulated as a site of hybridity, of experimentation, of unfixed or fluid definitional boundaries, one connected to the notions of place and geographic communities, impacted by power and struggle, and in a dialogic relationship with globalization and capitalism.

Critical regionalism is best thought of as a mindset or an approach rather than an empirical methodology. Powell (2007) calls it the "practice of critical regionalism," an apt description because it reminds the reader of both its utilitarian etymology (from architecture) and suggests that critical regionalism is a tool to help us achieve a goal. Critical regionalism, therefore, carries with it normative implications whereby "it matters not only *how* the map is drawn, but also *who* is drawing it and *why*" (Powell, 2007, p. 7, emphasis added). In this way, critical regionalism exposes the taken-for-granted assumptions and power dynamics engendered within the discursive construction of the local. A conceptual approach based on critical regionalism also helps to identify, examine, and celebrate alternatives to the status quo (Herr, 1996). Alternatives are necessary because the local is a complex and mercurial target, and cannot be harnessed by static definitions or reductive assumptions. It is therefore useful for media policy analysis to employ critical regionalism as an approach because it helps us better understand the relationship between local media, community, and places, and because it does not submit the local to an either/or question of communities of interest or communities of place. Instead, it provides a theoretical foundation for the identification of alternatives that already exist within regulatory discourse.

Critical regionalism in media policy analysis encourages a holistic approach to the local, rather than reducing it to a homogeneous site of consumption (e.g., a television market). It encourages us to seek out alternatives to the status quo of market fundamentalism and deregulation. Punctuating these instances are what I call "moments of critical regionalism," which occur when regulators are presented with alternatives, question taken-for-granted assumptions, consider a move away from static definitions, and seek nuance and complexity rather than status quo simplicity (see chapter 7). Critical regionalism puts us in the mindset to search for these moments, to flush them out, and to explore their utility.

As scholars of media policy, critical regionalism can help us in a number of ways: (1) it can allow us to better understand the supposed antagonism between communities of place and communities of interest; (2) it can offer a bridge between these two rhetorical positions by recognizing the role that communities of interest can play *within* communities of place; and (3) it can help us to identify moments within the discourse of media regulation where such solutions have already been proposed, but have been pushed to the periphery. Critical regionalism thus helps us understand that there have been periodic moments when regulators have had the opportunity to rethink their concepts and thereby engage in a more complex way with the substance of the local, but have failed to do so because it might challenge a preferred understanding of our contemporary media system. Using critical regionalism as a conceptual foundation, we can ask the following of policy and regulation: Where are alternative definitions of the local being proposed? What examples do we have of the spatial and social dichotomy being bridged? Who is proposing these solutions? And how are they reflective of a critical regionalist approach? In the following chapters, I demonstrate how the critical regionalism mindset can be applied to an analysis of localism in media policy.

Conclusion: Beyond the Status Quo

There is always more one can say about the local, and a single chapter cannot hope to encapsulate any more than a fraction of its meanings. Even so, unpacking the local through the lens of practice and critical theory provides us with several important insights into its social construction. Beginning from an understanding that the local is not a singular, static site, but rather a subjective, contextual, material, and mediated experience, I have mapped out key critical understandings of the local along with their strengths and weaknesses. I have argued that conceptualizations that reduce the local to a single site on a discursive map are inadequate because the local is at once places, communities, markets, relationships, resistances, and fetishes. It is also none of these things, because it is an empty signifier as a result of monopoly capitalism. Building from here, I have argued that before considering the role of the local in media policy, we need a more holistic way to theorize these problematic dynamics.

Critical regionalism is a useful conceptual tool in this endeavor because it seeks alternative renderings of the local engendered by critical and normative democratic ideals. It helps us understand the local in policy, practice, and theory, without "naturalizing, feminizing, or essentializing it" (Escobar, 2003, p. 40) and encourages conversations that focus on alternatives to the status quo. In the following chapters, I describe and assess how close local media policy is, and how far it still has to go to achieve this goal.

PART II

Regulating Localism

2

The Policies of Localism
Debates, Dilemmas, and Decisions in Local Television Regulation

> Following years of indifference "local TV"
> is suddenly being seen as worthy of attention.
> —Miller, 2009

The Paradox of Media Localism

In the spring of 2001, the FCC organized a panel of academics and policymakers to discuss the challenges of media ownership regulation. As the conversation turned to local media, Commissioner Michael Copps asked: "Is localism properly interpreted as local production of content, local selection of content, the production of information about local affairs or something else? And then what does the empirical evidence indicate about the relationship between local ownership of media and the extent to which content is local?" (FCC, 2001, p. 97). In two quick sentences Copps identified the crux of a debate that permeates not only regulatory discourse in America, but Canada and the UK as well: how media localism should be defined and regulated in the twenty-first century. Is localism about communities of interest and ethno-linguistic communities (e.g., Welsh speakers) or communities of place (e.g., Edinburgh)? What is a local program? Is it best to have local or network ownership? In short, how should we protect a practice that has been called a "touchstone value" and a "cornerstone" of our media ecosystem? Copps's statement also hints at the importance of media localism, both as a field of study and as an aspect of cultural production. As the introduction and first chapter of this book attest, media localism in Canada, the United States, and the United Kingdom is important as an element of community building and solidarity, as a catalyst for democracy and civic participation, and as part of the cultural industries. This holds true regardless of the growth of digital media technologies, the entrenchment of neoliberal capitalism, or the unfortunate decline of public broadcasting.

The case studies in this chapter recount changes to the structural regulation of local television from 2000 to 2012. In doing so, I shed light on the frustrating paradox of media localism: it is both a market failure and a public good. It is a public good in that it is nonexcludable, nonrivalrous, and contains positive externalities. It is a market failure in that it is underproduced, costly to produce, and provides little return on investment. The trend has been for regulators to relax local media policies, leaving market fundamentalism, or what Victor Pickard (2014) calls "corporate libertarianism," to replace the regulator as ensuring the provision of local news and information—the hallmarks of media localism. Nevertheless, regulators, public interest groups, and the public itself continue to extol the virtues of local news. To say that the stakes are high at this juncture is an understatement. Simply put, how much do we value local news? Regulators tell us they do, but their actions over the past decade belie their words.

To fully contextualize the implications of the structural regulation of media localism, I begin with an overview of the tension between public goods and market failures. I then turn my attention to the case studies. In America, structural regulations impacting localism fall under the larger debates over media ownership—a subject the FCC is mandated to review every four years. In Canada, the defining feature of structural regulation has been the debate over "fee-for-carriage" (FFC), or the requirement that cable providers compensate broadcasters for the retransmission of broadcasters' signals. In the UK, challenges posed by structural regulation befall the once dominant public service broadcasting system, seen particularly with the rising power of the ITV network. In sum, this chapter demonstrates how the local is bound so tightly to markets, technology, and the status quo that alternative views are effectively erased.

Of Public Goods and Market Failures

In the wake of the economic and authoritative crisis in journalism, scholars and activists have begun to use the term "public good" to describe the role of journalism in Western democracies (Pickard, 2014; McChesney & Nichols, 2010; Starr, 2011). Originating in the lexicon of neoclassical economics, public goods contain three primary characteristics. First, they are nonrivalrous, meaning "one person's use of or benefit from the product does not affect its use or benefit to another person" (Baker, 2002, p. 8). If one watches a local newscast, this does not preclude the ability for another person to watch the same newscast. This differs from, say, an apple: if I eat an apple, someone else cannot eat the same apple. Second, public goods are nonexcludable, meaning they "cannot be effectively excluded from use by consumers who do not 'pay for them'" (McChesney & Nichols, 2010, p. 101). With local news, for instance, we are able to have access without having to pay for it directly (for example, watching a newscast at a neighbor's home). Third, public goods possess positive externalities, or "the value some item has to someone who does not participate in the transaction" (Baker, 2002, p. 10). News and information benefit those who do not directly consume them. For instance, I may watch a newscast and then inform my neighbor of an impending city council vote. Public goods are thus democratically and "socially desirable" (Pickard, 2014). Other examples of public goods include national parks—noncommercialized spaces that we all benefit from regardless of whether or not we go (because we always have the possibility of going). Regarding journalism, its designation as a public good underscores the idea that news is much more than a commodity, but rather an essential component of democracy (Pickard, 2014).

The challenge for public goods is that they are often expensive to produce, provide little financial return, and are therefore underproduced by the private market. "Market failure" is the term given to the underproduction of public goods in the commercial market, and government intervention is often necessary to correct this failure (Pickard, 2014; Bator, 1959). Local journalism is therefore both a public good and a market failure. There are two competing discourses here: The first is that local news is a public good worthy of regulatory intervention. Not everyone has come on board with this normative assessment. The second is that local news is a commodity subject to the market. If we treat local news purely as a commodity, however, then the market has failed in delivering both quality and quantity (see Waldman, 2011). This is the paradox of media localism. Local daily newspapers have all but abandoned local investigative journalism, while television stations have replaced traditional newscasts with hours upon hours of breakfast television. In an era of light-touch regulation and neoliberal economic policies, regulators have been uncomfortable with intervening despite strong public support for local media. In chronicling changes in the structural regulation of local television from 2002 to 2012, first in the United States, and then in Canada and the UK, I demonstrate how we have been and continue to be in a state of uncertainty about the future of local news and local television.

United States: An Expensive Value

The 1996 Telecommunications Act (the Act) is the quintessential example of neoliberal policymaking in American media (Aufderheide, 1999). Based largely on the expectations of telecommunication companies, the Act drastically reshaped the American media landscape through the deregulation of broadcast ownership, the opening up of multivideo platform distribution (MVPD) markets (e.g., cable and satellite providers), and the equation of the market interest with the public interest (Aufderheide, 1999). The Act begat four regulatory actions from the FCC that have come to be known as the "local ownership rules":

(1) *Newspaper/broadcast cross ownership rule:* Prohibits owners of a television station from owning a newspaper in the same market (with the exception of certain grandfathered cases like the *Chicago Tribune* and WGN-TV).

(2) *Local TV ownership rule:* Limits a single company to owning a maximum of two stations in a market, given that the stations' Grade B contours do not overlap,[1] that both are not ranked in the top four in the market, and at least eight independently owned full-power stations remain after the merger.

(3) *Radio-TV cross ownership rule:* Operates on a scaling system, wherein the largest markets would "generally allow common ownership of one or two TV stations and up to six radio stations in any market where at least twenty independent 'voices' would remain post-combination."

(4) *Local radio ownership rule:* Allows one company to own up to eight radio stations in the largest markets (FCC, 2003a).

The Act also required the FCC to review its ownership regulations every two years (extended to four years in 2004), with a bias toward eliminating those no longer deemed necessary. Understanding the discourse and impacts of these reviews is crucial for the study of localism, because it is within these documents that regulations are proposed, altered, and eliminated.

2002: DISMANTLING THE SYSTEM

Of the FCC reviews to date, 2002's was by far the most contentious, as it proposed to drastically accelerate the pace of deregulation (McChesney, 2007). The process began in September 2002 with the release of a *Notice of Proposed Rulemaking* (NPRM), which outlined the Commission's agenda

(FCC, 2002). From the outset, the NPRM intimated confusion between geographies and markets at the FCC. At many points it conflated them by aligning the hallmarks of FCC policymaking—localism, diversity, and competition—with commercial markets. For instance, when asking questions about competition in the local broadcasting sector, the FCC noted that it is important to "define the geographic market for delivered programming and advertising" (par. 64). It further asked, "What are the implications of these different geographic market definitions for our competition analysis? Would the appropriate geographic market be different if we focused on viewership/listenership rather than advertising?" (par. 64). When asking about localism, the Commission sought comment on its definition and "whether we should define it more narrowly or more broadly" (par. 69). Such inquiry suggests that the Commission lacked more detailed analyses of the local media ecosystems in the country, but perhaps signaled a willingness to learn and listen. Still, the confusion was clearly apparent in determining the parameters of a geographic market. Is it the political boundaries of a city, community identification of a city (e.g., suburbs), the signal reach of an over-the-air station, or the market area of a cable company? This point is illustrated in the FCC's statement on localism: "Local geographic markets are particularly difficult to define because the footprint of a broadcast outlet is likely to be different than the geographic area covered by other media outlets, such as cable systems" (FCC, 2002, par. 85).

Outweighing the discursive issue of markets and geography was the relationship between networks and affiliates. Questions here revolved around how much power local stations should have over programming decisions. Concern for the autonomy of local affiliates was further voiced at the only public hearing for the 2002 review, which took place in Richmond, Virginia, in April 2003. Here, one broadcaster argued: "Localism has meant that viewers in North Dakota, Virginia, South Dakota, South Carolina and other states have been able to watch Billy Graham on their local stations. That, of course, would not have occurred if these stations had been owned by a network" (FCC, 2003b, par. 219).

While local stations have long championed the autonomy to opt out of network programming (known as the "right to reject"), the association between this ability with the concept of *localism* (rather than another term like "station rights") leads to an alignment between "local" and "conservative." Localism is associated with conservatism (such as Billy Graham's show) and framed as a reactionary approach to network decisions (such as NBC airing a controversial episode of *Fear Factor*). It recalls unproductive moments in the history of broadcasting when rural stations were thought to need modernization by the major media centers (Kirkpatrick, 2006).

Despite pleas to the contrary (primarily by Commissioner Copps) the FCC went ahead with its market-driven approach, proposing to increase the national television ownership cap to 45 percent and eliminate the ban on newspaper/television cross-ownership. The *New York Times* summarized the decision as "among the most far-reaching deregulatory steps taken during the Bush administration. It will permit a company to own up to three television stations, eight radio stations, a daily newspaper and a cable operator in the largest cities" (Labaton, 2003a). Throughout the proposals for deregulation, the Commission managed to "reaffirm [its] commitment to promoting localism in the broadcast media" where localism is defined as "ensuring that licensed broadcast facilities serve and are responsive to the needs and interests of the communities to which they are licensed" (par. 302). Undermining this sentiment, however, it added the caveat, "localism is an expensive value" (United States House, qtd. in FCC, 2003a, p. 25). Not surprisingly, commercial networks and the National Association of Broadcasters (NAB) jumped on this phraseology, and often reminded the Commission that because localism is such an expensive value, deregulation is necessary to promote synergies among commonly owned stations. The Commission took no issue with this position and even agreed that "media properties may allow their news and editorial decisions to be driven by the 'bottom line'" (FCC, 2002, par. 353). Further still, it argued that relaxation of ownership limits promotes the principles of localism for the reasons voiced by the NAB (economies of scope and scale). As with previous FCC decisions since the 1980s, this is a market-based approach to localism, one where the Commission rhetorically supports the principle, but would prefer to look for market incentives for the promotion of local reflection. Commissioner Copps, the voice of progressive politics at the FCC at this time, offers a demurral to these tactics: "Part of the blame was the private sector mentality that said . . . more and bigger is always better because you achieve all these wonderful efficiencies and economies and . . . enhance the bottom line. . . . And the result is less voices in the community, less localism in the community . . ." (personal communication, 11/20/12).

The FCC's release of the 2003 *Report and Order* (R&O), which codified the above proposals, immediately garnered the ire of public interest groups and consumer advocates. In his dissenting opinion to the R&O, Copps lambasted the Commission for failing to give due consideration to the public record by not taking into account the "overwhelming public opposition." As he continued, "I am convinced this is the wrong decision. It is wrong for the media industry, wrong for the public interest and wrong for America" (2003a, p. 18). Perhaps taking heed of Copps's stringent opposition, Congress passed legislation to reduce the national ownership cap from 45 percent to 39 percent in 2004, and the Court of Appeals remanded the ownership decisions back to the FCC for reconsideration. Specifically, the Court ordered the FCC to reevaluate its local television ownership rule, stating that the Commission erred in only counting television stations when determining how many independent "voices" existed in a market. Public interest advocates saw the court remand as a victory, and celebrated again when the Supreme Court refused to hear a case to reverse the lower court.

Now under pressure from public interest groups, Commissioners Copps and Adelstein, and Congress, Chairman Powell—champion of neoliberalism within the FCC—created the Broadcast Localism Initiative in 2003 to investigate the role of localism in the American mediascape (see chapter 5). While deemed a failure, its existence was nevertheless used as a scapegoat by the Commission to avoid addressing localism in the 2006 ownership review. Respondents who wished to remain anonymous echoed these sentiments, questioning the Commission's commitment to localism aside from rhetorical praise. For the time being, localism would remain an ambiguously defined concept, subsumed under the more manageable notion of "affiliate rights."

2010: A MORE CONSIDERED APPROACH

When the 2010 review came around, the Commission seemed to have learned from these earlier mistakes. The Notice of Inquiry (NOI), released in May 2010, demonstrates a more discriminating approach to localism (FCC, 2010b). To be sure, the FCC continued to advocate a strong deregulatory stance, calling again for the abandonment of cross-media ownership restrictions. But it also raised important questions about localism, television, and public goods. In many ways the inquiries made in the NOI and the corresponding NPRM were more far-reaching than those posed during the Localism Initiative (see chapter 5).

The point of the NOI was to review the four primary ownership regulations within the Commission's jurisdiction: local TV ownership, radio ownership, newspaper/broadcast cross-ownership, and radio/TV cross-ownership.[2] As with previous reviews, the Commission had to consider any regulatory changes in light of how to enhance its three policy goals: competition, localism, and diversity. Of localism in particular, the Commission asked about definitions and how best to promote "localism in the context of the media ownership rules" (FCC, 2010b, par. 54). More importantly, it sought comment on whether the "traditional localism goal [of fostering locally relevant programming] need[s] to be redefined in today's media marketplace?" (par. 54). Although dismissed by interview respondents, this seemingly innocuous question marks one of the first times the Commission acknowledged that the nature of the local might have changed in light of new social and technological patterns.

To that effect, the Commission sought comment on how best to assess localism, noting that it had traditionally relied on two measures: "(1) the selection of programming responsive to local needs and interests of broadcasters' communities of license, and (2) local news quantity and responsiveness" (par. 18). One discussion heretofore unheard of at the FCC since the passing of the 1996 Act was whether local news was "socially valuable in itself, regardless of variations in consumer interest in such programming? If so, would measures of civic engagement such as voter turnout or civic knowledge be useful to measure achievement of the localism goal?" (par. 58). This important query suggests the Commission pondered the merits of local news as a *public good* or even a *merit good* (a good that should be provided regardless of consumption habits) rather than as a market commodity.

This progressive set of questions, however, was undermined by a caveat in which the Commission voiced disinterest in hearing comments beyond "the structural media ownership rules" (fn. 101). The FCC justified its decision by noting that the Localism Initiative already covered these issues. Statements reflecting on larger epistemological issues, most notably the social value of local media and the definition of the local, were therefore notably absent. Instead, stakeholders stuck to the topic of ownership. The NAB (2010a), for instance, recalled the earlier argument that "localism is an expensive value" to advocate for the complete deregulation of broadcasting. In contrast, consumer and public interest groups like Free Press and the Prometheus Project argued for enhanced ownership requirements, including a restriction on Local News Sharing Agreements, which permits broadcasters to share equipment, staff, and stories and Shared Services Agreements, combining sales and other departments of local stations (Free Press, 2012).[3]

As it turned out, both private and public interest groups had cause for concern. The NPRM released at the end of 2011 suggested keeping most of the local ownership rules intact, but eliminating the newspaper/broadcast cross-ownership rule for the twenty largest markets as well as doing away with the radio/television cross-ownership rule (FCC, 2011a). A more robust definition of localism also seemed to be on the Commission's mind, as it recognized there might be multiple layers to localism that did not exist in previous generations, owing to the advent of digital technologies. Though the Commission failed to explain this statement, it did seek further comment "on whether, and how, to reevaluate localism to account for changes in the way consumers get local news" (par. 7). It is important to recognize, however, that local news is framed here as a benefit for consumers rather than for citizens.

Hidden within the NPRM is also an often-overlooked proposal to define the local in terms of the Nielsen Company's Designated Market Areas (DMAs) and do away with a definition based on the signal strength of over-the-air transmitters (Grade B contours). "A DMA is a geographic area defined by The Nielsen Company as a group of counties that make up a particular television market" (FCC, 2014b). Defining the local in terms of DMAs rather than signal contours was meant to be "consistent with today's marketplace" because "MVPD's [multichannel video programming distributors] generally will carry all the broadcast stations assigned to the DMA in which they are located" (FCC, 2011a, par. 37). Accordingly, because cable providers must carry all broadcast stations in their market area (rather than their geographic area), a definition based on markets rather than geography seemed more appropriate. This determination rests on the assumption that the market not only determines what qualifies as local, but is also the primary motivator for broadcasters to produce local programming.

DMAs have larger catchment areas than cities and often incorporate several municipalities into one market. For example, Philadelphia's DMA includes Wilmington, Delaware and Trenton, New Jersey. With the largest advertising market of the three cities, stations are more inclined to serve Philadelphia rather than the other two state capitals (Goldfarb, 2005). The NAB (2012) vehemently opposed the definitional switch to DMAs. Perhaps more surprising, it found a public interest ally in the Association of Free Community Papers. The NAB argued that using the DMA definition would hinder efforts of broadcasters to acquire newspapers (or vice-versa), noting the uncertainty that could come if "Nielsen changes its DMA markets, when the Commission modifies a DMA market, or in cases where markets are hyphenated" (p. 48). The Association of Free Community Papers (2012), meanwhile, argued that the market-based DMA approach serves only as a diluted proxy for "real communities." In their words, "In neither size, scope nor ownership could a DMA ever be confused with its municipal namesake, the City. Nearly half of all Americans live within the shifting borders of the twenty largest DMAs, and they live there as designated consumers, not citizens" (p. 11). Accordingly, ". . . The proprietary mapping of a Designated Market Area designed for broadcasters to bill Madison Avenue firms for advertising, is miserably flawed in parceling the dependent local television content. As gerrymandered borders for an open season on hunting and swapping media properties, the undemocratic foundation of DMAs are a disaster" (p. 12). This opposition serves to illustrate the difficulties of delineating geographic borders when it comes to what is local. More importantly, it raises the question of who is empowered to make these decisions—the FCC or Nielsen.

The 2011 NPRM presents a conflicted stance toward the failure of localism in American media regulation. On the one hand, the FCC tried to broaden the conversation to larger issues facing localism in the digital age: what is local, how to define it, how to assess it, and its place within democratic governance. On the other, it narrowed possible responses by focusing solely on ownership and reducing local communities to advertising markets. Replies to the NPRM followed suit by focusing on ownership rather than the larger epistemological issues that formed the subtext of the NPRM. As a result, the 2002, 2006, and 2010 Ownership Reviews, along with the 2004–2008 Broadcast Localism Initiative, failed to get to the heart of these important questions.

My examination of the past three media ownership reviews reveals how deeply entrenched market fundamentalism is within American communications policymaking and media localism. This is so pronounced that the Nielsen Company now sets the terms of debate around what is local and who is local through its power to define (and redefine as the case may be) DMAs. Still, the Commission has not been entirely without dissent on this issue. Buried in these reviews have been questions about whether local news is a public good or merit good: bold statements hidden in otherwise neoliberal documents. While it is doubtful that the FCC will answer its own question, the question itself demonstrates that media localism is a concept constructed through hegemonic processes, leaving spaces for alternatives.

Canada: The Fight for Fee-for-Carriage

The biggest difference between broadcast regulation in the United States and Canada is in the area of programming. While programming requirements are anathema to (certain readings of) the American First Amendment, the 1991 Canadian Broadcasting Act directs broadcasters to promote national, regional, and community identities. As a result, the Canadian Radio-television and Telecommunications Commission (CRTC) is empowered to mandate programming quotas. These requirements, known collectively as "Canadian content," are in place to ensure the production of Canadian drama, comedies, and news (among other categories), but have been on the wane since 1999 as Canada has followed its southern neighbor by pulling back from structural regulation. This regulatory roll-back has jeopardized local news in small and large communities alike. The focus of this section is on fee-for-carriage (FFC): regulations that would compel broadcast distribution undertakings (BDUs—cable and satellite providers) to financially compensate local broadcasters for the retransmission of the broadcasters' signal. Similar to the American "retransmission consent," FFC would provide local broadcasters with a second stream of revenue in addition to advertising. It would thus offer broadcasters greater economic security through a dual funding stream akin to those of cable networks. If media ownership defined the first decade of the twenty-first century in American media policy, it was fee-for-carriage that did so in the Great White North.

1999–2003: "A MAJOR BUILDING BLOCK OF THE COMMUNITY"

The 1999 Canadian Television Policy marked a neoliberal turn for an erstwhile protectionist regulatory body. Celebrating the financial health of local television, the CRTC removed hourly local news commitments, assuming local stations would continue production given the profitability of local news. Rather than have industry minimums, programming commitments would be up to broadcasters' discretion and approved by the CRTC during station license renewals every seven years. This occurred despite the acknowledgment that increased corporate consolidation had diminished the resources of local stations (Murray, 1999).

Trust in the market to provide local news would come to haunt the CRTC in later years, particularly with the growth of satellite television. With the introduction of satellite distribution in the mid-1990s, small-market stations often found themselves not being carried and therefore losing out on viewers and advertising revenue. At the time, direct-to-home (DTH) satellite providers were required to carry only one station per network, meaning, for instance, that viewers in Yorkton, Saskatchewan, might receive local stations from Vancouver but not from Yorkton. To address this market failure, in 2003 the CRTC proposed the creation of a Small Market Local Programming Fund (SMLPF) to support small-market stations impacted by their lack of carriage by DTH providers. The fund would go toward subsidizing "the creation, development and production of television programming," specifically local news (CRTC 2003, par. 135). This was accomplished through a 0.4 percent levy on the gross revenues of DTH undertakings and was in addition to the 5 percent of gross revenues that all BDUs were required to contribute to the Canadian Television Fund (CTF, now the Canadian Media Fund). Eligible stations had to be "small market, independently owned stations" serving populations of fewer than 300,000. Stations owned by the largest media groups (CTV, Global, TVA, CBC) were therefore ineligible.

Table 2.1: Small Market Local Programming Fund (SMPLF) Funding (2006–2014)

	2006	2007	2008	2009	2010	2011	2012	2013	2014
Amount (aggregate of eligible stations in $000s)	6,107	6,116	7,116	7,672	8,402	9,209	9,626	9,734	9,388
Funding as a % of total revenue	7.9%	8.3%	8.9%	10%	8.7%	9.1%	9.9%	10.2%	n/a

Source: Strategic Inc., 2014.

Table 2.2: Stations eligible for SMLPF

Station	City	Owner
CFEM-DT	Rouyn-Noranda, QC	RNC
CFJC-TV	Kamloops, BC	Jim Pattison Broadcast Group
CFTK-TV (ineligible as of 2013)[a]	Terrace, BC	Bell
CFTF-DT	Riviere-du-Loup, QC	Tele Inter-Rives
CFVS-DT	Val d'Or, QC	RNC
CHAT-TV	Medicine Hat, SK	Jim Pattison Broadcast Group
CHAU-DT	Carleton, QC	Tele Inter-Rives
CHEX-DT	Peterborough, ON	Corus
CHEK-DT (added in 2013)	Victoria, BC	CHEK
CHFD-DT	Thunder Bay, ON	Thunder Bay Electronics
CIMT-DT	Riviere-du-Loup, QC	Tele Inter-Rives
CITL-DT	Lloydminster, AB	Newcap
CKPG-TV	Prince George, BC	Jim Pattison Broadcast Group
CKPR-DT	Thunder Bay, ON	Thunder Bay Electronics
CKRN-DT	Rouyn, QC	RNC
CKRT-DT	Riviere-du-Loup, QC	Tele Inter-Rives
CKSA-DT	Lloydminster, AB	Newcap
CKWS-DT	Kingston, ON	Corus
CJBN-TV	Kenora, ON	Shaw Cablesystems
CJON-DT	St. John's, NF	Stirling Communications
CJDC-TV (ineligible as of 2013)[a]	Dawson Creek, BC	Bell Media
CJIL-DT (added in 2012)	Lethbridge, AB	Miracle Channel

a. CFTK and CJDC became ineligible after their acquisition by Bell Media in 2013.
Source: SMITS, 2014; CAB, 2013.

Such a complicated cross-subsidy system signals a tension between community, local, and nation within the Canadian mediascape. As the dissenters to the SMLPF complained, the original plan—which allowed DTH providers to deduct the SMLPF from their CTF contributions—diverted funds earmarked for national production to local news on commercial stations. Traditionally, the national has taken precedent within Canadian regulatory parlance (Ali, 2012a), but this outcome was far from certain in 2003. The question of where to position localism within the hierarchy of Canadian cultural production and regulation intimated by these 2003 documents was now front-and-center in a way that it had never been before.

The importance of local television was at the forefront of Commissioner Barbara Cram's objection to the 2003 ruling that implemented the SMLPF. Cram offered an eloquent plea for the preservation of local television, objecting to the idea that it was only the smallest stations that were failing. Instead, she saw a crisis within the entire local television sector and argued that all local stations were worthy of regulatory intervention: "Local television is one of the major building blocks of the community and of the Broadcasting system. It attaches people to others forming their community, building a sense of togetherness both in the community but also in the country" (CRTC, 2003a, p. 38). Cram positioned local television as a dynamic force within Canadian democracy. Echoing the national vs. local debate, she feared that "all television will become national and to a large extent disconnected with ordinary Canadians" (p. 39). In doing so, Cram reiterated the moral argument in favor of local news (e.g., solidarity, integration, democracy). Her dissent, however, also invokes elements of default localism and the fetish of the local: local television is romanticized to the point where localities and communities are taken as homogenous entities, devoid of class and social conflict, ethnically cognate and hermetically sealed from the concerns of capitalism.

The SMLPF highlights several tensions within Canadian local television regulation. First, it creates a hierarchy of localism, wherein small-market, independently owned stations are deemed the "most local" while large-market, network-owned stations are the "least local" and therefore the least deserving of protection. One commissioner even suggested that smaller independent operators perform localism better than their corporate counterparts: ". . . and sometimes, smaller operators, independent operators, can be quite nimble, whereas larger ones that somehow . . . are concentrated in the larger centers and perhaps miles away from the smaller ones . . . but maybe they just look at the books and say, 'Well we can't make it work. You know, so we end up selling it for a buck'" (M. Patrone, personal communication, 10/18/12). Second, it illustrates the strong interrelationship between broadcasters and BDUs, where changes in one industry cannot help but affect the other. This is evident in the fact that 90 percent of Canadians receive television through cable or satellite (CRTC, 2012a). The increased interdependence added fuel to a decade-long power struggle for control over the framework of Canadian television between the CRTC, broadcasters, and BDUs, with no party willing to give way.

2003–2008: A BROKEN MODEL?

For the next few years, the outward appearance of a stable broadcasting system masked intense internal political economic struggles. These came to a head in 2006 with Bellglobemedia's (owner of the CTV network and *Globe and Mail* newspaper) acquisition of CHUM Ltd., with its host of popular specialty cable networks (e.g., MuchMusic and Space) and second-tier Citytv and A-Channel networks. Not long after the bid, CHUM announced massive layoffs, including the complete cancellation of local news at Citytv (Norris, 2006). Despite noted opposition, the CRTC sanctioned the merger on the condition that Bell sell Citytv to avoid operating two stations in several large markets (it sold Citytv to Rogers Communications). Bell was permitted to keep the "A-Channel" network, which operated stations in smaller communities.[4]

In light of this merger and larger concerns for the structure of Canadian conventional broadcasting, the CRTC implemented a full-scale review of the regulatory framework for over-the-air (OTA) television in June 2006. It was called "one of the most crucial meetings of the Canadian industry since TV made the leap from black and white to colour" (Robertson, 2006a). Of all the factors considered, most important was the introduction of fee-for-carriage.

The press was awash with predictions that the outcome of the CRTC would favor fee-for-carriage, noting that it could deliver profits of up to $58 million per broadcaster through individual subscriber fees of fifty to seventy cents (Robertson, 2008a). Broadcasters were taken by surprise, then, when in May 2007 the CRTC denied fee-for-carriage. The Commission argued that broadcasters had not provided sufficient evidence that their industry was going through permanent structural change. The CRTC also denied a petition by broadcasters for the right to negotiate a fee for the retransmission of their signals beyond their community of license, known as "distant signals." BDUs had long valued the ability to market "time shifting" or the carriage of stations in different time zones, allowing, for instance, a Vancouver viewer to watch a live signal from Toronto (meaning a Vancouver viewer could watch *Grey's Anatomy* at 7 P.M. local time instead of 10 P.M. local time). Broadcasters countered that they should be compensated for this signal distribution. The Commission was not convinced. The CRTC thus remained skeptical to the claims of local broadcasters and more concerned with the mergers that had taken place.

Not surprisingly, within six months of this decision, the CRTC bowed to industry pressure and appended FFC to a review of BDU regulation. The Commission made this addition in November 2007, noting the symbiotic relationship between broadcasters and the systems that distribute their signals, and the "significant challenges" faced by local television (2007b, par. 6). That the CRTC reconsidered FFC on pressure from broadcasters, particularly in the press, underscores the defining importance of this issue within the regulatory landscape. It similarly highlights the economic challenges facing local television at this time. Indeed, at the start of 2008 the *National Post* reported that local broadcasting was in "crisis" (Shecter, 2008). Local media was hereby defined by this singular issue: fee-for-carriage.

Upon inclusion of FFC in the BDU regulatory melee, major media companies, including CTVglobemedia, Canwest Global, and the CBC argued vehemently in its favor, with CTV noting that "compensation for carriage is essential if CTVglobemedia is to sustain the level of service it provides to local communities and its contributions under the Broadcasting Act" (qtd. in CBC, 2008). In contrast, BDUs such as Rogers Communications, Bell-ExpressVu, Shaw, and Videotron threatened to pass on any fee directly to subscribers at an estimated average increase of $5 per bill. Rogers noted that consumers could see an increase in their bills of up to $8 per month if FFC was permitted (Lind, 2008). The only benefactors, BDUs argued, "would be the big broadcasting corporations themselves" (Smith, qtd. in CBC, 2008) because they could use the proceeds to either purchase more American programming or to pad the bottom line.

Rhetoric only intensified leading up to the October 2008 decision. In the press, cable companies argued that any imposed fee—a "TV tax"—would be an example of "robbing Peter to pay Paul" as it would divert revenues from commercial BDUs to commercial broadcasters (Lind, 2008). Broadcasters countered that BDUs "take broadcasters' signal, charge [consumers] for them, and pay [broadcasters] nothing" (Bell, 2008). In contrast, this period saw broadcasters appeal to the democratic importance of what was now being colloquially called "local television" (rather than "OTA" television). This would be the position of broadcasters from here on, in the press and in front of the regulator: Local news is vital to democracy and broadcasters need the added revenue to provide this democratic service. For them, "the future of local TV in Canada depends on it" (Sparkes, qtd. in Robertson, 2008b). As Paul Sparkes of CTVglobemedia editorialized: "Local newscasts do as much to forge the Canadian identity as any other form of story-telling, because after all, they chronicle our daily lives" (qtd. in Robertson, 2008b). The question put to CTV and all broadcasters by BDUs was whether they would reinvest any new profits into Canadian programming, or use them instead to purchase more American programming. One report noted that spending on foreign (re: American) programming rose from $603 million to $688 million between 2005 and 2006, whereas spending on Canadian programming fell by $36 million (Tillson, 2007). Added a respondent: "The challenge in which local broadcasting and therefore local news has faced over the past seven, eight years, is correlated very specifically to rising programming costs for American programming" (Anonymous, personal communication).

To say the hearings into the second consideration of FFC (which began on April 8, 2008) were intense is a gross understatement. Broadcasters squared off against BDUs, each claiming to have the best interests of Canadians at heart. After months of deliberation and rhetorical fights played out in hearing rooms and the press, the CRTC delivered its ruling on October 30, 2008. The Commission took pains to extoll the importance of local television—even calling it the "cornerstone of the Canadian broadcasting system" (2008b, par. 32). Despite such flattery, the ruling on FFC would come again at the dismay of broadcasters. The Commission noted that broadcasters needed to reevaluate their economic models, since "no business plans suggesting new sources of revenue were provided" (par. 332). While disheartening to broadcasters, this market-based rationale was consistent with the leitmotif of the ruling, which was based on "flexible regulation" and "industry solutions" rather than regulatory intervention. In an attempt to appease broadcasters, however, two new rulings were drafted. First, the CRTC granted permission for broadcasters to negotiate for the retransmission of their signals into distant markets. Second was the creation of a new subsidy program: the Local Programming Improvement Fund (LPIF) (see chapter 5). According to the vice-chair of the CRTC, the LPIF was a "tradeoff for value-for-signal retransmission consent fee.... We created [the fund] in part to help small markets ... to have the same quality of news gathering and information that Toronto has, for example" (T. Pentefountas, personal communication, 10/18/12). Despite the new subsidy, CTV announced it would cut 105 positions, while Canwest

Global eliminated 560 positions across its newspaper and broadcast holdings (Blackwell, 2008).

2009: CRISIS

With the LPIF in place and the CRTC emboldened by the recent *Diversity of Voices* (CRTC, 2008a) study, which concluded that the country had enough diversity in local editorial voices, one might assume 2009 would be a year of relevant tranquility. This could not be further from the truth, as it marked a year of station closures and the growing realization that local broadcasting was "broken" (Akin, 2009). Still, study after study concluded that local television remained a seminal component of Canadian media (Nordicity, 2008; Miller, 2009). As Nordicity (2008) found, "Broadcasters still recognize news as their best option to engage the local community, and as the most efficient vehicle among local programming options to generate local audiences, therefore ensuring some amount of local news diversity in each market" (p. 3). This did not change the fact that station revenues were stagnant, manifesting in a decrease of total news hours. As a result of the weak market and the added pressure of the global recession, CTV announced it would close stations in Windsor and Wingham, Ontario, in February 2009 (CTV would eventually save Windsor), and Canwest floated the idea of closing or selling stations in Victoria, Kelowna, Red Deer, Hamilton, and Montreal. CTV also cut newscasts at its second-tier /A\ Network (formerly "A-Channel") in March, resulting in the loss of 118 jobs. Broadcasters argued that the industry model was broken and fee-for-carriage was the only salvation to what the *Globe and Mail*'s Brian Laghi (2009) called a "sickness" in Canadian local television. For better or worse, broadcasters placed enormous faith in the market-based practices of FFC.

Rather than the normal seven-year license renewal for broadcasters, the CRTC granted temporary one-year licenses so it could comprehensively review the "deteriorating financial situation of conventional broadcasters" (2009a). Later in 2009, the Commission "harmonized" (re: decreased) local news requirements, with French-language broadcasters now required to produce five hours of original news programming per week, small-market English stations seven hours per week, and large-market stations fourteen hours per week (CRTC, 2009b). For the first time since 1999, broadcasters had actual quantitative benchmarks for local news, although these benchmarks were significantly lower than what was being produced. A third CRTC action to permit "group-based licensing" allowed the largest conglomerates to renew their OTA and cable networks simultaneously (CRTC, 2009b).

It was in the announcement for comments on this third regulatory action that the CRTC did an about-face regarding FFC, admitting that "a negotiated solution for compensation for the free market value of local conventional signals is also appropriate" (2009b, par. 37). After seven years, the Commission saw fee-for-carriage—or what was now being called "Value-for-signal" (VFS)—as an appropriate tool to assure sustainability in local broadcasting.[5] Bell Canada (owner of CTVglobemedia) immediately brought the issue to the Federal Court of Appeals, arguing it was not in the CRTC's power to permit VFS. As a result, the CRTC retracted its original statement, and instead simply stated that it was time "to consider whether or not a negotiated solution for the compensation for the fair value of local conventional television signals is also appropriate" (2009c). BDUs were clearly not giving up without a fight.

While the CRTC awaited comment from stakeholders on its proposal for group-based licensing (which concluded in 2010), three events irrevocably reshaped the debate. First, broadcasters and BDUs launched competing public campaigns regarding FFC/VFS. Second, an inquiry by the House of Commons into the future of local news was conducted. Third, an Order-in-Council by the federal government forced the CRTC to conduct public hearings on the feasibility of VFS. In the first instance, May 2009 saw the launch of the "Save Local TV" campaign from CTV and Global, complete with a Web site, station open houses, newspaper advertisements, and a YouTube video featuring "The Cable Song" sung by Canadian musician Dave Carroll (see introduction). Broadcasters strove to convince the public and the CRTC of the value of VFS. The campaign morphed into "Local TV Matters" in September 2009 when CTV and Global were joined by CBC, /A\, CHEK, V, and ntv. Local TV Matters lasted from September to November 2009 and signaled a clear rhetorical shift from "conventional" and "OTA" television to "local." In mobilizing a romanticized discourse of the local, broadcasters made efforts to stir public support by emphasizing the importance of local television for local news and Canadian democracy. Even the Commission and the press began to take on the more colloquial and much more loaded terminology of "local television" rather than its official moniker of OTA. Not to be left out, BDUs countered with their own campaign, "Stop the TV Tax," which lasted from October to December 2009. As can be imagined, the campaign framed VFS as a "tax" on consumers, arguing that "broadcasters are simply seeking more profit at the expense of consumers and that cable consumers already pay a fee in their bills for local programming" (Marlow, 2009). At their loftiest, these competing campaigns could be read as a battle between the public good of local news and the rights of consumers not to be overcharged. In reality, however, these campaigns represented a battle between opposing commercial giants wanting to curry regulatory favor and seek maximum profit. The campaigns rightly received the ire of the press. Viewers were "caught in the middle . . . bombarded with attack ads appealing to hometowns and pocketbooks" (Robertson, 2009a). Meanwhile, despite an increase in LPIF funding, three stations went dark: Wingham, Ontario (CTV), Brandon, Manitoba (CTV), and Red Deer, Alberta (Global). At the same time, Remstar, the new owners of Quebecois broadcaster TQS (which filed for bankruptcy in 2008), convinced the CRTC to dramatically lower its local news requirements. CTV also canceled newscasts in Victoria, London, and Barrie.

The battle between BDUs and broadcasters had the effect of drawing in the Canadian government on two separate occasions. First, the House of Commons launched its own hearings into local news in April 2009. Second, the government issued an Order-in-Council (OIC)[6] in October 2009, requiring the CRTC to launch public hearings and deliver a report on the viability of VFS. The government stood strongly opposed to any consideration of VFS, and directed the CRTC to only examine its impact on *consumers* rather than the industry as a whole (CRTC, 2009d). The CRTC's report was presented to the House of Commons in March 2010, with the Commission having received more than 190,000 public comments (CRTC, 2010a). The CRTC recommended the start of negotiations for value-for-signal, but not without hesitation. Explaining its equivocation, the Commission noted that while not immune to the recession, French-language private television continued to fare better than its English-language counterpart, which saw a decreased profit before interest and tax (PBIT) from a profit of 11.7 percent in 2005 to a loss of 9.1 percent in 2009. In contrast, Francophone broadcasters saw a PBIT decline from 13 percent in 2005 to 10.4 percent in 2009. Justifying VFS, the CRTC noted a recurring trend of regionalization in the production of local news. Examples of regional centers include CTV's Northern Ontario service out of Sudbury, a regional station that now serves an area larger than Texas. It was hoped that newly emergent hyperlocal stations such as CHCH in Hamilton and CHEK in Victoria would be popular replacements for these regionalized entities. Added Commissioner Tom Pentenfountas:

> I think there's always going to be a need for local. . . . And the international player can't compete with local, right? But I think there's a way of doing it without consumer money or government money backing that cost up, if you do it right. CHCH and CHEK are examples and I think there may be more

examples. There may be some of the network players that decide that, "you know, it's not worth it for me in this particular market." And I think that's going to actually offer opportunity for local expression because I think there will be a local player that could pick it up. (personal communication, 10/18/12)

To be sure, CHCH and CHEK represent anomalies as locally owned and community-focused *commercial* stations. Juxtaposing them with CTV's regional station in Sudbury illustrates just how much the larger epistemological tensions between localism, regionalism, and nationalism that permeate Canadian identity have carried over to the debate over value-for-signal.

The House of Commons Standing Committee on Canadian Heritage held its own hearings on local news in the spring of 2009 (Canada, 2009a). Its findings echoed many of those of the CRTC during the Order-in-Council proceedings. The House hearings, moreover, represent an excellent opportunity to investigate how the discourse of the local is mobilized by different actors. Themes in the hearings included the role of community television (which is owned and operated by cable BDUs) in filling the local news gap left by commercial broadcasters, the contentious definition of the local, and the role of Aboriginal and Francophone stations in producing local content.

Regarding definitions, witness testimony demonstrates the ambiguous characteristics of localism that occur when left ill-considered by the CRTC. Shaw, Rogers, and Cogeco (all cable BDUs), for instance, referred to their community channels as "local stations," while Quebec-based TQS defined "local" as anything produced outside the city of Montreal. A second consideration was whether Francophone stations could be considered local on the basis that they provide service to an ethno-linguistic *community*. Extending this further was the question of whether for the purposes of regulation, Quebec was to be designated a province, region, or locality. Aboriginal broadcasters, notably the Aboriginal People's Television Network (APTN) and Northern Native Broadcasting, also referred to themselves as "local broadcasters." As Jean LaRose, CEO of APTN, testified: "Our northern service is the most differentiated of our regional feeds. . . . Usually this programming is in Inuktitut or other aboriginal languages spoken in northern communities. This is a different way of looking at local programming. Programming that reflects Nunavut and Nunavik is local, from our point of view, even though the communities it serves are spread out over a region that represents a large percentage of Canada's land mass" (Canada, 2009b, p. 20). Stakeholders thus mobilize the language of localism when it suits their purpose. Arguably, assuming the mantle of "local" in this capacity was meant to rhetorically support Aboriginal broadcasters' petition for LPIF eligibility (see chapter 5). This demonstrates both the contextuality and the subjectivity of the discourse of localism in that it can be employed to suit the contexts and interests of whoever is speaking. It proved to be a successful tactic, as the House recommended that both Aboriginal and Francophone broadcasters be given access to the LPIF.

2010–2011: DECISIONS AND CONSOLIDATIONS

If 2008 was a year of neglect and 2009 a year of crisis, then 2010 represented a year of action. It began in March when the Commission released its determinations regarding group-based licensing. Here, the Commission continued its rhetorical support for localism by recommitting itself to the LPIF and supporting value-for-signal. The proposed VFS regime would mimic American retransmission consent, where broadcasters could choose whether to negotiate with BDUs for compensation *or* take advantage of the regulatory protections already in place, such as mandatory carriage, priority channel placement, and simultaneous substitution. While on first glance this may seem a victory for broadcasters, the CRTC backtracked at the last moment and asked the Federal Court of Appeals to determine whether it had jurisdiction to implement VFS. The court ruled in favor of the CRTC, but BDUs immediately appealed, leaving the ultimate decision to the Supreme Court of Canada.

While stakeholders anxiously awaited the Supreme Court decision, changes once again rocked the industry. These included the bankruptcy of Canwest Global and the sale of Canwest's broadcasting and specialty holdings to Shaw Communications. BCE meanwhile was given clearance by both the CRTC and the Competition Bureau to purchase its remaining stake in CTV. In return for these multibillion-dollar transactions, both of the new companies, "Bell Media" and "Shaw Media," pledged to increase local news, particularly in morning shows. These mergers resulted in the total vertical integration of Canadian media, where the four largest telecom providers (Rogers, Bell, Shaw, Quebecor) now owned the country's four largest commercial broadcasters (Citytv, CTV, Global, TVA).[7]

By the time the Supreme Court ruled against VFS in December 2012, the landscape of Canadian broadcasting had changed so much that the decision was effectively moot. The Court found that the CRTC did not have jurisdiction to implement VFS through powers allocated to it in the Broadcasting Act because VFS would directly contravene provisions in the Copyright Act by granting broadcasters the right to authorize retransmission of content, where no such right exists (Canada, 2012). Despite the Court's decision having little bearing anymore, the ruling still provoked the ire of BDUs/Broadcasters, who once again threatened to close stations.[8] A disappointing outcome of these protracted battles, therefore, is that localism has become an object of "regulatory ransom" for Canadian cable providers.

United Kingdom: The Localness of Public Service Broadcasting

When compared with the United States and Canada, the broadcasting system in the UK is both overly complex and inefficient for the delivery of localized content. Indeed, the system is based on *regions* covering large geographic areas, rather than city-based services. This derives from the construction of the ITV system in the 1950s, wherein regions were determined by the convenience of transmitters rather than consideration for cultural or community affiliation (Johnson & Turnock, 2005). When Ofcom was created in 2003, the structure of terrestrial broadcasting looked as such: BBC One (eighteen nations/regions); BBC Two (UK); ITV (fourteen regions); Channel 4 (UK); S4C (Wales); and 5 (UK). ITV is the main focus of media localism, as it is the only broadcaster mandated to provide regional content. Note already here the slippage between "local" and "regional." This will be a major discursive trend within Ofcom's commentary on what is called "nations and regions" within the UK broadcasting system. While "nations" refer to the devolved countries of Scotland, Wales, and Northern Ireland, "region" has come to mean anything from a "nation" to a large geographic area, like those covered by the ITV affiliates (e.g., "Anglia"). This confusion makes unpacking the UK regional broadcasting system exceptionally complex (Johnson & Turnock, 2005).

From 2009 to 2013, there were (and still are) fourteen ITV licensed regions, which provided news for thirteen regions and short news segments for thirteen subregions (see table 2.3). While regional makeup has remained consistent, the news areas have shifted dramatically. In 2009, for instance, ITV merged several of its newscasts in England to maximize efficiency and economies of scope and scale. Where it once produced seventeen individual newscasts it was now reduced to nine, with short opt-outs for sub-regions (Fitzsimmons, 2009). In the process it also expanded the geographic footprints of these news regions, which, coupled with ITV's desire to reduce regional news quotas, translated into less localized news.

Table 2.3: ITV Franchises and News Regions (2009–2013)[a]

Franchise Region	Geographic Area	Sub-Regions	Owner
Anglia	East England	Anglia East Anglia West	ITV plc.
Border	England/Scotland border and Northwest England	Border Tyne Tees	ITV plc.
London[b]	London	—	ITV plc.
Central	East, West, and South Midlands	Central East Central West	ITV plc.
Channel[c]	Channel Islands	—	Channel Television
Northern Scotland	Northern Scotland	—	STV
Granada	Northwest England and the Isle of Man	—	ITV plc
Wales[d]	Wales	Wales	ITV plc.
Meridian	South and Southeast England	Meridian East Meridian South	ITV plc.
Central Scotland	Central Scotland	—	STV
Tyne Tees[e]	North-East England	—	ITV plc.
Ulster	Northern Ireland	—	UTV[f]
West Country	West England	West Westcountry	ITV plc.
Yorkshire	Yorkshire and Lincolnshire	North South	ITV plc.
ITV Breakfast	National Breakfast Time Broadcasting	—	ITV plc./ Disney
ITN	National news provider	—	ITV plc.

a. In 2013 ITV radically restructured its news-gathering operations to focus more on local content. The most dramatic change was the separation of Tyne Tees and Borders into once again separate news regions and the inclusion of an opt-out segment for Scottish news on ITV Borders (Ofcom, 2013c).
b. The London license is divided between weekday and weekend franchises. Both are owned by ITV Plc.
c. In 2013, ITV plc. purchased the Channel franchise from Channel Television.
d. In 2013, the region known as "Wales and West" was separated. Wales become its own license area and "West" merged with Westcountry to become "West Country" (Ofcom, 2013c).
e. In 2009 Border and Tyne Tees were merged into a single region for news (Fitzsimmons, 2009).
f. In October 2015 ITV plc. announced that it would acquire UTV (ITV, 2015).
Sources: ITV 2013; Fitzsimmons, 2009.

As newly minted regulator, one of Ofcom's first projects was to conduct a series of inquiries into the state of public service broadcasting in the UK, particularly with regard to the crisis of local news. Ofcom's first public service broadcasting review took place in 2004–2005 and consisted of three phases. The second "Public Service Broadcasting Review" ("PSB review") took place in 2007–2009 and also consisted of three phases and reports. This section investigates these reviews as vehicles for regulatory intervention into media localism in the UK.

2004–2005: THE FIRST PSB REVIEW

Ofcom was well aware of ITV's precarious position when it conducted its first PSB review in 2004 (Ofcom, 2004a). One of its primary areas of focus therefore was regionalism within the PSB system. The first phase, released in the spring of 2004, was intended to better understand the framework of the PSB system, and provide a direction for following reports. The first report focused heavily on regional production outside London. Ofcom observed not only the dearth of regional programming, but also the specific lack of *local* news. Still, Ofcom noted that the primary PSB goal of ITV should be to focus on *regional* news and UK productions. At the time, ITV had a quota to air five hours and thirty minutes of regional news per week (per region), along with twenty-six minutes per week of regional current affairs programming, and two hours and thirty-four minutes of other regional programming. The importance of the terrestrial channels in the UK cannot be overstated with "over 85% of viewers in multichannel homes still watch[ing] something on one of these channels every night" (p. 43). Despite some decline, terrestrial PSB channels remained incredibly popular at the dawn of the twenty-first century, so much so that Ofcom favored public intervention over deregulation championed by ITV. For instance, it suggested that PSB possess qualities of a *merit good* whereby "individuals themselves can get more value from a programme, for example, in terms of news and information than they realize" (p. 72). An approach based purely on market fundamentalism would not permit such positive externalities because viewers do not always "appreciate that value [and therefore] would not necessarily choose to pay for such a programme in an open market" (p. 72).

Phase Two was released in September 2004 following a consultation period after Phase One (Ofcom, 2004b). Commentators focused primarily on the importance of regional news to viewers and the value of regional plurality. This echoes the normative role of local news in a democracy—solidarity, integration, and deliberation. In Wales, though, concern was for national Welsh content rather than geographically localized content, suggesting an important bridge between localism and language. Another point was that the BBC should be more involved in the production of news content for what had come to be called "the nations and regions." Inspired by these regional concerns, Phase Two was dedicated to understanding television specifically in the nations, regions, and *localities* (e.g., Scotland, Anglia, Manchester). The report contained three primary themes: regional production and the lack of localized news; a belief that digital technologies will improve localization; and the role of minority language programming in the devolved nations.

In the first instance, Ofcom agreed that the geographic framework of the ITV network was based on "an artificial construct, dictated by the 1950s TV transmission map." As a result, ITV regions in England were bloated. The Meridian region, for instance, is twice the size of Denmark (p. 50). Viewers understandably critiqued ITV "for being insufficiently local" (p. 5). Local identification was deemed a defining feature of quotidian life in the UK, echoed by the finding that "people's attachment is greatest to their own neighbourhood, the settlement they live in (village, town, or city), or to the nation as a whole, and that regional attachments, while present, are relatively weak" (p. 49). This poses serious problems for a system based on regionalism. The drive toward more local programming was also complicated by the observation that more needed to be done to promote minority languages (Welsh, Gaelic, Irish, Ulster Scots), along with greater sensitivity to programming in the devolved nations, where viewers tend to prefer programming reflective of their nations. Parallels can be observed here between the devolved nations of the UK and their respective minority languages (e.g., Wales/Welsh) and the Canadian province of Quebec, where rhetorical slippage occurs between national, regional, local, and community programming. Should Welsh-language programming, for instance, fulfill national, regional, local, or community mandates? Intuitively, we may assume that in this context local means both the language community of Welsh and the political entity of Wales, but its regulatory definition is unclear.

Acknowledging that localities often comprise disparate communities brought together under a single geographic unit, Ofcom sought comment on "what geographical units would make most sense ... if we were starting to develop regional programming from scratch?" (p. 48). Local OTA television was brought up as a potential solution, particularly given the extent to which viewers are attached to their neighborhoods. Ofcom, however, noted the challenges of local television in the UK, specifically the technological deficiencies of analogue broadcasting and the lack of sustainable business models. There is a discrepancy between the failure of localized television services to garner market support and the desire among UK residents for these services, wherein "60 percent want more TV made specifically for and about their regions [and] over 30 percent disagree with the view that there are enough regional programmes in the schedule already" (p. 33). Digital media, it was believed, held the potential to rectify this paucity: "[Local digital and broadband services] could meet audience demand for more local news services. But they could also play a wider role than this in building well informed and cohesive communities, enabling participation in local decision-making, stimulating interest and involvement in local issues and supporting local entertainment" (p. 54). Ofcom thus placed great faith in the development of digital technologies to rectify the market and regulatory failures of local terrestrial broadcasting.

Capitalizing on this digital utopianism, Phase Three proposed the development of a multimedia Public Service Publisher (PSP) dedicated to local content (Ofcom, 2005). This was the first of many proposals to correct the market failure of local media. The "PSP," as it came to be known, would have a remit to deliver local content through broadband Internet (such as online video streaming). This was again in recognition of the fact that "geographic communities and identities are still vitally important in the UK, despite growing social mobility and diversity" (p. 14). While Ofcom continued to see ITV as an important purveyor of local news and encouraged increased participation of the BBC, it also clearly recognized the need to move beyond these incumbent services and embrace digital broadband technologies.

2008–2009: THE SECOND PSB REVIEW

It was in the spirit of what we might call digital localism and certainly of digital utopianism that Ofcom launched its second PSB review in 2008, this time with a focus on multiplatform delivery (Ofcom, 2008a). Regionalism was again high on the list of priorities, particularly with respect to ITV. ITV argued that the benefits of being a public service broadcaster would be outweighed by the expenses by 2012. In other words, its expenditures on mandated programming (such as regional news) would no longer be offset by the benefits of being a PSB—such as preferred channel placement on cable and satellite. Ofcom conceded that this would be the case for ITV in Wales and STV in Scotland in 2009/2010. Ofcom's biggest fear was that ITV would hand back its PSB licenses and abandon regional television altogether.

As a result of this fear, Ofcom entertained propositions by ITV to lower its regional commitments for news and non-news programming. ITV also proposed to merge regions to save on production costs. Specifically, the network proposed merging the regions of Border and Tyne Tees (northwest England and southern Scotland), and West and Westcounty (west and southwest England). It also wanted to phase out subregional news such as Yorkshire north and south.[9] In essence, ITV wanted to dissociate itself from news provision other than in the largest regional groupings. Ofcom denied the latter request, but reached a compromise with ITV that would be published in the second and third phases of the second PSB review. That it would concede to requests from ITV demonstrates the degree to which Ofcom was desperate to continue having ITV produce some form of regional news.

As we know, Ofcom placed great faith in the abilities of digital media to solve these regional failures and to introduce a local element into the UK media ecosystem. It hailed the Internet as a space for hyperlocal (or the unfortunately labeled "ultralocal") Web sites, which "provide citizen journalism and a forum for local discussion at a level of geographic and community granularity which is impossible for TV, and currently uneconomic for the printed press" (2008a, p. 58). Two outstanding issues, however, curtail this optimism. First, the potential withdrawal of ITV from regional news would be a severe blow to any attempts at sustainable local news in the interim period before suitable online vehicles are developed. Second, the blurred discursive boundaries between local and regional make it extraordinarily difficult to develop any form of coherent local media policy: "The distinction between regional and local is to some extent blurred. One person's 'local' is their street or immediate community (something that has been described as 'ultra local' in some quarters), whereas others see 'local' as applying to their town or city (as per local TV station Channel M in Manchester) or indeed to their county (as is largely the case in the BBC's local radio map). And perceptions of localness in metropolitan areas may be very different from those in more rural locations" (Ofcom, 2008a, p. 125).

A concurring report by research firm Essential Research (2008) noted the instinctive feeling that viewers possess in defining what is "local," but "defining 'the region' was less clear-cut for most and generally involved rationalization, rather than instinctive reaction. Many commented that the distinction between 'local' and 'regional' was an arbitrary one" (p. 12). These reactions parallel Ofcom's own troubles in delineating between these two terms. Oddly, despite the very real concerns over social groupings, community definitions, technological changes, and corporate concentration, Ofcom perceived the regional/local dilemma as a short-term problem, placing great faith in the digital to solve any and all challenges and issues. Acknowledging, for instance, that regional news fell into the "very unprofitable" category for incumbent PSBs, Ofcom held out tremendous hope for the creation of a commercial market for local online content, asserting the "great potential for broadband delivery of local content services" (2008a, p. 82) and encouraging the "consideration of other forms of public service content" for national and regional content, particularly when it comes to indigenous languages (p. 80).

Phase two of Ofcom's second review picked up on this market and regulatory failure, and addressed the challenges of ITV (Ofcom, 2008b). Consistent with neoliberal rhetoric, Ofcom agreed with ITV that the conglomerate should be permitted to "*rationalise* its regional news delivery in England and the Scottish Border" and thus approved a series of regional mergers that would see seventeen separate news programs reduced to nine (2008b, par. 1.52). This was complemented by a suggested relaxation of the minimum number of hours of regional news, from 5.20 hours per week to 3 hours and 45 minutes a week. Ofcom also allowed ITV to "hub" certain regional newscasts, permitting two different newscasts for two different regions to be produced in the same location, therein decreasing ITV's local presence even further. Through the tactic of regulatory ransom of threatening to hand back its PSB remit, ITV succeeded in reducing its commitment to regionalism. As we might expect, there was significant public resistance to the proposed mergers, particularly the amalgamation of the Borders and Tyne Tees regions. A palpable concern was the elimination of the popular Cumbria-based newscast *Lookaround* in the Border region. A campaign was organized to "Save Lookaround," which convinced ITV to continue to produce the show, albeit in an abridged format.

The third and final phase of the second PSB review found Ofcom acquiesce to ITV's planned reduction to its regional commitments, with Ofcom granting the following:

- Merge news regions in England, southern Scotland, and Wales
- Reduce the volume of regional news requirement to 4 hours per week
- Reduce the quota for non-news in England to 15 minutes per week
- Reduce the quota for non-news in Wales and Scotland to 1.5 hours per week and two hours per week in Northern Ireland (2009b, p. 79)

Ofcom also agreed to permit a regional news-sharing partnership between ITV and the BBC to further reduce ITV regional production. In sum, it agreed to all of ITV's deregulatory demands. Despite an acknowledgment that something needed to be done to bolster localism in the media system (see chapter 5), the conclusion of the review saw Ofcom backtrack by simply stating that more work was needed.

Conclusion: Default Localism

What can we make of Ofcom's actions over the past decade in conversation with those of the FCC and CRTC? Three themes immediately become apparent in such a comparison. The first is the mobilization of the romance of the local. Regulators and commenters alike enjoy referencing the local and marshaling it out as something that should be saved and protected. "Save Local TV" and "Save *Lookaround*" are two excellent examples. Seldom, however, do we ask ourselves what exactly is in need of saving. Is it local television as a business, local newscasts as a genre, or localism as a normative idea? Is it a combination of all three? Furthermore, are we speaking solely of communities of place, or do communities of interest and ethno-linguistic communities factor in as well? Regulators seem to be focused on the first in this list, but mobilize the latter two to justify policies—both regulatory and deregulatory. What we are constantly told, however, is that the local is unquestionably a good thing, requiring both protection and attention—a taken-for-granted assumption that is never challenged and seldom explained.

The second theme is the tension between the public good and the market interest (disguised within the discourse of the public interest). This draws again on the dichotomy of normativity and neoliberalism. Should regulation be focused on enhancing local voices or bolstering local business? Or should it be focused on both? For the past few decades, the emphasis has been on ensuring profitability for incumbent media companies. As the examples of Canadian BDUs and UK-based ITV demonstrate, media conglomerates have not been shy to wield their enormous capabilities to hold regulators and the public at ransom: "give us what we want or we will close local stations." Localism, after all, is "an expensive value." This is a new type of regulatory capture that I have dubbed regulatory ransom. Though cities like Toronto, London, or Boston might not suffer greatly if one of their many local news outlets is closed, these are not the cities whose local media ecosystems are at risk. Instead, it is the smaller markets—Red Deer and Cumbria—that suffer most when big media companies threaten to close local stations.

Thinking about the romance of the local and the tension between the public good and the market interest in concert, we see a clear trend of default localism, where the local is invoked but seldom explicated, and if defined it is immediately equated with a commercial market. This discursive trend feeds into the development of a political economy of localism, one where default localism serves to mask alternatives such as organizing local stations by local communities, or ensuring local news and language programming, and set the parameters for acceptable discourse. Recall the FCC limiting discussion of localism in their 2010 regulatory review solely to issues of ownership. The question we need to ask ourselves at this point is what alternatives already exist within the framework of domestic media systems that may stem the tide of the evacuation of localism? The next chapter investigates this question through an assessment of community media and its heretofore-unacknowledged contribution to media localism.

3

The Communities of Localism
Community Television in the Digital Age

> Small is still beautiful, and we need to continually establish ways to theorise and analyse how the local interacts with its boundaries and contexts.
> —Carpentier, 2008

"Listen to the Sounds of Winnipeg"

In January 1975, the inaugural issue of *Access: Winnipeg's Public Access Television Newsletter* was released. Its publisher, VPW (Videon, Public Access, West of the Red River) had already been on the air as a public-access cable television channel in Winnipeg, Canada, for three years, producing upward of fifty hours of local programming per week. The goal of the newsletter was to get the word out about community television. Said then–program manager Dorthi Dunsmore in the first issue: "Public Access Television is an open invitation to people to tell their own stories in their own ways.... If you wish to join us in front of your television set or in front of our cameras, you are very welcome" (Videon, 1975, p. 1). Ten years later, Winnipegger Guy Maddin was one of the people to join VPW and tell his story in his talk show, *Survival!* Maddin would go on to become one of Canada's most celebrated independent directors.[1]

Much has changed in the world of community television in the forty years since the publication of *Access*. What was then seen as an important, if not quaint, vehicle "to enrich community life by fostering communication among individuals and community groups" now seems anachronistic in the age of social media (CRTC qtd. in Videon, 1975, p. 1). Nevertheless, community media remain the most local of any local media, and are seminal components of local media ecosystems. They exist, however, on the periphery of media regulation and conversations of media localism. Community media also struggle to compete in an era of user-generated content: if anyone with a smart phone is technologically capable of making media, I asked elsewhere (Ali, 2012b), is there still a need for community media?

Supporters have been quick to rebut accusations of obsolescence, arguing that community media foster a sense of place by providing a physical location for gathering, learning, and production (Howley, 2005). Over the past decade, for instance, community television stations have rebranded themselves as multimedia community media centers. These community media centers have expanded their original mandates from the basics of television production to include everything from citizen journalism to digital media literacy skills, high-speed Internet access for community residents, resumé construction, computer training, and in some cases even radio and theater production (Breitbart et al., 2010; Fuentes-Bautista, 2009). They have assumed the roles and responsibilities previously occupied by commercial media outlets (e.g., local news) and traditional community centers (e.g., computer and job training), particularly in low-income areas and urban centers. In sum, while existing in a world of digital media tools, the crisis of journalism, and a widening digital divide, community media contribute to community, localism, and place through the use of "old" and "new" media (Ali, 2014).

Regulators in the United States, the UK, and Canada have been slow to assess community media, particularly community television, which falls under their jurisdiction. This neglect denies regulators the opportunity to learn from the discourses and experiences of community media. The primary aim of this chapter, then, is to recover community media's place within the local media ecosystem. Regulators need to pay more attention to the dynamic practices that are occurring under the heading of "community media" and "community television."[2] Community media need to be fully integrated into a holistic conceptualization of local media among policymakers, regulators, and local media stakeholders. A second goal of this chapter is to demonstrate that it is within conversations about, and discourses of, community media where epistemological issues of the local and its relationship to local media become most pronounced. We get a better picture of what it means to be local in the digital age by listening to the experiences of community media producers and organizations. Inspired by critical regionalism's search for alternatives to the status quo, I demonstrate how it is in these conversations where the local is questioned and alternatives voiced.

Community media is a contentious term, equated and contrasted in equal measure with other forms of media production such as "alternative media" (Atton, 2002) "citizens' media" (Rodriguez, 2001), "radical media" (Downing, 2001), and "participatory media" (see Rennie, 2006). Regardless of label, the basic tenet of community media is that it is produced "of, by and for" members of a community, rather than by professional media makers. Nossek (2003) highlights three fundamental characteristics of community media: participation, access, and self-management. To this, some scholars have noted that community media's attachment to geographic communities, rather than communities of interest, is also a defining hallmark. Howley (2005) brings these two threads into conversation in his definition of community media: "Grassroots or locally oriented media access initiatives predicated on a profound sense of dissatisfaction with mainstream media form and content, dedicated to the principles of free expression and participatory democracy, and committed to enhancing community relations and promoting community solidarity" (p. 2). Community television, or as it is also known, public access television, falls under this larger umbrella of community media. The bulk of community programming in North America is delivered through cable systems (meaning one needs a cable subscription to watch the programs) and is predicated upon the ideas of public access and participation.

Canada has the longest historical engagement with community television, but recent decades have seen increased neglect by the Canadian Radio-television and Telecommunications Commission (CRTC). Still, of the countries that comprise this book, only Canada has a dedicated community media policy. This policy was revisited in 2002 and again in 2010, and is slated for review in the winter of 2016. The Canadian section of this chapter investigates the 2002 and 2010 community media policies, along with debates about community media in the House of Commons. American community television, or as it is officially designated, Public, Educational, and Governmental ("PEG") access television, is similarly neglected by policymakers. Given that the United States does not have a distinct set of community television policies, this section looks at events. More specifically, I assess statewide franchising, cable franchise regulations, and a dispute between PEG, AT&T, and Comcast. The UK case departs from its North American counterparts most notably because community television is not fully realized. This is not to say, however, that community media is nonexistent. To the contrary, community radio has been a success story. Hyperlocal media, particularly Web sites dedicated to local news (e.g., *Kings Cross Environment*) and civic needs (e.g., Stoke-on-Trent's *Pits 'n Pots*) have also grown dramatically (Radcliffe, 2012). The UK section of this chapter thus spends more space discussing these radio and online practices rather than television.

In recalling the regulatory events that shaped community television from 2000 to 2012, I illustrate how Canadian community channels are filling the voids left by local stations, how American PEG stations are facilitating new digital skills sets, and how British community radio and hyperlocal spaces are bridging the discursive and experiential divides between communities of place and interest. It is in the discourse of community media where the boundaries of what it means to be local are pushed and alternatives to the status quo offered. Consequently, community media embody the moments of critical regionalism described in the introduction. There we learned that critical regionalism is a theory that encourages us to think beyond geography when contemplating the local. It is in this search for alternatives where we learn to treat the local holistically as both a place-based *and* socially constructed site. Community media embody this foundation. Their incorporation into formal conversations about media localism at the regulatory level can only serve to strengthen our knowledge of local media ecosystems.

Canada: Community's Recovery

Canada is the birthplace of community television, dating back to the 1960s and the National Film Board's *Challenge for Change* program. The world's first community television center also opened (briefly) in Thunder Bay, Ontario, in 1970 (Howley, 2005). In Canada and the United States, community television is distributed primarily on cable, with an understanding that cable distributors should contribute to local programming. The CRTC's 1971 community television policy statement encouraged cable companies to provide for a "locally programmed channel" based on the belief "that a diversity of local programming best reflects community needs and interests" (p. 16). It subsequently received a huge boost of recognition in 1991 when "community" was recognized as one of three pillars of broadcasting in the *Broadcasting Act* (along with private broadcasting and public broadcasting) (Canada, 1991, §3[1][b]).

The community channel itself is based on programming produced by members of the public ("public access"). As the Commission noted in 1990, "The community channel has been described as the electronic equivalent to neighbours talking over their backyard fence" (CRTC, 1990, sec. 6). Until 1991, the carriage of a community channel was mandatory for all cable systems. That year, the CRTC relieved the smallest cable systems ("Class 2"—fewer than two thousand subscribers) of this requirement, and in 1997 made the carriage of community channels entirely optional. Public access would also be optional, and most cable companies ended up not only financing the channels, but also running them as de facto local stations using professionals rather than community members. Under current regulations, cable providers must contribute 5 percent of their gross revenues to support Canadian productions, and for the largest cable broadcast distribution undertakings (BDUs), up to 2 percent of these contributions can be directed toward "local expression" (e.g., local programming) through the funding of a community channel (CRTC, 2010b). This means that community channels are wholly dependent upon cable companies for channel placement, staffing, and funding.

2000–2002: A NEW MILLENNIUM, A NEW POLICY

After the deregulation of BDUs in the late 1990s, community television effectively collapsed. The Canadian Association of Community Television Users and Stations (CACTUS)—the de facto association for English-language community television—reported that since 1993, thirteen community channels had closed in New Brunswick alone (CACTUS, 2010). Recognizing the impact that deregulation and corporate consolidation was having, the CRTC announced plans in 2000 to revisit its community television policies for the first time since 1987.

To undertake this review, the Commission joined two separate policy frameworks—community television and low-power television—into a single proposed "policy framework for community-based media."[3] It is here where for the first and only time the Commission inquired into the nature of "community" in Canadian media and society:

> As a result of consolidation, the service areas of many cable systems are growing larger. These often include many distinct "communities" within the larger area.... The Commission seeks comment on the following:
> (1) How should the Commission define "community" with respect to the community channel—only in geographic terms, or also in terms of ethnicity, culture and language?
> (2) In the case of large cable systems, is there a valuable role in serving a broad regional "community"? If so, how can the reflection of smaller localities within the region be assured? (2001a, para. 22)

The first question considers the existence of community of interest *within* communities of place, thereby acknowledging the many social layers of a geographic locality. The second question of regionalization parallels an American debate over the issue of statewide franchising (see below). In essence, the Commission asked whether community television channels, which had traditionally served narrowly tailored geographical places, should be required to serve an area as large as a province because their cable company parents desire a larger geographical footprint. If so, what would this mean for the regulatory definition of community? Would it have to become expanded to include communities of interest? While these questions ultimately went unanswered, their existence within an official docket suggests a more considered approach to the challenges of localism and community.

This early document sought comments on the proposal of an integrated community media policy, and a later 2001 document outlined the proposed plan. The Commission emphasized the role that public access should have at community media outlets, and asked whether satellite distributors should be licensed to carry their own community channels based on communities of interest rather than geography (CRTC, 2001b). The CRTC reiterated that the main goals of the community channel remained consistent with previous community channel policies, chief among them: citizen participation and public access, training, advisory boards, viewpoint diversity, reflection of the ethno-linguistic groups in the community, and the coverage of local events. Underscoring the desire to increase the quality and quantity of local programming on community channels, an important step was to remove the ambiguity as to what actually constituted a "local program." This was necessary given that at least 60 percent of a community channel's programming lineup had to consist of local programming. To clear up any confusion, the CRTC defined "local community programming" as: "... programming that is reflective of the community, and produced by the licensee in the licensed service area or by members of the community in the licensed service area. Programs produced in other licensed areas within the same municipality will also be considered local programming" (par. 50). While applying only to community channels, this was the first time that the Commission defined a local program (for either community or conventional television) and clearly based its decision on geographically licensed areas.

Within a year, the CRTC released its final policy framework for community-based media, reifying many of the proposals from 2000 and 2001 (CRTC, 2002). The Commission recognized the paucity of both local programming and community-produced programming (as opposed to programming produced by the staff of the cable company). As such, it retained the 60 percent minimum of local programming and mandated a minimum of 30 percent of programming time be devoted to "access programs" (programs produced by the public). There was a concerted effort to ensure that community channels served a geographic area smaller than a region (e.g., central Saskatchewan) along with a recognition that these channels would *complement* rather than *compete with* commercial over-the-air (OTA) stations. A third decision was to treat community channels in Montreal, Toronto, and Vancouver differently from other localities. Community channels in these cities would have to demonstrate "their plans and commitments at license renewal time as to how they will reflect the various communities within their licensed areas in these urban centres" (para. 39). Unlike smaller cities or towns, Toronto, Montreal, and Vancouver were thought to have a greater number of communities within their territorial borders that should be served by community stations. The Commission therefore codified the heterogeneous composition of these largest Canadian cities, but neglected to do so for the rest of Canada. The smaller the community, according to the CRTC, the more homogeneous the programming could be—a pronounced illustration of default localism and a striking contrast to critical regionalism. Recall that critical regionalism reminds us to take a holistic approach to places, rather than rely on taken-for-granted assumptions of how a community should be comprised and the media required to serve a community's informational and communicatory needs.

One explanation for the failure to recognize diversity in non-metropolitan areas is the lack of empirical data on Canadian local media ecosystems, including community television (see CACTUS, 2010). The 2008 *Diversity of Voices* (CRTC, 2008a) proceeding, for instance, cataloged only professional "voices" (including community television) and did not account for online hyperlocal media. It also did not assess the dynamics *between* media outlets. If we believe Friedland's (2001) argument that community solidarity, deliberation, and civic engagement are related to the strength of a community's communicative integration, then this dearth of knowledge has important consequences. For instance, it is difficult to determine broadcast minimums for local newscasts without knowing which organizations and platforms are already providing local news.

2002–2009: DILUTED POLICIES, DISCURSIVE AGENDAS

Any concern for small communities dissolved in the following years, as more and more cable companies sought regional licenses and amended commitments to their individual community channels. For instance, the Commission approved a series of requests by cable companies to operate video-on-demand community channels, rather than formal studios and stations.[4] Winnipeg-based MTS Allstream asked that its financial contributions toward "local expression" be directed toward a video-on-demand service it called *Winnipeg on Demand*. MTS also pledged to "encourage participation of Francophone, Aboriginal and cultural community groups" and "promote community access to its outlet" (CRTC, 2007c, par. 8). An unacknowledged problem is that this form of "localism on demand" disembodies the practice of community media, because it eliminates the need for a community media center (Ali, 2012b). While it may be more efficient for the cable service, it dilutes one of the founding principles of community media—the bringing together of citizens in the practice of media production.

Paralleling these regulatory requests were discursive arguments brought by cable companies as part of their ongoing dispute with broadcasters. This came to a head in the 2009 House of Commons inquiry into local television (see chapter 2). Here cable companies mobilized the charged rhetoric of "the local" to argue that their community channels effectively served as replacements, not complements, to local stations operated by private broadcasters and the CBC. Cable companies such as Rogers, Shaw, and Cogeco vehemently expressed their community commitments through the running and programming of the community channel. Commented Rogers: "Community broadcasting paid for by cable companies is quickly becoming the most respected source of truly local television in Canada. At a cost of $30 million a year, Rogers' 33 television stations offer far more local programming than commercial over-the-air stations anywhere" (Canada, 2009c, p. 2). Shaw argued that "the government and the CRTC must fully embrace the potential of community channels to provide diversity of voices through local news and local programming that reaches various geographic, cultural and linguistic communities" (Canada, 2009d, p. 13). Cogeco added that its community channel in North Bay, Ontario, increased its local news programming to fill the gap left by the departure of a local commercial station.

Four issues are present in this conflation of community and local television. First, there is a clear push by cable companies to emphasize their commitments to community programming and to have it included in discussions of localism. One hypothesis for this strategy is that BDUs wanted to position the community channel as a replacement for the conventional local channel, and thereby dilute broadcaster claims for fee-for-carriage (see chapter 2). The second issue is the political-economic concerns of this discourse. Cable companies attested to the value of their channels to Canadian communities, while at the same time asking that their community channels have access to local advertising markets (which is restricted). This would further render community channels de facto local channels. One even argued for "a dedicated local community and access programming fund" (Gauthier qtd. in Canada, 2009b, p. 13).

There are two sides to this coin, however, because public interest advocates—such as Michael Lithgow of CACTUS—argued that the Local Programming Improvement Fund (LPIF—see chapter 5) should be expanded to include community media (under the condition that community channels are no longer controlled by cable companies). It must be remembered that *community* broadcasting is the third pillar of Canadian broadcasting as enshrined in the Broadcasting Act. As such, community channels may have a legitimate claim to funding. The issue, however, is whether cable companies were arguing in earnest for local voices, or if they were strategically positioning themselves against broadcasters in the larger fight over FFC. The evidence here suggests the latter. CACTUS, for instance, argued that community members should control the community channels (like in the United States) to facilitate actual public access programming. The emphasis on access was echoed by a respondent from the CRTC when asked about the definition of "localism"—a term that does not exist in Canadian regulatory parlance: "So I don't know if localism includes the notion of community expression as well or just a reflection . . . by the broadcasters. But that's the other aspect . . . with community programming is that it's not just a reflection by broadcasters of the community served, it's also an opportunity for residence so that community [sic] can actually express their own tastes, wants, whatever" (P. Foster, personal communication, 10/17/2012). To be sure, community channels do an impressive job of informing Canadian communities, but there are unacknowledged power dynamics at play. One interview respondent who wishes to remain anonymous expressed dismay at the notion of "monetizing" the community channel: "to my mind, the desire to monetize, the corporate desire to monetize the community channel, to become a real corporate channel is a potential loss." CACTUS also lamented the regionalization, professionalization, and commercialization of the community channel. Who controls the community channel is thus of paramount concern for a diversity of voices and is a topic of great contention within regulatory discourse.

The third issue apparent in this testimony is the discursive difference between "community" and "local." As we might remember from chapter 1, local often implies territorial spatiality, while community suggests less geographic and more socially based relationships. Community stations, however, are expected to produce local programming, suggesting adherence to local-as-place. As we know, however, the local is much more than simply "place." This dovetails with the fourth issue, the role of the community channel within the Canadian mediascape. As one MP asked a community cable representative during the House of Commons hearing: "Are you filling a void, or are you becoming that third pillar?" (Canada, 2009b, p. 20). In other words, the MP asked whether cable operators were committing to the traditional ethos of community media as being distinct and access-based, or simply attempting to mimic local stations.

This rhetoric was not lost on my interview respondents, many of whom supported an increased role for community broadcasters. CRTC Vice-Chair Tom Pentefountas, for instance, pondered whether the community channel should step in to fill the void left by the departure of a local commercial station: "If something does go south on these stations that benefit from public money, if you wish, that community television could take over and that the service to the community will always be met" (personal communication, 10/18/12). The House committee agreed, concluding that community channels should be included in any and all funding programs.

2010: COMMUNITY ON DEMAND?

Community television was again front-and-center some months later when the Commission revisited its community television policy framework in 2009. This review was the direct result of the *Diversity of Voices* proceeding, which expressed concern with the regionalization of community television (CRTC, 2008a). The goal of the inquiry was to address this concern, revisit the objectives of the 2002 framework, and discuss the impact of new technologies on community media. One of the more interesting questions posed was whether a separation between "community programming and the local programming provided by conventional television broadcasters" was necessary (CRTC, 2009d, par. 20). This reflects growing interest among policymakers over whether community channels were a replacement for local channels or a separate pillar of Canadian broadcasting. The CRTC also inquired whether community cable channels should have access to the LPIF (see chapter 5), local advertising, and the role of the Internet "as an avenue for community expression" (CRTC, 2009d, par. 37).

Responses to the consultation were unusually plentiful for a community media proceeding, suggesting the investment of both cable companies and public interest groups. Early on, for instance, CACTUS launched a public campaign to "put community back in Community tv [sic]" and argue for citizen control. As perhaps expected, cable companies focused heavily on the role their channels play in local communities, often filling the void left by broadcasters. Shaw Communications (2010) said that community television was "the new reality of local television" and the most important source of local programming for Canadians. Referencing the "crisis" of conventional broadcasting described in chapter 2, Shaw argued "if there is any crisis in local programming, community channels will provide the solution" (p. 5). Rogers Cable Communications (2010) argued that its community television stations had a finger on the "local pulse" of communities. Both Shaw and Rogers also favored the idea that cable companies and not citizens groups should control the community channel.

Bell Aliant (2010), a subsidiary of Bell Canada, came out strongly in support of video-on-demand for community television and for allowing satellite (DTH) companies to distribute community channels (Bell is also a DTH provider). SaskTel (2010) also cast its vote in favor of video-on-demand. It also supported the "zoning" of community channels, which allows one regional channel to serve a larger geographic area in place of several community-based operations. The Saskatchewan-based BDU argued: "Operating individual outlets for local expression in small communities is uneconomical and problematic for BDUs and other community programming undertakings. This has hampered the expansion of BDU-operated outlets for local expression in small towns and cities in Saskatchewan and across Canada" (par. 12). SaskTel argued that it should be able to benefit from the economies of scale (not unlike commercial networks) that would allow it to hub community channels, considering "Many small towns and centres in Saskatchewan share related views and social interests" (par. 14). SaskTel mobilized the rhetoric of community service and diversity of voices to argue against having a community channel in each of its licensed areas. This line of argumentation assumes the homogeneity of Saskatchewan communities to justify SaskTel's actions, negating a more nuanced approach to localism and community that comes with an ethos of community media as a geographically based practice.

Public interest groups and broadcasters opposed this zone-based approach. This was particularly evident in the testimony of St. Andrews Community Television (2010), an over-the-air station in New Brunswick, which argued forcefully against "super-community channels." CACTUS (2010) went furthest of all in its recommendations: Citing the number of station closures that have occurred owing to policy changes, it urged the Commission to instigate community member control of all community channels. CACTUS also opposed the idea that community channels and local stations should compete against one another. "In a competitive environment" wrote CACTUS, "it is unnatural to expect large regional and national private cable companies to be able to administer 'community' channels with that [sic] each community's unique interests at heart" (p. 142). The organization offered numerous recommendations, such as a Community Access Media Fund, and a new designation for community television that would specifically recognize community member engagement: "community access-television." It also argued strongly in support of the geographic basis of community media: "The Internet is an international cyber-community of individuals isolated in their homes. It's not a real geographic community. Real people need to meet in real places to tackle the real issues of their actual homes" (par. 489). This is an argument we have heard before: the Internet is not local. One of my interview respondents echoed this opinion:

> The Internet is a wonderful vehicle for allowing those communities [of interest] to develop. And to me that's very organic. And people with those kind of interests, you know, people that like knitting more ... they'll seek each other out. So I think that the commission's decision there was, no, let's stick with the geographic. That's how it's said in the Act. And ... that's the objective we're trying to achieve is to give our community, a geographic community, the ability to provide a platform for local expression. ... Communities of interest I think, as I say, they can take care of themselves in a way, for sure. (P. Foster, personal communication, 10/17/12)

We see here the familiar dichotomy between communities of interest and communities of place engendered by communication technologies reemerging in conversations of community television policy. This brings forth important definitional issues of the local and of community, particularly when we think of authenticity. How much should we hold on to the local-as-place? Geographic communities here are positioned as more "real" than other types of communities—a discursive strategy echoing Joseph's (2008) romance of communities (see chapter 1).

The CRTC's final ruling ultimately omitted any discussion of the nature of community or of the local, concentrating instead on the functional issues of regulation (CRTC, 2010b). While its findings sided with the arguments of cable companies, it extolled the importance of community television and observed that in many small towns "community television is almost always the only source of local programming" (par. 45). Contrasting this statement, the Commission noted that it would review zone-based community channel proposals on a case-by-case basis (rather than rejecting them outright). It also denied community channels access to the (then-active) LPIF, encouraged video-on-demand, and would "consider at licence renewal proposals by BDUs to allocate a portion of their local expression contributions to community programming to new media" (par. 80). Though this last consideration may not seem detrimental, the Commission did not qualify whether this referred to new media operations attached to the community channel or to separate "new media" operations; the latter would divert funds previously earmarked for the community cable channel.

Commissioner Michel Morin dissented from this ruling, voicing concern that BDUs were the ones controlling community channels. Not licensing community channels to community groups (thereby keeping them in the hands of cable companies) "is tantamount to a denial of adult status to community groups, since it is still the BDUs that will be determining the content of access programming" (CRTC, 2010b, p. v). Community channels, he argued, are a public good, and the country needs to restructure its community television sector in this light. Despite Morin's arguments, Canadian community television remains in the hands of cable companies, and therefore remains a political economic bargaining chip for BDUs. What we have seen in this section is that there have been moments when the CRTC has thought outside the status quo of cable company control. Indeed, the Commission considered alternatives in the form of communities of interest within communities of place, therein recognizing that local communities are more than markets for cable or broadcasting. Still, it fell back on default localism, agreeing with cable company demands, putting greater pressure on community stations to provide regional content and keeping the public at arm's length.

United States: Community's Relevance

Unlike Canada, the United States lacks a coherent policy framework for public, educational, and governmental television. Instead, PEG regulations are found in myriad pieces of legislation, cable regulations, and judiciary rulings. Despite not having a dedicated community television policy, or having given it much regulatory thought recently, both Congress and the FCC were at one time keenly interested in the reflection of local voices on cable (Linder, 1999). During the congressional debates on the 1984 Cable Act, it was stated: "Public access channels are often the video equivalent of the speaker's soapbox or the electronic parallel to the printed leaflet. They provide groups and individuals who generally have not had access to the electronic media with the opportunity to become sources of information in the electronic marketplace of ideas" (US 1984a, p. 4667). Earlier attempts in the 1970s saw the FCC require that *all* cable companies carry multiple public access channels (Linder, 1999). These progressive provisions were eliminated after the Supreme Court ruled they infringed on the free speech rights of cable companies (*FCC v. Midwest,* 1979). It would not be until 1984 that PEG was officially sanctioned through the 1984 Cable Act.

The 1984 Cable Act gives authority over cable to local municipalities, whose rights of way cable companies use to lay wires. Cable companies must solicit a franchise from each municipality (Local Franchising Authorities or "LFAs"). LFAs are entitled to compensation in the form of 5 percent of the gross revenues of the cable operator derived from the specific municipality (a "franchise fee"). LFAs may also request funding and channel space for PEG. Franchise fees go directly to the municipality, with some (or all) proceeds allocated to the nonprofit group(s) organized to run the PEG stations. While the 1984 Act may have legitimized PEG, it also required citizens to actively petition the cable company for a channel and funding, rather than guarantee it. Though it did not change this burdensome requirement, the 1992 Cable Act did strengthen PEG's legitimacy by mandating that PEG channels be carried on the basic cable tier, along with the local stations in the market. Though an official quantitative survey has never been conducted, the Alliance for Community Media (ACM) estimates that there are as many as three thousand PEG groups and five thousand PEG channels in the country (Goldfarb, 2008).

2005: A JURISDICTIONAL LEVIATHAN

Following the deregulation of the multivideo platform distribution industry (MVPD—cable and satellite operators) in the 1996 Telecommunications Act, telecom companies (e.g., AT&T, Verizon) began to compete directly with cable companies (e.g., Comcast, Time Warner Cable) for pay television and Internet provision. In an effort to gain a foothold on previously occupied territories of cable, new entrants began pressuring state governments to remove the franchising authority from LFAs and give it to the state. This would allow new entrants to seek permission from one centralized entity (the state), rather than individual communities, thereby hastening the licensing of new competitors. This practice is known as "statewide franchising."

Several particularly damaging results of statewide franchising are that the state often fails to allocate adequate funding for PEG, reduces PEG commitments for MVPD operators, or in some cases, eliminates PEG funding altogether. By 2011, more than twenty states had imposed some form of statewide franchising. While laws differ by state, community media advocates argue that on the whole they are a significant threat to the survival of PEG organizations. According to American Community Television (ACT), ten states (Florida, Georgia, Idaho, Iowa, Kansas, Missouri, Nevada, Ohio, South Carolina, and Wisconsin) have zeroed-out PEG funding either by a prescribed date or upon franchise expiration. These actions leave "as many as 500 PEG access channels in jeopardy" (ACT, nd). Other states require new entrants to match incumbents' PEG expenditures, such as Texas (until expiration of the franchise) and Michigan (for life) (Miller & Van Eaton, 2007). Still others, like California and Virginia, set "minimum or maximum levels of PEG support, in terms of a percentage of revenues [of the cable operator]" (Goldfarb, 2008, p. 6). One draconian law in Kentucky (KRS 136.660) prohibits municipalities from collecting franchise fees and any in-kind services, therein eliminating the primary source of funding for PEG stations in that state. Unique in the country, some communities in Vermont receive the entirety of the franchise fee, while others have been able to negotiate so that the fee is divided between capital and noncapital expenditure requirements (see Vermont, 2007, §8.417, Vermont, 2005, ACM, 2010, p. 9). This inchoate legislative landscape at the state level leads to significant unevenness in the PEG community. Its complete neglect at the federal level is even more troublesome, as it serves to limit the abilities of PEG groups and in some cases (when PEG organizations have been forced to close) has removed a voice in local media ecosystems—an ecology that is already collapsing (see chapter 4).

Texas was the first to enact statewide franchising in 2005 (Util. Code Ann §66.003). Though the law requires MVPD operators to contribute 1 percent of their gross revenue for PEG capital support, a study by the University of Minnesota found that "many local franchise agreements had providers [also] paying operating and staffing expenses. These payments may no longer be made under state franchising" (Fealing et al., 2009, p. 13). As a result of this decision to only allocate PEG funding for capital expenses, PEG organizations in Austin saw a funding decrease of $2.5 million, while a channel in Dallas closed (Fuentes-Bautista, 2009; Waldman, 2011). In a 2008 survey of 204 PEG organizations, ACM found that 20 percent reported a decrease in funding and seventeen communities in eight states "reported a loss of access to PEG facilities" (p. 1). While these results must be taken with a grain of salt because of the source and the unscientific nature of the survey (Goldfarb, 2008), the FCC reported similar findings from a survey of 165 PEG centers, half of which noted a decline in funding while "100 community media centers had to shut down during that period [2005–2010]" (Waldman, 2001, p. 300). Though the FCC tried to avoid direct intervention into the issue of statewide franchising, its actions, documented next, demonstrated a favorable attitude to the practice.

2007: "SUFFICIENT" ENOUGH?

Although the FCC refused to intervene in statewide franchising, it did intervene during a dispute between LFAs and MVPDs. In 2005 the FCC opened a docket exploring the possibility of enacting Section 621(a)(1) of the 1996 Act, which "prohibit[ed] franchising authorities from unreasonably refusing to award competitive franchises for the provisions of cable services" (Goldfarb, 2008, p. 4). The FCC had received complaints that LFAs were making unreasonable demands on MVPDs and the docket asked if 621(a)(1) should be activated to hasten the entrance of new competitors. This docket proved highly contentious, as it brought to light the FCC's jurisdictional powers and challenged the ability of LFAs to negotiate with cable companies on behalf of their constituents. These events recall our conversation earlier in the book about political localism, where tensions exist in the American mindset between nationalism and localism. This debate is echoed in telecommunications policy with the question of who should have authority over cable connections: the city, the state, or the federal government.

PEG was an important topic in the first round of responses to the *Notice of Proposed Rulemaking* (FCC, 2005). One of the key questions was whether the franchise fee included funding for PEG or if PEG expenses should be over-and-above the 5 percent. The 1984 Cable Act specified that PEG capital costs like building construction, channel placement, and equipment did not count against the fee, but was ambiguous about noncapital costs like salaries and training. Some cable companies did pay for noncapital costs on top of their prescribed franchise fee (Goldfarb, 2008). Public interest groups including the National Association of Telecommunications Officers and Advisors (NATOA) supported LFA rights to determine cable franchises and conditions. NATOA (2006a) also argued that the FCC had no jurisdiction in this matter because it fell under the purview of Congress. One of the key points NATOA made was that PEG channels exemplify how LFAs serve the needs of their communities—something that could not be done if the FCC mandated a "one-size-fits-all" approach to cable franchising (p. iii). NATOA interpreted Section 622(g)(2)(c) of the 1934 Communications Act (as amended by the 1996 Telecommunications Act) to mean that *all* PEG expenses were excluded from the franchise fee. Cable companies demurred, arguing that noncapital expenses should be deducted from the franchise fee. This would have immediate consequences for PEG, because their revenue stream is dependent on the fees negotiated by the LFA. A related question then, is how does the definition of a franchise fee shape our view of the local? In other words, how much is the local worth? This also illuminates a larger debate over who should provide for the information needs of American communities. PEG advocates argued that this responsibility should remain with local groups and local media, while cable companies preferred a uniform national market.

The FCC's (2007a) decision would not prove favorable to PEG organizations. In keeping with a market-based approach to telecommunications policy, the Commission argued that LFAs were implementing "unreasonable barriers to entry into the cable market" by taking too long to grant franchises, imposing "unreasonable build-out mandates," and imposing fees above the 5 percent maximum (p. 3). The Commission bowed in the direction of statewide franchising, which "appear[s] to offer promise in assisting new entrants to more quickly begin offering consumers a competitive choice among cable providers" (p. 9). The FCC thus grounded its support of MVPD operators in the rhetoric of consumer choice and competition. Citing the problem of the interpretation of the franchise fee as a central issue, the FCC interpreted "capital costs" to mean, "those costs incurred in or associated with the construction of PEG access facilities" (p. 51). This definition excludes noncapital costs (such as salaries), which many cable companies had been paying above the 5 percent fee. Another decision, this time favoring new cable entrants (and disadvantaging PEG), came from the interpretation of the word "adequate." As the FCC noted, "Section 621(a)(4)(b) provides that a franchising authority may require 'adequate assurance' that the cable operator will provide 'adequate' PEG access channel, capacity, or financial support" (p. 52). Ambiguity around the word "adequate" resulted in myriad franchise conditions. As a result, the FCC issued an interpretation of "adequate" to mean "satisfactory or sufficient" and not "significant" (p. 52). Consequently PEG organizations and LFAs were left "with a large degree of uncertainty about what assessments they may impose on cable franchises over and above the franchise fee" (Goldfarb, 2008, p. 5). It demonstrates how community television is beholden to telecommunications regulation, caught in the middle of battles between LFAs, MVPDs, and the FCC.

Commissioner Adelstein dissented to this decision on the grounds that it encroached on local jurisdiction and "turn[ed] federalism on its head" (FCC, 2007a, p. 99). As it turns out, the ruling spawned so much ambiguity and confusion over franchise fees that eight months later, a second R&O was necessary for clarification (FCC, 2007b). Here, the Commission reiterated that only immediate capital costs are excluded from the franchise fee, and "payments made to support the operation of PEG access facilities are considered franchise fees and are subject to the 5 percent cap" (p. 6). Adelstein (joined by Copps this time) again dissented from this ruling. Despite these fervent dissents, however, this remains the most recent ruling the FCC has made regarding PEG, signaling considerable neglect on behalf of the regulator.

2008: AT&T AND COMCAST

While the FCC worked to hasten competition, telecommunications companies were busy prepping to compete with incumbent cable operators. A key driver in this expansion was AT&T, which went head-to-head with Comcast in several municipalities. To compete, Comcast began rolling out its digital cable network and in the process went ahead with the digitalization of PEG channels. In doing so, Comcast moved some PEG channels off the basic analogue service and onto a digital tier in the nine hundred–channel range, requiring those wanting to view PEG programming to lease a digital converter box from Comcast (the first year would be provided free) (Goldfarb, 2008). This action brought about the ire of PEG organizations in Dearborn, Michigan, who filed a petition of declaratory ruling with the FCC in 2008 claiming that Comcast was violating the 1992 Cable Act, which mandated PEG channels be on the basic analogue tier (FCC, 2008b). Petitioners argued that "channel slamming" (placing channels on a high tier) was a clear example of how cable operators discriminate against PEG (FCC, 2008b, p. ii). Joining Dearborn was the city of Lansing, Michigan, followed quickly by ACM, both of whom filed petitions for declaratory rulings against AT&T. Lansing and ACM argued that through its "U-Verse" multichannel video system, AT&T had moved PEG channels to an on-demand platform, making them hard to access and outside the basic package of local channels that all MVPDs are required to provide (FCC, 2009a, 2009b).

The FCC amalgamated these two petitions and began receiving public comments in February 2009. Public interest groups such as Free Press argued in favor of the plaintiffs, describing PEG as an empowering venue for public participation and calling its content "overwhelmingly local" (p. 15). NATOA (2009) furthermore contended that AT&T's "PEG product" treats PEG programming like YouTube, thereby diluting the role PEG plays in local communities. In contrast to this democratic discourse, AT&T (2009) took a juridical approach. It first argued that its service was not in effect a "cable service" because it uses Internet protocol television (IPTV) and is thus exempt from *cable* legislation. Failing this, it argued that it was compliant with the Cable Act already, because "federal law imposes only modest PEG requirements on cable operators" (p. 3). Interestingly, AT&T also argued that its product served to enhance PEG viewing by offering local content to different municipalities through an on-screen menu where users can select programming from a number of localities. This brings up an important question about PEG and localism: is the value of PEG in its content (it which case place matters little) or is it in the practices and production of this content (in which case place matters a great deal) (Ali & Conrad, 2015)? Scholars tend to agree with the latter, noting that providing a "place for the placeless" is as important as providing a "voice for the voiceless" (Ali, 2012c). As of yet, policy and regulation has not taken note of these embodied experiences and the "sense of place" facilitated by community media centers (Ali, 2012c).

In the mist of this heated rhetoric, Dearborn and Comcast reached a compromise, and Dearborn retracted its petition in 2010. Based on this compromise, when Comcast purchased NBCU it made two PEG-related commitments: (1) Comcast would desist from transferring PEG channels to the digital tier until all channels were relocated to the tier; and (2) Comcast would develop on-demand platforms for PEG to complement the conventional channel (NATOA, 2010a, p. 3). The AT&T case, however, remains outstanding, and in filings to the *Information Needs of Communities* inquiry (see chapter 4) PEG advocates demanded FCC action.

While regulatory documents imply a tension between the traditional platforms of PEG and the digital media world in which it now resides, Fuentes-Bautista (2009) argues that the analogue and the digital should work in concert within community media practices: "The key question is not whether YouTube, videoblogs and social networking replace broadcasting or cable television as media technology, but how citizens and localities can use the complete set of electronic media tools and distribution systems to expand and support activities for community building and citizen use of new technologies" (Fuentes-Bautista, 2009, p. 49). PEG advocates understand this ecosystem approach, as well as the need to continue to act as community centers and not reduce themselves to file-transfer protocol systems or online communities. The adherence to place, Rennie (2006) argues, is the seminal difference between "amateur" and "community" media. To this, former Commissioner Michael Copps adds that it is about regulation and community media coming together:

> They're struggling often without resources and trying to make sense of all this and where can they really have an impact on localism. . . . I'm distressed at

the experience lots of PEGs have been through with the cable companies. . . .
But it is a time of transition for them, and I don't have a lot of easy answers.
I'm supportive of making sure the cable companies treat them right and
supportive of the FCC using its jurisdiction to make sure that they're in the
neighborhood with other kind[s] of similar channels. But there has to be a lot
of creative thought in PEG too. . . . I hope there's room on both the traditional
media and the new media for PEG. . . . (personal communication, 11/20/12)

The survival of PEG, then, is not just a technological issue, nor is it solely about regulatory protection or digital media practices. Rather, a holistic approach is necessary to ensure its survival as a place for gathering, training, and production.

United Kingdom: Community's Moment?

The UK has a weak track record of sustaining community television. One explanation has been the poor take-up of cable across the country, thus depriving viewers the opportunity for cable-based community channels. The dearth of community television, however, is not without trying (Hewson 2005). Cable developed in the UK in the 1950s, and in 1972 Greenwich Cablevision launched an experimental community cable channel in southeast London (Nigg & Wade, 1980). Five similar channels were subsequently launched by other cable companies, though Nigg and Wade (1980) argue that the channels "were born out of a search for profits" rather than a sense of community solidarity (p. 25). The UK has always been a nation of terrestrial television, however, and cable never took hold the way satellite would in later years (Crisell, 1997). As a result, by 1976, many of these pilot channels were terminated (Nigg & Wade, 1980; Hewson, 2005).

The greatest boon to community television came in 1996 through a provision in the Broadcasting Act that allowed for a new class of local television called Restrictive Service Licences (RSLs). In 1998, the Independent Television Commission (ITC, precursor to Ofcom) awarded RSLs to Leicester and Manchester, and by 2001, nine stations were in full swing (Blanchard, 2001). Like their cable community channel brethren, however, many of these operations would prove unsustainable, and by 2009 only four RSLs remained in operation (Ofcom, 2009a; Ali, 2012c). Moreover, RSLs were never required to operate on a nonprofit or public-access basis, and at the time, were regarded more as Britain's attempt to do "local" rather than "community" television (Timescape, 2009). Hewson (2005) argues that this lack of participatory impetus is significant because "the idealization of 'the local' or 'community' *per se*, without a grounding in local participatory activity easily leads to commercial capture" (pp. 33–34). Commercial capture became reality some years later with the emergence of the local digital television program service (L-DTPS) (see chapter 5).

COMMUNITY TELEVISION

By the early 2000s, concerns were being voiced for the survival of the RSLs. The *Times* of London, for instance, reported that in 2002, of the twenty-six RSL stations in operation, only one was turning a profit (Jackson, 2002). In a 2005 report on local and community television, Hewson (2005) cataloged only eight RSL services: Solent TV on the Isle of Wight; Thistle TV in Lanarkshire; Midlands Asian TV in Leicester; SixTV in Oxford; Channel 9 in Derry; Channel M in Manchester; York TV in York; and Northern Visions Television (NvTv) in Belfast. In addition to these was a prelaunched station in Cardiff and three cable and broadband channels: Channel Seven in Immingham, Tenantspin in Liverpool, and c21Vox in Birmingham. By 2009, only four RSL stations and two digital channels could be identified by Ofcom (2009a) and Timescape Productions (2009): Channel M (Manchester), NvTv (Belfast), Leicester, and York, Channel Seven (Immingham) (cable), and MonTV (Monmouthshire) (online). Though these organizations all labeled themselves "community television," only NvTv was based upon the traditional notions of public access and nonprofit (Ofcom, 2009a).

With the launch of local television in 2013, the Restricted Service License was eliminated. Despite the disappearance of these localized services, Damian Radcliffe, former manager of nations and communities at Ofcom and expert on hyperlocal media, thinks that community television will continue in some capacity: "I think they'll always be offering something different . . . they'll be providing a more localized tier of news and information that will be different and distinct from local television, which will be covering a much bigger geographic patch. So I see the two as being very complementary, sitting alongside one another and each adding value to the media ecosystem" (personal communication, 1/20/13). Radcliffe intimates something akin to the geographical tiering seen in the United States and Canada, with community media targeting smaller geographic units (possibly within larger geographic centers) and local television targeting entire cities. He also noted that sentiments among community media organizations are mixed about the prospect of local television: "I think it's a mixed bag, that some of them are very excited and see it as a once in a lifetime opportunity to get involved with something that will broadcast straight into people's living rooms, and those kinds of opportunities don't come across very often. Whereas others are dubious because they just can't see the business model." For the community television stations still in existence, getting involved in the L-DPTS means applying for a license. To date, only two have done so: NvTv won its bid to operate in Belfast, while Channel Seven won the license for Grimsby.

COMMUNITY RADIO

Community radio began in earnest in 2001 with a pilot project of fifteen stations spearheaded by the Radio Authority (precursor to Ofcom). Two years later a report was commissioned to assess the future of what was then being called "Access Radio" (Everitt, 2003). This report would help galvanize the regulatory and legislative action needed to officially sanction community radio in the UK. According to its author, Anthony Everitt, the choice of using "access" rather than "community" was deliberate because "community" could mean both radio *by* the community and radio *for* the community. "Access Radio," it was thought, connoted the traits of community participation better than "community radio" (pp. 29–30). One of the pivotal concerns was the relationship between "communities of interest" and "communities of place": "while it is true that everyone is in the nature of things geographically based, where people live is no longer how many people define their social or individual identities. For an increasing number, place is where they happen to be at a given time, as traditional family structures weaken and social and job mobility becomes increasingly common" (Everitt, 2003, p. 30). Access Radio and the criteria used to evaluate its performance needed to be sensitive to these changing dynamics of place and community. The project and report underscored the idea that geographically based communities consist of layers, and are not the homogeneous markets defined by commercial interests. For instance, in debating whether the future of Access Radio should be one of geographic contingency or something more expansive, Everitt noted, "it is appropriate for the Radio Authority to include communities of both interest and of place in its criteria for eligibility for Access Radio status" (p. 31). This perspective nuances our definitions of what it means to be local. Understanding that Access Radio will have a circumscribed radius (5 km.), the report acknowledged that different communities populate even the smallest geographic spaces, but all remain linked to that place. This gets to the heart of a critical regionalist ethos for media regulation, for it offers an alternative to the status quo thinking of local markets, and suggests the fusion of place, culture, identity, and language that go into localism.

Attention to the nuance of place was also influential in drafting the Community Radio Order in February 2004. After the draft was published, Ofcom engaged in a series of consultations to better understand the regulatory implications of community radio. Changing the name to "Community Radio" from "Access Radio," Ofcom established four "core elements of community radio" based on criteria established by the Community Radio Order:

- It is primarily for social gain rather than commercial reasons
- It serves a particular community—a neighbourhood or community of interest
- It is not provided in order to make a profit
- If offers the target community opportunities to participate in the station (2004c, p. 3)

The four criteria made clear that community radio would have specifically targeted audiences, be they communities of place, of interest, or both. The draft also proposed a community media fund, and suggested restrictions on advertising if a community radio station was located in the same community as a commercial station. This was suggested to ensure that community broadcasters would not siphon off scarce advertising dollars from local commercial broadcasters (Ofcom, 2004d).

Parliament officially passed the Community Radio Order in July 2004, which contained a definition of community that recognized the intersection between communities of place and interest:

(2)(1) "community" means—
(a) the persons who live or work or undergo education or training in a particular area or locality, or
(b) persons who (whether or not they fall within paragraph [a]) have one or more interest or characteristics in common. (UK, 2004)

This definition incorporates both communities of place and communities of interest, and allows for the fluidity engendered by the mobility of people and technology. In no other policy action do we see a more considered approach to what it means to be local.

Ofcom's final statement on the Licensing of Community Radio in September 2004 echoed this discursive flexibility while also requiring tangible commitments (Ofcom, 2004d). This included a broadcasting radius of 5 km., and establishing a Community Radio Fund of £500,000. Despite some early setbacks, by 2012 the community radio sector boasted 198 stations and 254 licenses

(Ofcom, 2012a). While most stations serve general audiences in a community of place (59 percent), others serve "smaller communities of interest" within geographic localities (Ofcom, 2011a, p. 3). Community radio is a vital component in this nascent local media ecosystem, and its legislation and regulation offers a breakthrough in dynamic ways to think through what it means to be local. Advocates for community television are not wrong to suggest that any attempt to create a community television sector should look to community radio for precedent (see Ofcom, 2006, p. 25). That said, as the L-DTPS is unveiled, a community television system has become a distant thought.

HYPERLOCAL MEDIA

Joining community radio in the community media landscape is the emerging sector of online hyperlocal media (Radcliffe, 2012, 2015). Unlike the radio sector, Web sites are unlicensed and do not have to adhere to any community regulations or standards. Nonetheless: "Hyperlocal media normally provides news and content at a more grassroots level than most traditional media can achieve. It can help to define local identity, fill gaps in existing content provision, hold authority to account and broaden the range of media available to audiences" (Radcliffe, 2012, n.p.). Hyperlocal is defined as "online news or content services pertaining to a town, village, single postcode or other small, geographically defined community." As such, it assumes a more delineated definition than that of community radio (Radcliffe, 2012, n.p.). Ofcom has also employed the term "ultralocal" to describe these services, but "hyperlocal" is the term that has best caught on. In 2012, there were more than five hundred hyperlocal Web sites, the most common being those that "address specific gaps in local news or information provision" (n.p.). This also pertains to linguistic gaps, suggesting a relationship between localism and language. While certain language groups are protected by regulation (e.g., Welsh and Gaelic) and have dedicated media streams, other prevalent languages, such as Sylheti (of which there are approximately 200,000 speakers), do not. As Radcliffe noted: ". . . there's huge potential for these services to offer localized programming for new communities, new geographic communities or linguistic communities across the UK who perhaps are not served by existing media provisions" (personal communication, 1/20/12). Hyperlocal online services are increasingly valuable and recognized as dynamic parts of Britain's local media ecosystems. Nonetheless, Ofcom acknowledges that the entire array of hyperlocal, ultralocal, and community media outlets face the significant challenges of "funding and visibility" (p. 42).

Conclusion: Community Lost?

Jean Luc Nancy (2006) tells us that we should not pine for the "community lost" because the idea that communities come fully formed only upholds bourgeois ideology. To the contrary, community is a constant work-in-progress. For our purposes, however, the loss of community media would be a tremendous blow to local media ecosystems. Still, Nancy's idea that community is a constant work-in-progress—"infinite lack of infinite identity" (p. xxxviii)—resonates with the evolving practices and discourses of community media. Three points are important to take away from this chapter. First, beyond the hype of rhetoric from cable companies and policymakers, we actually know very little about the contemporary practices of community television, and even less about how they interact with other local media outlets. There are also definitional differences between community and local that remain under-investigated by regulators and scholars. Second, there is much to be learned from the regulatory discourse emerging from both supporters and opponents of community television. Indeed, it is here where we have been presented with numerous alternatives to the status quo of default localism—from a layered understanding of local-as-place, to new funding models, to innovative regulatory initiatives. Third, what we have unveiled is a clear political economy of localism. Here, the desires of incumbent cable companies (and emergent video distribution companies) serve to drown out the voices of community television. Community media play a dynamic role within local media ecosystems and are more necessary than ever given the reduction of media localism in the commercial and public sectors, and the ever-growing propensity toward discourses of globalization and glocalization. To ensure the survival of community media, however, we require a thorough understanding of the ecosystems in which they exist. This is the topic of the following chapter.

4

The Ecosystems of Localism

A Holistic Approach to Local News and Information

> ... [I]n an age of globalism people feel the need for stronger not weaker connections to the communities in which they live.
> —Hunt, 2010

Information Needs

Let us return to Moscow, Idaho, an early adopter of the Buy Fresh, Buy Local campaign. I noted that Moscow has one public television station and no commercial stations. The city does however boast a local daily newspaper (the *Moscow-Pullman Daily News*), and a handful of local and college radio stations. Taken together, these media outlets begin to paint a picture of what we might call Moscow's "local media ecosystem" or "local media ecology." In this chapter, I analyze key studies of local media ecosystems in the United States, United Kingdom, and Canada to better understand how regulators talk about local news, how they define the local, who they include in this definition, and how they interpret the role that public and private organizations play in the current and imagined media ecosystem.

Concern for local media ecosystems has manifested in exhaustive studies in both the United States and the UK, prompted by the precipitous financial declines of traditional news organizations, concerns over the quality and quantity of local news, and concerns over the types of news reaching communities. Between 2003 and 2012 the FCC and Ofcom undertook omnibus studies of local media, investigating not only the local media that fall under their jurisdiction (e.g., broadcasting/cable/satellite) but also newspapers, online sites, community media, mobile platforms, journalism schools, and foundations—any entity that contributes to the production of local news and information. The understanding being that it is "impossible to understand the information needs of communities . . . without taking a holistic look at all media . . ." (Waldman, 2011, p. 9). Ofcom released its study, *Local and Regional Media in the United Kingdom,* in 2009, while the FCC released its iteration, *The Information Needs of Communities,* in 2011.[1] As the preeminent studies of local media in the United States and the UK, these two reports constitute my American and British case studies for this chapter.

Canada is the outlier, having never conducted a review of its local media ecosystems despite suffering from the same crises of economics, quality, and authority of journalism. In its place, the House of Commons Standing Committee on Canadian Heritage conducted a review of Canadian broadcasting in 2001–2003, with an eye toward understanding how the industry was meeting the aims of the 1991 Broadcasting Act. Chaired by Member of Parliament (MP) Clifford Lincoln, the "Lincoln Report" is the most comprehensive review of Canadian broadcasting ever undertaken, and stands as the Canadian case study for this chapter. The report focused on the role that broadcasting plays in the creation of Canadian national identity, but also took great pains to underscore the important contribution of local media to the Canadian media system and Canadian democracy. Despite the comprehensiveness of the report, I argue that Canada is in need of a comprehensive study of its local media ecosystems, one that does not focus only on broadcasting (Burgess, 2011; Ali, 2016b).

The above studies of local media ecosystems provide important contributions to a fuller understanding of what it means to be local in the digital age. This is particularly evident in the attention paid to definitions of the local, and to the importance placed on a holistic approach to media localism. By "holistic approach," I mean engendering a belief that all media organizations (and not just mainstream outlets) at various levels of distribution and circulation contribute to the functioning of a local media ecosystem. This chapter reminds us that local news contributes not only to democracy but also to community solidarity, civic participation, and community awareness. "For democracy to work, community is necessary," writes Friedland (2001, p. 358). For community to work, moreover, information and communication are required.

Unfortunately, all three studies in this chapter share the fate of neglect and dismissal. Given the concerns voiced by regulators, industry, and government over the health and vibrancy of local media ecosystems, the lack of impact of these studies is both lamentable and problematic. That the press also failed to bring attention to these important proceedings suggests that localism may not be as high atop the policy priority list as regulators have promised. If a goal of the CRTC, FCC, and Ofcom is indeed to foster robust local media ecosystems, these reports and any future iteration require visibility.

Ecologies and Ecosystems

The terms "ecology" and "ecosystem" are loaded with ideological meaning, but as I demonstrate in this section, they are employed deliberately and referentially. They take their definitions from the field of biology, particularly from the work of Arthur Roy Clapman, who "coined the term *ecosystems* in the 1930s" (Scolari, 2012, p. 220). An ecosystem "is a network of relationships between elements inside an environment" (Scolari, 2012, p. 220). In addition to serving as useful metaphors, I also use "local media ecosystem" and "local media ecology" as emic terms, meaning that they are used by stakeholders themselves. The Waldman Report (2011), for instance, writes of "local media ecosystems" while Ofcom (2009a) discusses the "local and regional media ecology."[2]

Drawing from both the etymology of the term and its emic usage, a local media ecosystem is the network(s) of media outlets and the interconnections between them within a community of place. This definition privileges a holistic approach to local media, understanding that: "Policy-relevant research must capture the increasingly complex functioning of local media systems in ways that fully account for the role played by *all* relevant stakeholders, the interconnections and interdependencies that exist among media platforms" (CPRN, 2012, p. xi). We need to understand that everything from commercial television stations to newspapers to hyperlocal sites and blogs contribute to how citizens receive local news and information. This demands not just a nominal assessment, but also a network assessment in order to understand, as the Communications Policy Research Network (CPRN) notes above, the interconnection and interdependencies between stakeholders.

Friedland (2001) offers a more conceptual definition of what he calls "communication ecologies," which denote "the range of communication activities that link networks of individuals, groups, and institutions in a specific community domain" (p. 360). As we recall from chapter 1, Friedland proposes the theory of a communicatively integrated community, arguing that media from all levels and layers of distribution and circulation are necessary. His typology, reproduced here, depicts his "community communication ecology":

Table 4.1: Community Communication Ecology

Level	Location	Medium
System	Global, national, regional	Systemwide media: national networks, national newspapers, elite journals, global computer networks
Macro	Metropolitan	Metro newspapers, metro broadcast media, metro Internet portals, metro public media, cable systems, metro alternative media
Macro-meso	Metropolitan/community	Zoned editions, cable access, specialized community media (e.g., ethnic radio), civic Internet portals
Meso-micro	Neighborhood	Neighborhood newspapers, newsletters
Micro	Neighborhood/interpersonal	Newsletters, point-to-point communication (telephone and email), interpersonal network discussions.

Source: Friedland, 2001, pp. 381–82.

Friedland's article was published in 2001, and as such, we see some absences in his typology, most notably social networks, which would no doubt exist at the system level; mobile locative technologies (e.g., GPS, check-in apps), which would exist at the meso-level; and hyperlocal blogs, which exist at the meso-micro level. Nonetheless, his typology is useful in appreciating the fact that all outlets and platforms play a role in the local media ecosystem.

Recently, a holistic approach similar to Friedland's was used by the New America Foundation's Media Policy Initiative, which, at the height of the crisis of journalism in 2009, conducted five "information community case studies" (Scranton, Pa.; Seattle, Wash.; Minneapolis–St. Paul, Minn.; Research Triangle, N.C.; and, Washington, D.C.) with the goal of understanding the "(1) availability of relevant and credible information to all Americans and their communities; (2) capacity of individuals to engage with information; and (3) individual engagement with information and public life of the community" (Durkin & Glaisyer, 2011, p. 1). These studies not only mapped the structure of the local media ecosystem, but also their uses and functions. They considered contributors such as print media, commercial television, public television, Internet media (including hyperlocal blogs), radio, news aggregation sites, social media, libraries, broadband connectivity, and local government Web sites. By recognizing local media as an ecosystem, we can better understand the local imagined community, the local public sphere, and how community structure and social integration are performed through communication.[3]

United Kingdom: "Buy local, live local, go local"

Ofcom's *Local and Regional Media in the United Kingdom* (Ofcom, 2009a) was part of a series of reports contemplating the future of media in the UK. This included the public service broadcasting reviews (see chapter 2), the *Digital Britain* report (2009), which outlined the government's broadband and digital strategy, and the Department for Communication, Media and Sport (DCMS) *Sustainable Independent and Important News*. Ofcom's report contained three major themes: how to define the local, the "threat" of the Internet and digital media to traditional media, and the roles of public and commercial media. Though the title of the report signals *media* as the central focus, the primary issue was clearly local and regional news. This was evident at the outset of the report, which outlined what it considered to be the requirements for a local media ecosystem:

- A wide choice of local content, covering news, information and community life
- Available across traditional media platforms (TV, radio, newspapers) ... but also through the internet
- Delivered by a healthy and vibrant commercial media sector, but also from organizations employing a range of different ownership models, including public sector and not-for-profit
- Underpinned by a spine of strong and independent local journalism
- Delivering public interest outcomes to citizens and consumers (p. 5)

Though the public system so prevalent in the UK was not ignored, it was to the commercial system that Ofcom looked to fill the gaps in local content and achieve these normative and economic goals.

DEFINITIONS: GEO-SPATIAL AND SOCIO-GEOGRAPHICAL

As with previous reports, a considerable number of pages were devoted to the contemplation of what was local and what was regional—a notably "complex" undertaking as both are subjective and contextual (p. 15). Ofcom rested on a definition of the local that aligned it with geographical enclaves "at the sub-UK and sub-nations level" (p. 15). This decision was based on an understanding that the UK political system rests on local representation and authorities. From this, Ofcom identified five types of geographic media:

- Ultra-local—The individual's immediate geographic community
- Local—The individual's city, town, or local district

- Regional—[A]ssociated with either metropolitan, the county or broader geographic area, e.g. East Anglia / West Midlands.
- National—[A]ssociated with the devolved nations, i.e. Scotland, Wales, and Northern Ireland, particularly due to their strong sense of cultural identity and devolution at the national level
- UK—[T]he UK as a whole (p. 20)

This typology takes into account not only the local and regional levels, such as the content provided by ITV, but also differentiates between (devolved) nations and the UK. It does not, however, take into account communities of interest that may exist within and between these geographic units.

Despite the adherence to geographic localities, Ofcom acknowledged the subjective, contextual, and mediated nature of the local. The decision to align localism with geographic places was not made without consideration of alternatives. For instance, Ofcom admitted that defining the local is difficult, and that consumers struggle with this term: "our research suggests that this varies both by geography and (significantly) between individuals; there is no single or simple definition of what is meant by local, although the research suggests that over half considered their own village, town or city as being 'local'" (p. 19). Reflecting on the five tiers, Ofcom added that the "boundaries between 'regional,' 'local,' and 'ultra-' (or 'hyper-) local are blurred" (p. 20). This underscores Ofcom's general argument that the local is contextual, reflecting anything from a neighborhood to a "population of several million" (p. 20). That Ofcom treated the local as contextual and subjective further supports one of this book's main premises: the local is itself a heterogeneous concept on any scale.

ECOLOGIES

The next task was to describe and assess the local media ecology. Accordingly, 92 percent of all adults consume some form of local media, with newspapers and regional news (on ITV) being dominant sources. Some of the more significant findings in this section included the (surprisingly) small role played by commercial local television (RSLs—see chapter 3) and the lack of local news provided by ITV. Not only did ITV lack localized news on television, but the network shuttered its online local efforts in 2009. There was also an acknowledgment of attempts by the BBC to localize its content, and recognition (but not concern) of increased industry consolidation, particularly by ITV and local commercial radio. Community and ultralocal media platforms were also given due attention, with Ofcom recognizing their growth and their struggle for sustainable business models, staffing, and general visibility among UK media users. Ofcom differentiated "community media" from "ultra-local media," associating the former with all mediated platforms, while basing the latter primarily in web and text "as [ultra-local media] often targets a much smaller constituency and therefore is not always scalable in the way that radio and TV can be" (p. 42). The characteristics shared by community and ultralocal media underscore their benefits to a local media ecosystem because they localize programming to a greater extent than commercial media, fill the gaps left by commercial media, source out a variety of funding options, grant social capital, and address issues or areas too small for coverage by traditional media (Ofcom, 2009a).

TECHNOLOGIES OF THE LOCAL

A major concern was the decrease of regional news on ITV, and the network's threats to abandon its public service broadcaster status. Coupled with the closure of some local newspapers, Ofcom was unsurprisingly concerned about the amount of local news reaching citizens and consumers. While it is true the BBC was trying to enhance its local reach, Ofcom preferred a plurality of voices—particularly *commercial* voices. To this end, two regulatory measures were contemplated to quell this market failure: first, the launch of Independently Funded News Consortia (IFNC) to relieve the burden placed on ITV to produce regional news and to expand local news on multiple platforms (see chapter 5). Second came the introduction of local television through digital terrestrial television, cable, satellite, or broadband (see chapter 5). No matter what distribution mechanism, Ofcom decided that television needed to be part of the equation to increase local and regional news, because it remained the primary destination for news consumers. At the time, regional television was watched daily by approximately 80 percent of adults, and 49 percent get their regional news through television (p. 49). In contrast, the Internet stood at only 4 percent (p. 51). At the same time, Ofcom placed great faith in the abilities of digital technologies to deliver localized content to geographic communities: ". . . new technologies and new ways of thinking about 'localness' and content may combine to change conceptions of what it is to create and consume local and regional media. The prize is great: a sustainable and diverse local and regional media sector that is an integral part of healthy and vibrant geographic communities throughout the UK" (p. 138). This represents a more positive take on what Frau-Meigs (2011) calls the "re-territorialization of the Internet." For her, this term describes an attempt by nation-states to impose surveillance techniques on digital and online platforms. Ofcom intimates here that broadband infrastructure could be used to foster geographic communities and localness without the nefariousness feared by Frau-Meigs.

PUBLIC AND PRIVATE

Ofcom also tried to balance the public service rendered by media outlets in the provision of local news with commercialism and new business models. In its recommendations and conclusions, for instance, it debated the implementation of public subsidies, targeted tax breaks, trusts, charities, and "community interest companies," therein suggesting that it is not against state intervention (pp. 132–34). Nonetheless, the report's primary recommendations included calls for the deregulation of local radio and cross-media ownership (both of which would eventually happen). While Ofcom's general mandate is to encourage the development of both *citizens* and *consumers* in equal fashion, it is telling that the word "citizen" appears fifty-one times while the word "consumer" appears 144 times in the ecology report. Though by no means scientific, it nevertheless suggests the role of the consumer over that of the citizen (see Livingstone & Lunt, 2007). That the report concentrates heavily on the market capitalization of the media industries and stresses the commercial media system over that of public media supports the argument of an unbalanced citizen-consumer relationship, with a preferential tilting toward the latter. As such, Ofcom finds itself, like all regulators that have had a traditionally interventionist history, attempting to regulate an industry through the lightest means possible in an era of neoliberalization and globalization, all the while stressing the normative importance of local news and information. If the decline in regional television news is any indication, this balancing act has failed.

To the detriment of media policy reform, Ofcom's report received little attention and exists today only in the footnotes of other reports. In fact, not one single press article could be found that discusses the report. Its peripheral resting place underscores one of my central arguments that alternative contemplations of the local tend to exist on the outskirts of regulatory discourse, even those drafted by the regulator itself. The result of such neglect is that the data, opinions, and recommendations are quickly forgotten, if read at all.

United States: Information Needs of Communities

At the same time Ofcom was conducting its local and regional media inquiry, the Knight Commission on the Information Needs of Communities[4] released a report on American local media ecosystems titled *Informing Communities: Sustaining Democracy in the Digital Age* (2009). This report detailed normative concerns that had been circulating for years: there was a crisis in American journalism, and that crisis began at the local level: "The digital age is creating an information and communications renaissance. But it is not serving all Americans and their local communities equally. It is not yet serving democracy fully. How we react, individually and collectively, to this democratic shortfall will affect the quality of our lives and the very nature of our communities" (p. xi). Troubled by the findings of the Knight Commission, the FCC created its own task force to report on local media in January 2010. Originally called "The Future of Media and Information Needs of Communities in a Digital Age," the task force, headed by FCC Senior Advisor Steven Waldman, would "assess whether all Americans have access to vibrant, diverse sources of news and information that will enable them to enrich their lives, their communities and our democracy" (FCC, 2010c, p. 1). The initial *Public Notice* presented forty-two questions for comment, ranging from the needs of communities, to how to measure and map them, to different business models for local journalism, to questions about television, radio, cable, satellite, noncommercial media, newspapers, public access stations, the Internet, and mobile platforms.

HEARINGS AND COMMENTS

Over winter and spring 2010, the FCC's task force held two public hearings on the Future of Media (FOM)—one for commercial media and one for noncommercial media. At this time, written comments were also coming in, eventually totaling approximately 1,500—a far cry from the hundreds of thousands received during the ownership reviews (see chapter 2). Still, the comments and hearings reveal important trends within the American media landscape. For instance, in both hearings Public, Educational, and Government (PEG) access channels were given considerable attention, with one speaker in the first hearing pleading to "stop starving PEG," and Ellen Goodman—chair of the second hearing—discussing the unresolved tensions between community and public media (FCC, 2010d, 2010e).

The major commenters (those with comments exceeding two pages, which totaled 431) to the FOM proceeding proposed numerous solutions to the democratic deficits inherent with a market failure for local news. Notably absent from the list of commenters were commercial media groups, particularly broadcasters. Of the major commercial stakeholders, only the NAB, Belo Corp, Lin Media, the Radio Television Digital News Association (RTDNA), and Google submitted comments, while, Fox, Comcast, Time Warner, Walt Disney, and Microsoft submitted ex parte.[5] The lack of substantive comments by commercial stakeholders suggests the task force was not taken as seriously as the media ownership review. One hypothesis is that the task force lacked regulatory powers, and could only offer recommendations, which the Commission could (and did) ignore at its discretion.

Of the commercial media companies that did submit public comments, the dominant theme was a staunch opposition to further regulation. Noted Belo Corporation (2010): "Belo's stations provide excellent news and information content to the communities they serve not because of regulatory command, but because Belo's stations are integral parts of those communities and because public service is a central part of the Company's history, culture, and business model" (p. 8). This is familiar rhetorical terrain for us at this point, wherein the market—and not regulation—will assure localism in the public interest. The National Association of Broadcasters (NAB) echoed these comments, exalting broadcasters' commitments to their communities as a vital source of local journalism, and as a contribution to a "shared sense of community" (2010b, p. 12).

Contrasting with commercial stakeholders, public interest groups, public media groups, and PEG groups were well represented. PEG advocates were particularly vocal in their comments, with individual stations and national organizations such as Alliance for Community Media (ACM), Alliance for Communications Democracy (ACD), National Organization of Telecommunications Officers and Advisors (NATOA), and American Community Television (ACT) submitting substantial comments. What all comments—private and public, commercial and noncommercial—had in common was a discursive mobilization of the local to underscore their individual arguments. This illustrates the contextuality of the local and the way different actors can use the same language—localism, diversity, pluralism—to suit their respective ideological positions. PEG groups, for instance, focused heavily on justifying their existence in the digital age, arguing their organizations serve as community centers and that the Internet is not a replacement for either the content or physical meeting places offered by PEG. As ACD wrote, "A significant benefit of PEG centers is that people gather together in classes, volunteer on each other's projects, and connect with communities of interest in ways that cross class, race, and ideological divides" (Linder & Kenton, 2010, p. 7). ACD thus linked the role of PEG to communities of geography, communities of interest, and democratic participation. For ACD, the Internet is both "everywhere" and "nowhere," suggesting that while a valuable tool, it cannot replace the physical presence of the community media center (Linder & Kenton, 2010, p. 18).

Joining PEG groups were Free Press and the New America Foundation (NAF), which argued in their joint statement that the Internet has "not established itself as a viable alternative to the journalistic functions and resources provided by more traditional media outlets" (New America et al., 2010, p. 15). As a result, certain communities of geography and interest continue to have their information needs underserved. One such community is aboriginal Americans, whose media body—Native Public Media (2010)—argued that their programming is an example of community and local media (not unlike the rhetoric used in Canada), and therefore required more services to meet these needs. In sum, public interest groups dominated the comments filed to the FOM task force. However, many of their comments would go unheeded in the final report, which held intractably to the belief that the First Amendment prohibited government from intervening in American media: "government is simply not the main player in this drama" (Waldman, 2011, p. 6).

THE "WALDMAN REPORT"

The Information Needs of Communities was released in June 2011 to great anticipation in the media reform community. Unfortunately, many of its final recommendations fell short of expectation. The report began by acknowledging "an abundance of media outlets does not translate into an abundance of reporting" and noted a dearth of what it called "local accountability reporting" (p. 6). It also noted that while the Internet, digital, and mobile technologies have indeed changed the media landscape, "traditional" media continue to play an important role, particularly in the delivery of online news (p. 6). Like Ofcom, the FCC iteration delineated several types of geo-spatial news and information services. Unlike Ofcom, however, it refrained from explicating what it thought "local" meant, thereby relying on a form of default localism of assumption and taken-for-granted definitions. Still, it identified four types of news: (1) Hyperlocal (neighborhood based); (2) Local (municipal and state); (3) National; and (4) International. This is a departure from the FCC's 2010 media ownership review (see chapter 2) and the Commission's *Broadcast Localism Initiative* (see chapter 5), both of which spent more space contemplating media localism. Despite the flourishing of online hyperlocalism, moreover, it was determined that this alone would not fill the gaps in local accountability journalism (particularly investigative journalism) caused by the decline in local daily newspapers and reporting staff. Accordingly, "the Waldman Report" (named after the report's chief architect, Steven Waldman) estimated that it would take between $265 million and $1.6 billion per year to close the lacuna within news and information services.

ECOSYSTEMS

The Waldman Report represents the most comprehensive assessment of local media ecosystems ever undertaken in the United States. It assessed the declining profits and audiences of local news across media, but also made sure to take note of the innovations and experimentations that had taken place in both the public and private sectors. It also cataloged the interactions between these media, the role of policy and regulation, and the role of government, foundations, libraries, and journalism schools. The most precipitous drops had, of course, been experienced by newspapers, with an impressive list of newspaper closures taking up an entire page. Television stations saw a decline of 56.3 percent in revenues for local news, and a 62.9 percent revenue decline for local news in smaller markets (p. 74). Approximately 258 commercial stations and 68 percent of public television stations did not produce any local news (pp. 157–58). For public broadcasting, this was a surprising finding, given that public stations have often billed themselves as the last remaining local electronic media outlets in the American mediascape.[6] Interestingly, in spite of declining revenues, the raw hours of local news on commercial stations actually *increased* from an average of 3.7 hours per day in 2003 to 5 hours per day in 2009. These hours, however, reflected breakfast shows, and not an increase in accountability or investigative reporting (p. 64). This increase in raw hours masks significant deficits in local television news, such as the lack of investigative and in-depth reporting, the reduction of staff, an ongoing reliance on the "if it bleeds, it leads" credo, and the disturbing trend of advertisers dictating editorial content through "pay-for-play" arrangements (pp. 86–92).

Broaching the question of content diversity, a key question asked, but never answered, stemmed from a discussion of the role of the Internet (or lack thereof) in contributing to original local reporting, and the notion of local news as a public good: "Markets usually respond to consumer demand. *But what happens if consumers don't demand something they essentially need?*" (pp. 125–26, emphasis added). This is the fundamental dilemma for media in the public interest, and is complicated by the Internet, which allows those who do not wish to pay for news to do so.[7] This important question rests on a "thought experiment" that asks the reader to consider local news as a "merit good"—something that should be offered regardless of levels of consumption (Musgrave, 1959; chapter 7). The report did not follow through on this question, though it did explicate the relationship between public goods and market failures: "Why would consumers not want to pay for goods that are so beneficial? The short answer is: because they do not have to. They can receive the information or the benefit of the information's creation regardless of whether they have paid for it, essentially getting a 'free ride'" (p. 126). While acknowledging the political economic positioning of local news as a public good and as a market failure, the report committed to a doctrine of regulatory nonintervention, or as it put it, adhering to the "Hippocratic Oath of physicians, 'First, do no harm'" (p. 2). Believing that the First Amendment "circumscribes the role government can play in improving local news" (p. 6), the Waldman Report concluded that it will be the *commercial* media system that will deliver news and information to citizens. This staunch market fundamentalism can be summed up in one key heading: "how fast will commercial media markets evolve to fill the gap [in local reporting]?" (p. 263).

Exemplifying the central tenets of neoliberalism, individual citizens were encouraged to increase funding and support of public broadcasting and public media: "It is time for citizens to think of media as an important item on their menu of charitable choices . . . labor-intensive, civically-valuable reporting will not flourish unless citizens spend more on it, whether through donations to nonprofits, subscriptions to commercial entities, or a combination of both" (p. 355). The public is thus saddled both with supporting the private system by continuing to subscribe to and consume local news and with supporting the public system through increased donations. Private foundations were also encouraged to contribute more to support journalism at the local level. This celebration of the individual over the collective, the private over the public, and failure ascribed to the individual rather than the market, are apt illustrations of what Harvey (2005) calls the "neoliberal turn" in the modern nation-state. At its most extreme, it means that public media are being ransomed back to the citizen through the expectation of increased donations.

IMPACT

The Great Recession and changing consumption habits were identified as seminal factors in the reduction of local news. Other sources of blame included certain FCC policies that apparently discouraged local production. The Waldman Report targeted four FCC policies for revision or termination. These policy suggestions were largely benign, leaving many dismayed that the report had not been more aggressive in promoting progressive media

120 · REGULATING LOCALISM

reform (*Variety*, 2011; Stearns, 2011; see also Pickard, 2015). Specifically, the report recommended terminating remnants of the long-defunct Fairness Doctrine, which had been effectively eliminated in 1987.[8] The second recommendation was the termination of the *Localism Proceeding*, which had been ongoing since 2003 (see chapter 5). Apparently, the *Localism Proceeding* contained "several unworkable or unnecessarily burdensome ideas such as a requirement that all stations have around-the-clock staffing" (p. 347), though it had not produced a document since 2008 and was functionally disbanded. The third recommendation was the elimination of the paper logs that broadcasters were required to keep in order to comply with certain public interest provisions (p. 347). The fourth recommendation was that the FCC should "consider the potential effects of newspaper-TV station mergers on local news ecosystems" while undertaking the 2010 Ownership Review (see chapter 2).

Despite the comprehensive research agenda, many public interest advocates, including Commissioner Michael Copps, were underwhelmed with the recommendations (Pickard, 2015). As Copps remarked, the report "and its accompanying recommendations are not the bold response for which I hoped and dared to dream. Instead, the overarching conclusion of the Staff Report seems to be that America's media landscape is mostly vibrant and there is no overall crisis of news or information. But there *is* a crisis, as this Report tells us, more than one-third of our commercial broadcasters offer little or no news whatsoever in their communities of license" (2011, p. 1). In contrast, Commissioner Robert McDowell (2011) offered solace to those who feared the report had gone too far in recommending progressive tactics: "I want to stress that this is report is simply that: a report which, though generated by a hard-working group of agency staffers, has no binding effect. In other words, this report does not establish new FCC rules" (p. 1). McDowell foreshadowed the eventual fate of the Waldman Report—that it would not have much impact on the overall policies, regulations, or opinions of the FCC. Indeed, the report made few waves within the policymaking community and received even less attention from the mainstream press. Interestingly, though, it was the centerpiece of an article in the Canadian business newsletter *Wire Report*, which claimed "Canadian broadcasters can take lessons from FCC report on local news" (Burgess, 2011).

ADDENDUM: "CRITICAL NEEDS"

Less than one year following publication of the Waldman Report, in February 2012, the FCC sent out a call for bids to conduct a comprehensive literature review on the "Critical Information Needs of the American Public" (FCC,

2012). The winning bid was from a collection of scholars spearheaded by the Annenberg School for Communication and Journalism at the University of Southern California: the Communication Policy Research Network (CPRN).

At 124-pages long, the CPRN Report is an impressive scholarly literature review containing significant implications for media localism. In particular it identified local news and information as *public goods,* and noted that "the failure to provide them is, in part, a market failure" (p. v). It also defined a community in both "geo-spatial and demographic terms":

> Americans live in communities of place, despite the exponential penetration of new forms of digital technology into every corner of everyday life. Whether South Los Angeles or rural South Carolina, our needs for information are shaped by the places that we live in, our blocks and neighborhoods, cities or suburbs, and the people we live with. . . . The groups we are a part of also shape our information needs in many ways: by ethnicity, race or immigration; by religion; by occupation or income; by gender and family situation; our health or abilities. (p. iv)

This is one of the few American documents to fully recognize the symbiotic relationship between communities of interest and communities of place, rather than viewing them as antagonistic. From here, the CPRN identified eight critical information needs, spanning everything from emergency information, to health, education, transportation, economic opportunities, the environment, civic information, and political information (p. vi). It also echoed previous reports in arguing that the Internet is not a substitute for traditional media, and that all media must be assessed in concert. As with the Waldman Report, however, little has come of the CPRN report.

Canada: Cultural Sovereignty

Despite Canadian media industries suffering from the same challenges as those described in the United States and the UK, neither the government nor the CRTC have embarked on a comprehensive study of local media ecosystems and the information needs of Canadian communities (Ali, 2016b). Instead, the CRTC has focused its attention, almost myopically, on broadcasting, rather than embracing the belief shared by the FCC and Ofcom that a regulator should be aware of the entire media ecosystem.[9] The closest approximation of an ecosystem study came in the form of the 2003 report *Our Culture Sovereignty: The Second Century of Canadian Broadcasting* (Canada, 2003a). Its mandate was to assess the Canadian broadcasting industry in light of the goals set out in the 1991 Broadcasting Act. Of particular interest, as the title suggests, were provisions in the Act that promoted Canadian reflection and production. In other words, cultural sovereignty. Notwithstanding the reference to domestic sovereignty, the report represents the most focused review of Canadian local broadcasting ever conducted. It is also the only Canadian study to grapple with the underlying challenges of defining the local, the regional, and the community in a globalized and digital age. As with other case studies in this chapter, however, its recommendations and conclusions would fall on deaf ears, "gathering dust on a shelf at Canadian Heritage" (Raboy, 2006, p. 302).[10] Any effort to resuscitate the Canadian broadcasting industry needs to dust off this important report, and revisit many of its thoughtful conclusions.

THE "LINCOLN REPORT"

Commissioned on May 10, 2001, the Lincoln Report (as the report came to be known for its chairperson, Member of Parliament Clifford Lincoln) was "the first major look at the Broadcast Act since the [1988] Task Force on Broadcasting Policy" (Fraser, 2001). Taking two years to produce, it was tabled to parliament in 2003 and covered everything from the history of Canadian broadcasting, to the CBC, private broadcasting, aboriginal broadcasting, and educational broadcasting. A considerable portion was also devoted to local, regional, and community broadcasting. This included an entire chapter dedicated to the subject, and part of the chapter on the CBC dedicated to describing (and chastising) the public broadcaster's commitments to localism and regionalism.

One of the report's most important, yet seldom recalled, conclusions was the difficulty of delineating "community" and "local" from "regional" in Canadian media. The report initially defined local television from a technical standpoint, using the definition employed by the CRTC of signal contours and license areas. From this point of departure, the committee noted the complexities in defining "the local" when placed against "the regional." It poignantly commented, "part of the problem with the term regional is that one person's regional can be someone else's local, regional or provincial; and, depending on one's location, it can be all three" (p. 356). An excellent example of such slippage occurs in the province of Prince Edward Island, where, as one witness testified: "The problem with discussing the Island as an example is that the population is so small. It is a province, it is a unit, it is a unity, but the point that is being made here is that the question of what is local, what is provincial, and what is regional is blurred a little bit here. In

P.E.I. clearly you need to have what may appear to be local broadcasting, but it is also provincial broadcasting" (p. 356). Defining a locality from a region and a region from a province has enormous implications for Canadian media policy, including the regulation of quotas, market areas, licensing, and diversity of voices.

The report chastised the CRTC for failing to ameliorate these definitional problems: "The Committee is of the view that the CRTC's new community media policy does very little to resolve the definitional ambiguities and inconsistencies inherent in the existing uses of the terms community, local and regional" (p. 361). As the report continued, "as should be clear by now, finding satisfactory definitions of community, local and regional is difficult" (p. 362). In a subsequent chapter, it noted how considering Aboriginal broadcasting as an element of "community," "local," or "regional" broadcasting further complicates these already muddy waters (p. 378). One of my interview respondents added that the CRTC had "very little appetite to divorce the concept of community from geography" (anonymous, personal communication). While this may be true, the Lincoln Report demonstrates the inherent complications and complexities even when community and geography are assumed tethered. The report itself, however, offered no concrete definitions of its own, and instead advised the Department of Canadian Heritage and the CRTC to resolve these taxonomic challenges on their own (which they have not). The report pointed out the lack of a unified understanding of "key terms" and advised the CRTC to clarify its "bewildering array of policies." Accordingly, it recommended the development of a Community, Local and Regional Broadcast Policy. Included in this single "coherent policy" framework would not only be community, local, and regional media but also ethnic and minority-language programming and low-power and campus broadcasting. Never before—or since—has a committee or the CRTC recognized these kinds of issues in Canadian media policy and regulation.

PUBLIC AND PRIVATE

The CBC was another target for localism critiques, particularly for its controversial decision in 2000 to reduce local news and regional programming. The decision to concentrate production in major centers also drew substantive criticism: "As the Committee travelled across Canada, it became apparent that feelings run deep—especially outside Toronto and Montréal—whenever the issue of local, regional and national programming is mentioned. In particular, decreases in local CBC programming—which started in the early 1990s—raised many questions concerning the role and mandate of the national public broadcaster" (p. 203). Reference to these cities is not unfamiliar in Canadian regulatory parlance. The regional programming guidelines, for instance, specify that to qualify as "regional" a program must be produced more than 150 kilometers away from Vancouver, Toronto, and Montreal (CRTC, 1999). Adequate regional production is one of the central challenges in a country as geographically vast and sparsely populated as Canada.

One of the pivotal questions arising from the Lincoln Report was whether the CBC was mandated to serve neglected localities, as its regional and local responsibilities were left ambiguous in the Broadcasting Act. A related question is whether the CBC and its French-language counterpart, Radio-Canada, should do more to serve Canada's francophone populations, particularly those outside Quebec. This raises a larger epistemological question for public broadcasting, not only in Canada, but elsewhere: When the mission of public broadcasting is to unify a country, how should it respond to regional concerns? While recognizing the different roles that the CBC may play in a metropolis like Toronto and rural Saskatchewan, where "the CBC may be the only strong voice" (p. 217), the report recommended leaving local and regional programming decisions to the broadcaster.

The report also examined the local commitments of commercial broadcasters, noting that cuts to local programming have been severe. It criticized commercial broadcasters (particularly CTV) for consolidating many of their smaller operations into regional hubs, especially in northern Ontario and the Atlantic provinces. Interestingly, fee-for-carriage (see chapter 2) was briefly addressed as having the potential to solve these local programming issues. The report did not recommend this particular course of action. It did, however, make note of some of the success stories of local news, such as CHUM Media's Citytv station in Toronto, which "seamlessly blend[s] interactions with the local community into live and recorded programming" (p. 353).

Coupled with the recommendation to sort out definitional conundrums and create a unified local media policy, the report recommended that the Department of Canadian Heritage—one of two Canadian departments overseeing broadcasting—create a Local Broadcasting Initiative Program (LBIP) "to assist in the provision of radio and television programming at the community, local and regional levels" (p. 367). Anticipating the 2008 Local Programming Improvement Fund, the LBIP would be a community-driven fund, accessible to all local broadcasters including the CBC, to develop locally targeted programming and reduce some of the deficits in this genre. Ideally, the fund would be malleable to reflect the needs and interests of disparate Canadian communities, to be identified by the communities themselves. Though the fund was never implemented, its proposition demonstrates the palpable concern for the dearth of local and community programming, and signals an interventionist, rather than market-driven, approach to its solution—a contrast to the market fundamentalist approach of the FCC, and the neoliberal nod of Ofcom.

The Lincoln Report concluded with two dissenting opinions: one from the conservative political party, the Canadian Alliance, and one from the separatist, Québec-based party, the Bloc Québecois. The Bloc's dissent is particularly insightful, as it addresses the definition of a region for Canadian broadcasting: "One of the problems with the Broadcasting Act is that it does not have a definition of the adjective 'regional'; a 'region' may be assimilated with a group of provinces, one province or another region (part of a province). Quebec will never agree to being regarded as a region. This results in a confused understanding and application of the law" (p. 859). This highlights the political tensions of defining a region in Canada (not unlike the problems of defining Scotland, Wales, and Northern Ireland for the purposes of broadcasting law in the UK). The challenge leaves one to ask, as Friesen (2001) and Dunbar-Hester (2013) do, if such definitions are entirely useful. The Bloc, moreover, aligned the challenges of Francophone cultural production with those of First Nations peoples, arguing that both of these communities are neglected by a system predicated on centralization: "The Canadian broadcasting system seems to have gone off-course: it is now more open to the world but it is also too focused on major urban centres, and local and regional communities feel forgotten . . ." (p. 574). This view aligns with the one remarked upon in chapter 3, where the CRTC has tended to neglect smaller Canadian regions and communities in favor of the metropolitan centers of Canada. Though the Bloc Quebecois has now entered into political obscurity, questions around definitions of the local and regional (and of the role of Quebec in Canadian nationalism, for that matter) remain unresolved. The CRTC seems comfortable relying on default localism rather than opening up the conversation, as the Lincoln Report suggested.

LINCOLN'S LEGACY

When a report from a parliamentary committee is tabled, the Canadian government is mandated to respond within 150 days. The government's first response to the Lincoln Report, written by Heritage Minister Sheila Copps (no relation to Michael Copps), came in November 2003 and left much to be desired. As Raboy and Taras (2004) argue, the response "seemed to resist any notion that the system was in need of considerable overhaul" (p. 63). It contained mostly platitudes and vague commitments, while "largely ignor[ing] or put[ting] off to a later date" many of the report's more substantive recommendations (p. 63). For instance, in spite of the report's concern with localism, the government's response was simply the promise to "examine the wider issues the Committee raises" (Canada, 2003b, p. 5). Raboy and Taras (2004) aptly label this a "politics of neglect."

Despite some initial press coverage, interest in the report waned within a few months. As the broadcast industry magazine *Playback* commented: "Sank like a cinder block. Gone the way of the dodo. Fell off the radar. These are the phrases that spring to mind when one thinks of the Lincoln Report" (Davidson, 2004). Saved from this fate, the Report was given a second life when it was reintroduced to Parliament in December 2004, mandating a second government response. The second response, this time under a new Liberal Prime Minister, Paul Martin, was written by then-Heritage Minister Liza Frulla and released in 2005. It promised greater intervention and study of the broadcasting system (Canada, 2005). The response even suggested a comprehensive study of local media ecosystems focusing on the information needs of Canadian communities and the range of media platforms that Canadians consult (Canada, 2005). As Frulla wrote: "Canadians have made it clear that local and regional content is important to them. Local news is the most important type of news to Canadians, ranked over national or international news. If the Government is to respond to Canadians' needs, the focus must shift from the provider to the citizen, by looking at all of the various media that serve Canadians in a given community" (p. 7). Frulla's response received considerable press attention, much of it critical of the government's alignment with media moguls (*Toronto Star*, 2005). Though these critiques are not wrong, the response signals the government's most progressive pledge to the information needs of Canadians. Unfortunately, it would not have an opportunity to act. Another change of government, this time in 2006, ousted the Liberal party and replaced it with a minority Conservative government, which quickly forgot about the Lincoln Report. The report has thus completed the self-fulfilling prophecy predicted by many of "gathering dust" in the library of parliament (Raboy & Taras, 2004; Raboy, 2006, p. 302).

Conclusion: Gathering Dust

Each of the studies examined in this chapter underscores the normative importance of local news to the democratic health of the country, and took pains to demonstrate the lack of in-depth local news and information coming into and being produced out of individual communities. The US and UK reports also underscored the important need for regulators to understand local media ecosystems holistically, rather than concentrating on media within a specific jurisdiction.

Where the studies dramatically depart is in how they approach the larger epistemological question of defining the local. The American study took a conventional route, assigning terms on a scale of geographically delineated units—hyperlocal, local, national, international. While understandable, this delineation relies on an uncritical assumption of default localism that tends to treat the local as a homogenous unit of consumption of the news commodity rather than a complex ecosystem of communities and organizations. The UK presented the most considered approach, and while ultimately relying on a place-based definition, explicated its decision process and anxieties. The Canadian report, too, discussed the challenges of defining community, local, and regional, and critiqued the CRTC for its opaque treatment of these terms. Though the report did not offer any definitions of its own, it attempted to start a conversation about the nature of the local in Canadian society—a conversation that unfortunately was not continued.

Lamentably, a lack of impact is a shared feature of these reports. Despite the impressive volume of research and assessment, the resulting impact of these studies has been disappointing. The largest of the three—the Lincoln Report, at almost nine hundred pages—had a brief resurgence upon its reintroduction in 2004, but its recommendations, conclusions, and research have since been forgotten. Still, these reports remain important assessments of local media ecologies, and their findings should not fall into disuse or victim to regulatory amnesia that focuses on the new and the now. The next chapter looks at the concrete regulatory actions taken to positively intervene in the challenges of media localism.

5

The Solutions of Localism
Regulatory Approaches to the Crisis of Local Television

> Nobody in Cambridge is interested in the traffic jams in Bedford.
> —qtd. in Briggs, 1995, p. 631

A Twentieth-Century Medium

By the end of the first decade of the twenty-first century, localism was in trouble. "Crisis" became the watchword of the industry. A crisis of journalism was looming over news organizations, the business model for local television was broken, and local content was ailing or absent. Something needed to be done, or, at least, regulators needed to appear to be doing something to protect this element of the public interest. After all, if two constants emerged from the ecosystem reports of the previous chapter, they are that consumers value local television and do not want to see it disappear. This present chapter documents those "somethings" attempted by regulators, chronicling efforts by the FCC, CRTC, and Ofcom to address the many facets of the localism problem that have plagued the broadcasting industry and evaded policymakers for decades.

Responses to these challenges align with the political-economic realities of the respective countries. In the United States, a country firmly embedded within the structures of market fundamentalism and with distaste for regulatory intervention, a taskforce with very little real policymaking authority was announced in 2003. In Canada, with weaker neoliberal sensibilities but with great hopes for technological nationalism, the CRTC created a short-lived subsidy in 2008 to support small-market television stations. In the UK, a change in government in 2010 saw the termination of a widely supported multimedia local news project in exchange for a profit-driven local television service. These initiatives attempted to solve the problem of an analogue medium in a digital world: how to profit from local television.

Marc Raboy (1990) has called the history of Canadian broadcasting one of "missed opportunities" to create a robust, sovereign, and public system. This narrative can be applied to thinking about the processes of drafting regulatory responses to the crises of localism. No more so is this true than with the United States, which is where this chapter begins, and where an opportunity to foster an open dialogue on the nature, goals, and definitions of localism was ultimately stifled by regulatory malaise.

United States: "A thousand footnotes"

Unlike the UK and Canada, the American regulatory response to the challenges of media localism did not result in regulation, subsidy, or system change. Rather, it manifested in a study of "Broadcast Localism." This project represented a unique opportunity in American communications history to better understand the information needs of local communities and to evaluate the policies and epistemologies upon which localism was regulated. Perhaps not since the 1946 "Blue Book" had an opportunity been so available (Pickard, 2014).[1] Sadly, this potential remained unrealized. Though the project succeeded in mobilizing a grassroots base, a clear lack of regulatory support meant that it could never achieve what it was tasked to accomplish.

2003: THE ANNOUNCEMENT

On August 20, 2003, FCC Chairperson Michael Powell announced the creation of the Localism in Broadcasting Initiative. Clearly responding to the criticism garnered by the Commission's recent attempt to deregulate broadcast ownership (see chapter 2), Powell conceded: "we heard the voice of public concern about the media loud and clear. Localism is at the core of these concerns . . . and we are going to tackle it head on" (FCC 2003c, p. 1). This encouraging start was quickly tempered by a set of mixed signals. In the same speech that Powell acknowledged "a deep-seated anxiety in the American public about a commitment to local values and local communities," he did not shy away from noting his own "skeptic[ism] . . . that 'the only way you can serve a local community is by having a small station in a local community owned by a local owner'" (qtd. in Steinberg, 2003). While Powell was correct to identify an existential crisis within the discourse of American localism (see Braman, 2007), many would disagree that a station owned from afar serves a community equally as well as a locally based owner (e.g., Napoli & Yan, 2007).

The Localism Initiative would have three components. First and foremost, it would have a taskforce comprised of FCC staffers mandated to "advis[e] the Commission on concrete steps that can be taken to promote localism" (FCC, 2003c, p. 2). Toward this end, the taskforce's specific duties were to conduct hearings and commission studies. The second component was a comprehensive report, delivered by the taskforce within twelve months. The third component was a formal Notice of Inquiry issued by the Commission to investigate potential policy changes.

Though the taskforce garnered support from major industry groups such as the National Association of Broadcasters (NAB), many in the public interest community saw this as an attempt by Powell to quell his critics. Jeff Chester of the Center for Digital Democracy argued that Powell was "... trying to shore up his support in Congress" (Salant, 2003). Senator Byron Dorgan (D-N.D.) expressed confusion as to why the chairman would deregulate broadcast ownership only to study localism after the fact (Steinberg, 2003). Most vocal of the critics was Democratic Commissioner Michael J. Copps, who had long opposed the deregulation of broadcast ownership and was a longtime progressive supporter of the public interest. Copps called the announcement "a day late and a dollar short" and argued that if localism was so important to the FCC, then it should have been studied *before* the deregulation of the industry (2003b, p. 2). Copps recalled in 2012: "In my mind, it was a charade . . . because we had made such a ruckus . . . all of a sudden, I think Michael [Powell] . . . had to do something. . . . So, all of the sudden, we had this localism taskforce. . . . I don't think it was designed to make a difference" (personal communication, 11/20/12). Notwithstanding dissenters, the taskforce went ahead with plans for public hearings in Charlotte, N.C. (October 2003), San Antonio, Tex. (December 2003), Santa Cruz/Salinas, Calif. (March 2004), Rapid City, S.D. (April 2004), Portland, Me. (May 2004), and Washington, D.C. (June 2004). Much to the chagrin of media reform advocates, only four of these hearings would occur. The others would be pushed to 2008.

2004: THE HEARINGS

The hearings brought together invited panelists (primarily from the commercial broadcasting industry) and members of the public. With few exceptions, Commissioner Adelstein chaired the sessions, which began with a recitation on the value of localism to the American media system:

> Every community has its local needs, its local talents, local elections, local news, and local culture. And localism reflects the commitment to local news and public affairs programming, but it also means a lot more. It means providing opportunities for local self-expression, it means reaching out, developing and promoting local performing artists and other local talent. It means making programming decisions that serve local needs. It means making sure that the coverage reflects the makeup of the community.... Localism also means the station being responsive to the community in other ways, such as dedicating the resources to discover and address the needs of the community. (qtd. in FCC 2003d, pp. 19–20)

In a few short sentences, Adelstein defined localism far better and far more precisely than any previous attempt by the FCC. Nevertheless, he shied away from tackling the larger epistemological challenge of defining what is meant by "local." Still, his definition of localism clearly demurs with Powell's reticence toward the role that local communities play within the media ecosystem. Such praise, however, was not without qualification. After the first hearing in Charlotte, North Carolina, Commissioner Copps had to qualify this epigraph by reminding those presenting on behalf of television stations that "conducting blood drives and fundraisers for charities" does not constitute "the sum total of their public interest responsibilities" (qtd. in FCC, 2004b, p. 26). While recognizing these contributions, Copps pleaded with respondents to avoid "the temptation to catalog all of their nonbroadcast efforts" and instead "focus ... on the greater picture of what they are doing as trustees of the public's airwaves" (p. 27). This was echoed by a commenter in San Antonio who questioned why broadcasters were being praised for doing what was expected of them: "I think that praising broadcasters for giving to charities or covering local news is like praising my son for taking a bath, because that's something that they should be doing anyways" (FCC, 2004b, p. 210). Early on in this process we see hints that the definition of localism employed (or taken for granted) by the Commission—that of a station being responsive to community needs—did not adequately satisfy the public's expectations. Dunbar-Hester (2013) praises this ambiguous quality of localism, calling it a "discursive boundary object," and focusing on the benefits of such a malleable definition. At that particular moment, however, it seemed that a lack of definition was more a source of frustration than of innovation.

The connection between localism and ownership was the main driver of the hearings, but an important secondary topic was that of definitions, followed by implications for minority audiences, particularly in promoting minority language and local news. This suggests that localism is more than the immediate geographic community, but also encompasses the communities of interest *within* the community of geography, including ethno-linguistic groups. Such was the argument heard in South Dakota, where Native American representatives pushed for greater positive representation of their communities on local airwaves (FCC, 2004c). In Monterey, one speaker suggested that local programming be defined "as programming of interest to the local community, regardless of the source" (FCC, 2004d, p. 51). Another suggested that news about Mexico or El Salvador should be considered local if it is "important locally" to the Hispanic population (p. 51). These comments certainly suggest a more encompassing regulatory definition of localism. Though the Commission has long agreed that local programming is not solely about locally originated programming, its track record indicates that it prefers local origination.[2] This was noted by a speaker in Monterrey who explained that Class-A stations are the only category of license that has a local-origination mandate (three hours per week).[3] Like the minority interest speakers, this respondent argued that the definition of local programming needed to be expanded "so that when we do local interviews at the state capitol, that this could be a local program for our stations" (p. 139). A more expansive regulatory definition of localism may indeed allow for more "community communication" (FCC, 2004a) particularly with regard to minority communities. How these changes might occur, however, was not discussed.

2004: THE NOTICE

The final public hearing, which was by far the most spirited (Hillard & Keith 2005), took place on July 21, 2004, in Monterey, California. Earlier in the month the FCC released its long awaited (and year late) *Notice of Inquiry In the Matter of Broadcast Localism* (NOI) to formally interrogate issues of localism (FCC, 2004a). This could not have come at a more crucial time for local broadcasters, with Pew (2004) reporting a decade-long decline in audiences for, and investments in, local news. The NOI reaffirmed the Commission's definition of localism as one in which "licensees must air programming that is responsive to the interests and needs of their communities of license" (p. 1). Departing from the FCC's normal deregulatory ethos, the NOI—for perhaps the only time—sought comment on the possibility of redefining localism. It is worth quoting the NOI at length to fully understand these unique propositions:

> Does "local" programming best serve [community needs]? If so, what would qualify as "local" programming? Locally originated or locally produced pro-

gramming? Or should locally oriented programming, meaning programming of particular interest to the local community, count regardless of its source? ... Difficulties associated with defining "local" programming present geographic questions as well. We also note that programming that is not specifically targeted to the local community may still serve the needs and interests of the community ... (FCC, 2004a, p. 7)

Here, the Commission sought comment on definitions of the local, local programming, local origination, and the geographic orientation of the localism principle—all issues that had frustrated previous Commissions and observers alike.

In public comments to the NOI, a predominant theme was exactly this definitional quandary, in particular the divide between locally originated programming and locally relevant programming. Community-based organizations including the National Federation of Community Broadcasters (NFCB) and the Alliance for Community Media (ACM) favored locally originated programming, noting the market failure in the genre. Other small organizations like the Community Broadcasters Association (CBA), which represents Class-A stations, argued against any definition that mandates local origination. Instead, they suggested a more expansive definition that would "include a test of 'significant local interest' in a program's content" (2004, p. 4).

This latter group was joined by a set of strange bedfellows that comprised both the market-oriented NAB and the public broadcaster National Public Radio (NPR). NAB (2004) favored the deregulatory precedent set by the FCC, specifically arguing that "competition forces localism" (p. 3). They furthermore argued against local origination, noting, "programming need not be produced locally to be locally relevant" (p. 24). To do so would violate the position the Commission took in the 1980s that "programming does not have to be originated locally to qualify as 'issue responsive' ..." (p. 24). The NAB also disagreed with the FCC's proposal to reinstate the "ascertainment regulation" of mandated community dialogue, believing that stations already served their communities according to market demand. The market, not regulation, was what drives broadcasters to be responsive to their communities. This objection was echoed by NPR, which also argued against ascertainment and local-origination stipulations. Like the NAB, NPR (2004) argued that its stations were "fundamentally rooted in local communities," but, unlike commercial broadcasters, NPR stations were driven not by the market, but rather by "social and institutional factors" to serve their communities (p. 21).

One of the most detailed comments came from the Brennan Center (2004), which favored media reform but also seemed to walk the line between opposing sides. Their primary concern was the geographic definition of localism, and they offered a clear interpretation of the localism principle to reinforce their arguments: "Serving local communities—'localism'—is a fundamental goal of American broadcast policy. Localism means providing residents of local communities with diverse cultural programming, opportunities for self-expression, and access to the solid, in-depth public affairs programming about local and national affairs that is essential to democracy" (p. iii). Unlike NPR and NAB, Brennan argued for a geographically based definition, one that would also take into account communities of interest within geographic boundaries. They were particularly concerned that local communities were being defined as *markets*, rather than as political or cultural communities. As we know, the FCC uses "Designated Market Areas" (DMAs) (created by Nielsen) to demarcate community boundaries. Markets are larger than the communities of license for a station, and can easily be extended through retransmitters. This allows stations to cater to larger audiences. According to Brennan, the needs of individual communities get lost when they are subsumed into larger and larger markets. The larger the footprint of a station, the more diluted local reflection becomes. To correct this, the Brennan Center recommended more attention be paid to the licensing of nonprofit media to "serve the needs and interests of diverse social, economic, ethnic, and racial groups *within* local communities" (p. v., emphasis added). Noting, as the Center did, that localism and diversity are inextricably linked (cf., the NAB, which linked localism and the market), Brennan advocated for an expanded definition of localism, but one still within the confines of geographic parameters.

These comments represent a clear example of the conversations occurring within the peripheries of localism regulation that offer alternatives to the spatial/social dilemma. Localism is a topic that divided commentators not only along ideological lines (commercial vs. noncommercial) but also within what have traditionally been thought of as homogenous groups (e.g., nonprofit media). One of the difficulties for the Commission, therefore, was weighing these arguments and attempting to craft a solution to what Cox Broadcasting (2008) now called the "localism problem." Unfortunately, stakeholders would have to wait four years for any such decision-making to occur.

2005: THE DMA

The NOI would be the last official foray into localism for four years, during which time a presidential election, the resignation of Michael Powell, and the promotion of Republican Kevin Martin to chairperson all forced changes at the FCC. Other issues also diverted the Commission's attention, including another review of media ownership (2006) and a slew of court battles related to the 2002/2003 ownership review (United States, 2004a). During this interim, however, the localism issue was not dead and certainly not forgotten. Senators Byron Dorgan and Trent Lott argued that the Commission should delay its 2006 review of media ownership until the localism docket was complete (Triplett, 2007). A Senate bill floated by Dorgan in late 2007 even proposed to force the issue upon the FCC (Triplett, 2007). The Commission itself also did not entirely forget about the localism proceedings. To the contrary, it used it as an opportunity to skirt important ownership questions, concluding that the 2006 ownership review did not have to include matters of localism because those were handled in a separate docket (FCC, 2008c).

While the FCC put localism on the backburner, the Brennan Center's concern that local communities were being subsumed into markets was revived in an insightful (yet seldom referenced) document drafted by the Congressional Research Service (CRS) (Goldfarb, 2005). Its primary focus was the challenge of defining the local for broadcasting, cable, and satellite services. The report highlighted the confusing definitions of the community of license (with narrowly drawn boundaries), signal reach (a much larger geographic area), and the DMA (an even larger geographic region). Concern here was for those who reside within a DMA, but outside the city of license. Residents of these geographic areas are often unserved or underserved by their local stations because "the licensee's explicit public interest obligation is limited to serving the needs and interests of viewers within the city of license" (2005, p. 1). An illustrative example is the PBS affiliate WHYY, licensed to Wilmington, Delaware, but serving the entire DMA of (and located in) Philadelphia, Pennsylvania. With a substantially larger population, Philadelphia is the station's target market, but at the expense of smaller cities in the DMA: Wilmington (Del.), Camden (N.J.), Trenton (N.J.), and Atlantic City (N.J.). While the FCC created a "secondary obligation for the licensee to serve the needs of viewers outside the city of license but within signal reach" (p. 70), the CRS found that in practice this obligation was not being met. The report thus detailed the heretofore-unnoted market failure of local broadcasting in serving *all* communities within the DMA.

Cable regulation further compounds this geographic confusion, particularly for residents whose DMA straddles two states. Cable providers are required to carry only those stations whose signal contours align with the cable service area. This "must carry" regulation stipulates that a cable system can only carry channels local to the DMA and cannot import outside signals (United States, 1992). If a cable subscriber resides in a DMA that straddles two states, but lives in the state that does not have the city of license, they will not receive any in-state stations. So, if a subscriber lives in Wilmington (and therefore within the Philadelphia DMA) they cannot receive signals from other Delaware stations through their cable provider, because the cable provider is only legally able to provide local stations from the Philadelphia DMA. This leaves viewers who reside outside the state where the city of license is based without local or even state news, and poses significant complications for the mandate of localism to serve specific geographic communities. It furthermore poses democratic challenges: When residents are only able to receive out-of-state "local" information through their cable systems, informational and communicatory neglect is inevitable.

Though unspoken, the underlying issues are clearly those of definition, markets, and communities of place and interest: How does a local station decide who its communities are? How does it serve these communities? And how do federal regulations hinder or support these determinations? This gets to the heart of the localism question: What is local, what is a community, and what is local television? The CRS outlined certain steps Congress could take to mitigate these territorial tensions, particularly because "market incentives" for stations often diverge from the goal of serving all communities within the DMA. Suggestions included requiring the FCC to address this issue in the Localism Initiative, or to mandate cable providers to carry the "multicast" signals of broadcasters if each stream targeted a "previously unserved geographic portion of the broadcaster's serving area" (p. 29).[4] To date these issues remain unresolved.

2007: THE RESTART

Amid calls from Congress and commissioners, Chairperson Martin reinstated the localism proceeding in 2007 and called for hearings in Portland, Maine, and Washington, D.C., in June and October, respectively. The Washington hearings—the last of the Localism Initiative—would be particularly damning for the FCC, with critique coming from both commissioners and respondents. Tensions escalated the week before the October 31 event, when Copps and Adelstein criticized the Commission for only announcing the hearing a week before. In his opening remarks at the hearing itself, Copps restated his many concerns and challenged the FCC to actually do something with the data that had been collected. Witness testimony reflected these concerns, and exposed the failure of the localism project to bring about meaningful change. Marc Cooper of the Consumer Federation went further by critiquing the handling of this docket: "despite the fanfare . . . the initiative simply disappeared from the recent research studies. ... It should not disappear into a thousand footnotes in a final order on media ownership" (FCC, 2007c, p. 48). Cooper's comments would prove prescient after the release of the Notice of Proposed Rulemaking, almost five years after the launch of the initiative.

2008: THE PROPOSAL

A Notice of Proposed Rulemaking is meant to be a stepping-stone to more concrete actions for federal agencies. It is a set of proposals to be publicly debated so the agency can make informed decisions. The FCC's (2008a) *Report on Broadcast Localism and Notice of Proposed Rulemaking* (NPRM) certainly fulfilled the first part of this definition, causing tremendous debate among stakeholders. The Commission received more than 83,000 public comments to the localism docket. More surprising than this great number was the slew of proposals from the Commission itself to stem the decline of local programming. Three recommendations stand out for being particularly interventionist from this otherwise hands-off regulator. First, it was observed that stations no longer engaged in discussions with viewers about the needs and interest of their communities. As a result, the Commission proposed to revive a version of the ascertainment rules that had been attached to station licenses before the 1980s to promote "communication between licensees and their communities" (see FCC, 1971). The proposed update—a "community advisory board"—would require stations to meet regularly with community advisers in order to better understand the "local needs and issues and seek comment on the matter" (p. 23). These conversations would help stations determine the needs and interests not only of the city of license, but also the outlying communities that receive their signal.

The second recommendation asked whether market-based practices should continue to decide the nature of local programming. Comment was sought on a proposal to create a more stringent license renewal process, whereby stations that met a minimum requirement of locally oriented programming would have their license renewal expedited. This proposal revived a rule that existed in the 1970s, where stations that aired a certain percentage of local programming were fast-tracked through the license renewal process (see FCC, 1973, 1976). A key point of debate here concerned measurement. Should local programming be assessed by prescribed hours of programming, percentage of programming hours, genres of programming, and/or local origination?

The third recommendation was to reinstate a version of the "Main Studio Rule" that had fallen by the wayside during the deregulatory push of the

1980s, and would require stations to be physically located *within* their community of license, not simply around their community of license, as had been permitted since 1987 (see FCC, 1998). In theory, this would allow for greater public access—an important component of the public interest—although critics have questioned whether the rule actually achieves this goal (Silverman & Tobenkin, 2001).

The Commission received trenchant objection to these proposals. Again unexpected were the bedfellows created by this opposition. Public, private, noncommercial, and religious broadcasters alike balked at the recommendations. The Main Studio Rule was a particular target for dissenters, who argued that moving stations within the community of license would be tremendously expensive, would not create tangible community benefits, and would cause "substantial burdens" (NPR, 2008, p. 1; APTS, 2008; NFCB, 2008).

Echoing the noncommercial groups, commercial broadcasters contended that the FCC was going against years of deregulatory precedent by digging up former regulations. The NAB, Cox, Clear Channel, NBC, and Ion Media all objected, arguing that the FCC had "no legitimate basis for adopting" these rules (Clear Channel, 2008, p. 21). Broadcasters also rallied against the rekindled ascertainment requirements, arguing that their stations already performed community needs assessments and function as "a public voice for local community and charitable organizations" (NAB, 2008, p. 3). Cox (2008) went so far as to argue that the "localism problem" was a creation of the FCC. The broadcaster argued that market incentives already demanded that stations serve the needs of their communities, and therefore there was no need for federal intervention.

Another point of agreement between commercial and noncommercial broadcasters was a critique of the regulatory definition of the local. Many noted that the Commission had failed to adequately define the local, leading to confusion and ambiguity. Clear Channel, for one, argued that the Commission did not have the authority to define local programming, and any attempts to do so would violate broadcasters' First Amendment rights to make programming decisions. Its argument hinged on the spatial/social divides so common in regulatory discourse: "Is 'local' programming locally produced programming, or programming that is locally oriented, or both? What is the geographic scope of a 'locality'—a community of license, a city, a county, a state, or a region? What if, as is often the case, programming addressing an issue of statewide, regional, national, or international importance is of interest to the local community?" (2008, pp. 56–57). This comment highlights the immeasurable complexities of defining localism in the twenty-first century, and the stake all media organizations have in the local as conveyers of a public good. Despite the obvious willingness of stakeholders to comment on these matters, the FCC did not act on any of its proposals, thereby missing an opportunity to engage with these questions. The end result, as Marc Cooper predicted, is that the Localism Initiative exists only as "a thousand footnotes" in other documents (FCC, 2007c, p. 48).

The Broadcast Localism Initiative's lack of impact suggests an overall neglect of localism by the FCC. Meanwhile, a reliance on DMAs as the measures for what is local fails to account for adjacent communities and communities of interest. That localism has remained an unresolved issue within American regulation since the creation of the broadcasting system in the 1920s (Kirkpatrick, 2006) suggests both the need for it to be openly discussed and the unlikelihood that such discussions will occur outside the beltway and stock market.

Canada: The Life and Death of the Local Programming Improvement Fund

The years leading up to the creation of the Local Programming Improvement Fund were acrimonious for Canadian local television. The 2007/2008 global financial crisis wreaked havoc on local advertising, while the industry was (and still is) engaged with the structural challenge of remaining relevant in the digital age. Whether local stations would survive past the first decade of the twenty-first century was a very real concern. In concert with these economic shifts was the ongoing petition for fee-for-carriage (FFC), which would see broadcasters compensated by cable and satellite companies (collectively, "Broadcast Distribution Undertakings" or BDUs) for the distribution of their signals (see chapter 2). The CRTC struck down broadcasters' petition for FFC in 2008, but did concede on two points. First, it permitted broadcasters to seek compensation from BDUs when their signals are transmitted out of market (known as "distant signaling"). Second, it created a subsidy to assist small market stations in the production of local programming.

2008: A TRADEOFF

At first glance, it appears that the subsidy contradicts the market-based logic prized by the Commission. However, the CRTC was unprepared to see the conventional broadcasting industry fail. Recognizing that local stations were under increased financial pressure and that this pressure was particularly acute for small-market and French-language stations, the CRTC created the scaffolding for a cross-media subsidy to assist local programming at nonmetropolitan television stations. This was justified on the basis that healthy "local stations that will enrich the diversity of information and editorial points of view" were in the public interest of Canadians (CRTC, 2008b, par. 348). It did not hurt that major broadcasters—CTV, Global, CBC—were threatening to close stations without some form of assistance (preferably FFC). Called the Local Programming Improvement Fund (LPIF), the subsidy would be financed through a 1 percent levy on the gross profits of the broadcasting activities of BDUs. BDUs were already required to contribute 5 percent of their gross profits to Canadian programming, and this contribution was raised to 6 percent, creating an initial fund of approximately $60 million (Cdn.). Eligible stations included both public and private stations serving "nonmetropolitan" markets, meaning those cities where the "population with a knowledge of the official language of the station (i.e., English or French) is less than one million" (par. 360).[5] BDUs were strongly discouraged from raising subscriber rates to accommodate the new levy.

The CRTC set out three objectives for the fund: to ensure the availability of local programming—local news programming in particular—for smaller communities; "to improve the quality and diversity of local programming broadcast in these markets;" and to "ensure that viewers in French-language markets are not disadvantaged by the smaller size of those markets" (par. 359). While the language of the LPIF promoted the development of local programming, the driving factor was to support local news. To qualify for the fund, eligible stations would already have to be producing original local news. Recurring LPIF grants would be predicated on an incremental increase in the stations' local programming expenditures. Funds could be used at the discretion of the station, but would have to be directed toward the production of additional local content, or enhancing existing content. The Canadian Association of Broadcasters (CAB) was seconded to administer the fund and create its technical framework. The Commission furthermore stipulated that to be fair to French-language broadcasters (which operated in the smallest markets), one-third of the total fund would be reserved for them. Last, the CRTC laid out speculative criteria on which to evaluate the LPIF no more than three years following its commencement:

1) The number of original local new stories
2) Evidence of increased audiences to local news and other local programming
3) Evidence of increased resources allocated to local newsgathering
4) Evidence of the increased diversity of local programming offered
5) Other quantifiable evidence of audience satisfaction. (par. 380)

The LPIF was to be fully operational for the start of the 2009/2010 broadcast year.

Though not what broadcasters wanted or asked for, the CRTC considered it a tradeoff for refusing fee-for-carriage. Still, a definitional problem is immediately apparent in the initial framework: the difference between "local programming" and "local news." The Commission seemed driven to protect local news, but for reasons unexplained allowed the more ambiguous "local programming" terminology to enter into regulation. This omission was not lost on dissenters. Two Commissioners dissented from the LPIF plan. Peter Menzies's dissent hinged on the lack of evidence demonstrating demand for local television. Menzies was unconvinced that the CRTC had proven "that this is a public good sufficiently imperiled to warrant intervention against these forces" (p. iv). In line with this neoliberal skepticism, Menzies worried that the subsidy would create "a co-dependency between the regulator and industry" (p. vi). Instead, he advocated for a market-based approach, whereby "those willing and able to compete will do well, while those more inclined to invest their time bickering over who gets what will be challenged" (p. vi).

Menzies may have been unconvinced by the cultural and democratic conclusions reached by the Commission, but he raised important concerns about the definition of local news, something the Commission had not resolved: "Is a person on the street interview with local people conducted by a local reporter still considered local news if the topic under discussion is the sub-prime crisis in the United States or an earthquake in China? ... Given that stations in provincial and territorial capitals and even in the national capital ... all qualify, is the news coming from their legislatures local news or otherwise?" (p. ix). Two important and interrelated issues are raised here: First, the debate between locally produced programming and programming of local relevance. Second, the definition of the local: Are provincial matters to be considered local for the purposes of the LPIF?

Michel Morin's dissent fell closer to regulatory matters than to epistemological concerns. For Morin, the question came down to the aforementioned problem between "local programming" and "local news." He contended that the LPIF should have been demarcated solely for local news, and not the more encompassing "local programming." To align LPIF with the ambiguously defined "local programming" could unleash a "virus" that "could contaminate the entire Canadian system via the Local Programming Improvement Fund" (p. xi).[6] Unlike Menzies, Morin would have supported the LPIF had it not been for this detail.

2009: AN EXPANDED FUND

During the months leading to 2009, the press was agnostic toward the LPIF, preferring instead to focus on the Commission's decision to once again refuse FFC. Broadcasters, too, seemed indifferent. In fact, the only noticeable comment came from vice-president of media for the Communications, Energy and Paperworkers Union, Peter Murdoch, who enthusiastically stated: "This fund is only a first step, but does send a clear message to Canadian broadcasters about the need to meet their obligation to local viewers" (Vlessing, 2008, p. 6). Unfortunately, the opposite was about to occur.

While the LPIF was being established, the impact of the cyclical and structural economic shifts in the broadcast industry manifested themselves in a slew of layoffs and the threat of station closure. CTVglobemedia cut 105 positions and announced the closure of stations in Wingham and Wheatly, Ontario, and Brandon, Manitoba. CanWest Global announced that it was either selling or closing its second-tier "E" network, which operated stations in smaller communities such as Hamilton, Red Deer, Kelowna, Victoria, and the larger market of Montreal (Robertson, 2009b, 2009c; Blackwell, 2008; Laghi, 2009). "Profits at Canada's major commercial TV networks" wrote Grant Robertson of the *Globe and Mail*, "had fallen more than 90 per cent" in 2008 (2009d). In response to what was now clearly a "crisis" in Canadian broadcasting (Robertson, 2009c), the CRTC announced that stations would only be issued one-year licenses (as opposed to the traditional seven-year license renewal) so it could evaluate these drastic market shifts (CRTC, 2009e). It also announced hearings for April 2009 to review license renewal procedures, the LPIF, and contributions to Canadian programming more broadly.

The report to emerge from these hearings proved remarkably important for the LPIF and for the Canadian broadcasting industry as a whole (CRTC, 2009b). First and foremost, BDU contributions to the LPIF were increased from 1 percent to 1.5 percent, which would raise the fund from $60 million to $102 million. Second, as recounted in chapter 2, the CRTC enacted "harmonized local programming levels" for stations across the country. English-language metropolitan stations would now be required to broadcast fourteen hours per week of local programming, and nonmetropolitan stations would need to broadcast seven hours per week. French-language services saw a more tailored approach. TVA, the country's largest French-language broadcaster, was given station-specific requirements. Its Quebec City affiliate, CFCM-TV, would have to broadcast eighteen hours of local programming a week, while smaller stations would have a quota of five hours per week. To be sure, many stations were already broadcasting hours of local news well above these minimums, however this provided the Commission with a benchmark to assess license renewals. Whether stations are continuing to meet their previous local programming requirements remains to be seen. Nor do we know whether these new levels have created a "ceiling" rather than a "floor." Still, those stations wanting to receive LPIF funds would have to demonstrate that they met the harmonized levels. To further assist local stations, the incremental expenditure requirement was also eliminated. Like the other changes to LPIF, this change was in recognition of the economic instability of the industry, and was an attempt to stabilize the financial resources of stations. In short, the LPIF became a way to stabilize existing commitments, rather than to increase programming.

To enforce these new quotas, definitions of local programming and "local presence" were established. A local program would now be defined as: "Programming produced by local stations with local personnel or programming produced by locally-based independent producers that reflects the particular needs and interests of the market's residents" (par. 43). With this definition, the Commission skirted the local origination/relevance dichotomy by including both locality and community interests. This definition, however, demonstrates a turn to default localism whereby the CRTC relied on tautological reasoning, defining local programming as that produced by local stations.

"Local presence," meanwhile, would be "encouraged" but without firm guidance as to the role it would play vis-à-vis LPIF. Based on a proposal by CTVglobemedia, local presence was defined as:

- Providing seven-day-a-week original local news coverage
- Employing full-time journalists on the ground
- Operating a news bureau or news gathering office (par. 45)

Evident here is the discrepancy between the harmonized "local programming" commitments that do not directly reference local news, and the "local presence" commitments that rely specifically on news. The Commission seemed unconcerned with this discrepancy, demonstrating the inconsistency of expectations when it comes to localism.

Rhetoric used to rationalize these new commitments also seemed to conflict with desired outcomes. On the one hand, the CRTC explained that corporate consolidation has "detached" "large media companies ... from the local communities they serve" and scolded broadcasters for their lack of local commitment (par. 49–50). On the other hand, these sentiments contrast with the relaxed local programming requirements and increased BDU contributions, both of which are geared toward propping up stations, regardless of whether they serve their communities.

2009–2012: THE LPIF YEARS

The LPIF began distributing funds at the start of the broadcast year in September 2009. Months into its first term, the CRTC's worst fears were realized in the closure of stations in Brandon, Manitoba (CTV), Red Deer, Alberta (Global), and Wheatley, Ontario (CTV). Over the next three years the industry would be also rocked by a series of monumental events, including the bankruptcy of CanWest Global in 2009, the acquisition of CTV by BCE in 2010, and the 2010 sale of the Global Television Network and CanWest's specialty services to Shaw Communications. These changes meant that Canadian media, already heavily concentrated, would become even more so, with the four largest telecommunication providers (Bell, Shaw, Rogers, Quebecor) owning the four largest private broadcasters (CTV, Global, Citytv, TVA). In sum, when the CRTC announced the LPIF review in the final days of 2011, the Canadian mediascape had changed dramatically.

The CRTC's *Notice of Consultation* (2011a) established parameters for hearings and public commentary to review the performance of the LPIF. The Commission sought comment on the overall success of the fund, the incremental expenditure condition, eligibility and allocation formulas, BDU financial contributions, and the larger question of "whether the LPIF should be maintained, modified, or discontinued" (par. 24). A final important question was the impact that vertical integration was having on local programming. The Commission rightly asked, "to what extent, if any should the nature of a station's ownership structure within a vertically integrated entity be considered in terms of LPIF eligibility?" (par. 42). This question is crucial given that the recent mergers described above had created a funding feedback loop, whereby BDUs were contributing to a fund that was serving stations owned by the same BDUs.

According to the Commission, stations on average showed a .5 percent profit margin in 2009–2010, in contrast to the -5.9 percent profit margin experienced in 2008–2009. Expenditures on local programming had risen by 9.8 percent, suggesting at least moderate success of the LPIF. The CRTC also released data on the amount of local news produced by stations receiving LPIF funds. Like the expenditure reports, this data demonstrates moderate success in at least stabilizing programming commitments:

Table 5.1: Hours of local news (per week) pre-LPIF and with LPIF by ownership group

Group / Groupe	Pre-LPIF	With LPIF
0859291 B.C. Ltd. (CHEK-TV)	23:08:12	50:28:31
2190015 Ontario Inc. (Channel Zero)	34:39:09	66:12:43
Newfoundland Broadcasting Company Ltd. (CJON-TV)	17:07:22	18:36:58
Astral Media Radio G.P.	9:07:02	9:56:53
591987 B.C. Ltd. (Corus)	12:19:52	19:25:11
CBC/SRC		
English	6:50:30	9:04:47
French	5:15:39	6:42:20
Shaw Television L.P.	14:59:35	14:36:09
Bell Media (CTV)	15:57:52	15:59:23
Jim Pattison Broadcast Group L.P.	16:15:31	19:27:45
Newcap Inc.	4:40:01	5:30:53
RNC MEDIA Inc.	2:11:19	4:19:32
Rogers Broadcasting Ltd.	9:24:31	10:20:03
Thunder Bay Electronics Ltd.	7:45:59	9:25:01
Télé Inter-Rives	6:03:27	9:53:48
Groupe TVA	5:32:41	6:59:49
V Interactions	0:00:00	3:03:30

Source: CRTC, 2011b.

2012: THE HEARINGS

The LPIF hearings took place the week of April 16, 2012, and proved to be a microcosm of the entire Canadian local media landscape. Here, broadcasters and public interest advocates in favor of the fund squared off against BDUs who opposed it. The one exception was BCE, which not only supported the LPIF but reversed its position on the CBC, agreeing now that the public broadcaster should remain eligible.

Two themes dominated the hearings: the role of regulation as market intervention, and the ambiguity of definitions. Both remain unresolved. The first theme questioned whether it was the CRTC's responsibility to prop up an industry where no sustainable economic model existed. As Commissioner Menzies asked: was there an argument strong enough to support public intervention for a "20th century model at a time when times are changing?" (CRTC 2012b, par. 3883). In response, independent programmers and independent broadcasters like the Alliance des producteurs francophones du Canada, On Screen Manitoba, the Jim Pattison Group, and CHEK-TV, and even large broadcasters such as CBC and CTV (BCE), argued for the necessity of the LPIF. CHCH-TV, a newly repurposed hyperlocal station in Hamilton, formally owned by CanWest, argued that LPIF funding was integrated into their business plan, and likened LPIF to "a support wall that reinforces a building while it is being renovated" (par. 1121). CBC argued that it was entirely because of the fund that it was able to keep its affiliate in Windsor, Ontario, on air. The broadcaster characterized the LPIF not as a subsidy but as a "contribution" made by BDUs to support Canadian programming (par. 2467). While the CBC shied away from threatening to close stations, it did note that without LPIF it would be forced to seriously cut back on local and regional programming.

Like the CBC and CHCH, BCE argued that LPIF has been essential in supporting stations within the CTV and CTVtwo networks, noting that ten of the nineteen stations that are eligible for LPIF funding "would have been unprofitable [without LPIF]. Even with LPIF funding, 6 were unprofitable" (par. 506). Appealing to cultural values, Bell argued that its local stations "are integral to the local identity of these communities" and as such, needed resources to continue to provide culturally and democratically vital programs. Like the CBC, BCE's testimony also came with an ultimatum, wherein without LPIF, it would close small-market stations. Unlike CBC's more veiled threats, however, BCE's forthrightness suggests the regulatory ransom that can come with the power of a consolidated company. LPIF, in sum, was both a necessary tool in broadcaster's business models and an element of leverage against the CRTC.

The overall sentiment expressed by the Commission was one of skepticism. On numerous occasions commissioners doubted the CRTC's role in supporting the industry through subsidy, and worried that market intervention could halt innovation and experimentation. Commissioner Patrone discussed the danger that subsidies could breed regulatory dependence, while others voiced concern that the LPIF distorts the "natural evolution" of local programming and markets. Accentuating this distrust of subsidy and a preference for the market, commissioners floated the idea (which would eventually be adopted) of phasing out the fund. Skepticism was also the position taken by BDUs (with the exception of BCE), who, in their ransom tactic, fully acknowledged that the LPIF levy was being passed on to subscribers through increased subscription rates. We might label this "consumer ransom" as opposed to the "regulatory ransom" of BCE. Consumers would see their cable bill increase if LPIF was maintained.

As we may have come to expect, the second theme was definitions. Calls for adequate definitions came primarily from Commissioner Morin, who again voiced concern for the unacknowledged differences between the more general "local programming" and the much more specific "local news." There was also confusion over what "local news" actually meant, with BCE's Kevin Goldstein citing differences between a "local newscast" and "local news segment": "We need to actually decide as to whether what we are talking about is local newscasts or local news segments within a newscast.... A local newscast has a number of different components to it. It has purely local news, it has regional news, it has national news of relevance to the local community" (par. 836–39). These questions went unanswered, with some stations counting news segments and others counting newscasts in their LPIF filings, thus distorting any potential quantification.

A second definitional quandary was the epistemological issue of what should count as a local station. As a representative from CHCH-TV noted, "there is a real fundamental difference about what is local when you are a local station without network affiliates across the country and what is local when you are a network" (par. 1276–77). This comment was echoed in the president of CHEK-TV's response to a question about local news thresholds: "First of all, I applaud [the CRTC] for recognizing that there is local and local and local, local. Could I also suggest that there is local, local, local, local: locally produced, locally directed, locally presented and locally relevant" (para. 1347). This excerpt underscores three crucial issues. First, the unfortunate lack of vocabulary we have to describe local media practices, aside from relying on tautological explications of default localism (a local station produces local programming that is local). Second, it suggests a hierarchy of localism, with the most local stations being those that are independently owned, and unaffiliated with a larger network. Though the witness was clearly trying to prove a point about the various interpretations of the word "local," this excerpt suggests that the best local stations are those that are "local, local, local, local"—a nonsensical definition. Third, it includes local labor practices into the definition of localism, something seldom considered by regulators. To this, the president of CHEK added, "what we do is local. We have a new control room, we have a new master control—we have people there. *It's like a real TV station.*" (par. 1362, emphasis added). This adds to our working definition the ideas of authenticity and proximity: the closer one is to being local, the closer one is to being authentic—a "real" TV station.

2012: LIFE AND DEATH OF THE LPIF

The CRTC released its LPIF report in August 2012. Despite four full days of hearings, and 1,352 public comments, the report clocked in at a total of seven pages, and fourteen short paragraphs. The decision was to phase out LPIF by 2014. The CRTC argued that the LPIF had achieved its mission of stabilizing the industry, and as such, was no longer needed, particularly because BDUs were raising subscription rates to compensate for the levy. In the CRTC's words, stability in the broadcast industry "has ultimately been achieved primarily at a cost to Canadians who pay the subscriber fees from which the LPIF is derived" (2012c, par. 15).

There is an evident market orientation to this explication, one resting on "consumer interests" and a rationale based on the "cost to Canadians." It represents a point of departure for the Commission's move to rhetorically place the individual consumer and consumer rights at the forefront of its deliberative processes, rather than the public, or more recently, the consolidated media corporation. Veiled in the guise of consumer sovereignty, the decision to eliminate the fund calls into question the CRTC's commitment to local news and information and underscores a tension between consumer rights and the public good.

Back to the point, the Commission expected BDUs to reduce their bills in line with the elimination of the LPIF, and to credit any overbilled customers. The phase-out was to occur incrementally over three years, with the fund completely eliminated by September 2014. This time frame was to "provide conventional stations with sufficient time to adapt to the evolving broadcasting environment" (CRTC, 2012c, par. 17). In sum, the CRTC argued that with increased vertical integration and the partial recovery of the advertising market, it was time once again for the market to assume its dominance over the Canadian broadcasting industry. Consistent with this market-based justification, the corresponding press release framed the decision as a victory for consumers, and saw the CRTC recommit itself to the role of "consumer advocate" (CRTC, 2012d).

Broadcasters were naturally against this decision, with CBC/SRC President Hubert T. Lacroix quoted as being "astonished" upon hearing the news (Pedwell, 2012). He was not the only one to express dismay. *Globe and Mail* columnist Ora Morison (2012) wrote that this decision "will save cable and satellite TV subscribers about the cost of a coffee a month, but threatens to put struggling local stations out of business." The Commission itself was also divided, with three commissioners dissenting. Elizabeth Duncan favored the retention of the fund, but one returned to the original 1 percent BDU contribution and incremental expenditures. Suzanne Lamarre argued the Commission failed to perform its due diligence on the evidence presented. She contended that regulatory capture had taken hold, noting that the final report addressed only sixty-five of the 1,365 interventions, thereby failing to account for the 95.2 percent of interveners who supported the fund. Louise

Poirier focused on the potential consequences to minority-language communities, and local economies, and expressed doubt about whether consumers would truly emerge as "the big winners" (CRTC, 2012c, p.vi). The lack of interest demonstrated by the CRTC in engaging in these discussions and those noted above indicates a disturbing trend of neglect toward localism in the Canadian system.

UK: No Porn, No Psychics, No News?

In contrast with the FCC and CRTC, the challenges of local television were relatively unfamiliar to Ofcom when it took the helm of communication regulation in 2003. Up to that point, British broadcasting had operated primarily as a centralized system, anchored by the BBC. To be sure, ITV, the commercial OTA network, was comprised of regional affiliates knitted together to form a network, but the creation of the ITV regions was one of technological convenience rather than political or cultural sensitivity (Johnson & Turnock, 2005). By 2003 this loose federation of stations had faltered, as ITV plc. consolidated the bulk of the network under its ownership. The BBC, of course, has regions too, but the other public service broadcasters—Channel 4, "5," and S4C—are national. Still, while the business of local OTA may have been unfamiliar to Ofcom in 2003, the lack of regional and local television news certainly was not.

2006: DIGITAL LOCAL

In its 2003 review of public service broadcasting (see chapter 2) Ofcom singled out local and regional news as an area of critical concern, but it would take another three years to fully investigate the state of local digital media. The 2006 report, *Digital Local,* was worth the wait. It focused not only on the mediated experiences of localism for citizens and consumers, but on a much larger and much more elusive question: What does it mean to be local in the United Kingdom? Without a strong system of local electronic media, this was not a question that needed to be answered by a British regulator, until now. This marked the only time when all options were on the table, and Ofcom held out high hopes for a new locally tailored service (whatever that may be) to fill the democratic and cultural gaps in the UK media system. In no other document has Ofcom, or any regulator for that matter, gone to such strides to understand the local. Ofcom even went so far as to consider whether geographic places were the appropriate frame of reference for local media: "In this context [weakening of geographic ties and the strengthening of social ones] it might be argued that local communities are no more nor less important from a policy perspective than wider communities of interest, and that we should be looking more broadly at 'community' services. Is there any particular reason for focusing on local content services, compared to (for example) services for particular ethnic or religious groups?" (2006, p. 19). Communities of interest were therefore considered alongside place-based communities as potential targets for more tailored information services. We see here an attempt to think productively across the spatial/social divide that has harassed the development of localism policies in other countries.

After due consideration (demonstrated by the considerable number of pages dedicated to the subject) Ofcom decided that place-based communities remained an appropriate foundation for local media regulation because "most people still rely on local communities, services and businesses for most aspects of their day-to-day lives" (p. 20). Even with this commitment to geographic place, Ofcom admitted that any such definitions were always contextual and multilayered: "What counts as 'local' when we buy a pint of milk, go to work or vote for an MP may be three very different things" (p. 2). "Local" here is tied to places, but it is also forged out of social relations, context, and discourse (cf. Massey, 1993, 1994; Powell, 2007). Deciding that the local should be tied to geographic places also required another question: How local is local? Ofcom settled on a pluralistic approach, employing a broad definition of the local that "pertain[s] principally to a geographic area" but recognizing that this geographic area could span "anything from a few thousand homes (e.g., neighbourhood), through a town or rural area with a dispersed population, to a large metropolitan area with a population of a million people or more" (p. 22). The next step was to consider which media would best serve these contextual and complex communities.

A platform-neutral approach was taken, with a goal to "understand what local content and interactive services could be in [the] future, rather than what they are now, or have been in the past" (p. 1). Seminal was the provision of local news and information, which would be the hallmark of any new local service. Four media platforms were considered: digital terrestrial television (DTT), digital satellite, digital cable, and broadband (IPTV). Satellite and cable were quickly dismissed because of the inability to adequately localize satellite data streams, and the intense infrastructural needs of cable. While perhaps leaning toward IPTV for its low overhead costs and interactive potential, Ofcom was reticent to declare a favorite. It was less hesitant about economic sustainability. Ofcom was firmly convinced that the market should not be left alone to determine the future of local programming, considering that "many of the potential benefits of local services are social benefits that are unlikely to be taken into account by the market: social cohesion, democratic engagement, better-informed and more active citizens" (p. 68). Given these many unknowns, it was ultimately concluded that the next few years should be for innovation and experimentation, rather than hard-and-fast decisions.

2006–2009: BBCI AND IFNC

Digital Local was quickly shelved after its release, and by 2010 DTT seemed inevitable despite Ofcom's push for innovation and experimentation. The intervening years, however, did see two alternatives depart from this trend: the BBC's localized services and the Independently Funded News Consortia (IFNC).

An early pilot was the £25 million BBCi Hull project, an interactive local online news and information service (see Davies, 2004; BBC 2002). The BBC framed it as "local interactive TV" and the 2003 pilot project in the northern city of Hull saw heavy monthly usage. Building on this success, the BBC proposed to launch fifty to sixty such services offering "ten minutes an hour of genuinely relevant local news and information" first over broadband and then DTT (BBC, 2004, qtd. in Ofcom 2008a, par. 3.6). Despite its success in Hull, BBCi was never realized, as local commercial newspapers and radio groups succeeded at convincing the BBC Trust that the public broadcaster's presence in local news would distort the market for commercial competition (Mair, 2013b; Davies, 2004). The concern for market distortion was revived some years later when local newspapers used it as justification to stop another BBC attempt at online local news in 2008 (Martin, 2008; Ofcom 2009, BBC Trust, 2009).

The second interim project saw much wider support. The Independently Funded News Consortia (IFNC) was first proposed in the Department for Culture Media and Sport's (DCMS) Digital Britain report, which outlined Britain's plan for broadband and digital services. The proposal sought to create a network of news companies, partially financed by the public, which would assume many of the responsibilities of providing local news on multiple platforms, including television on ITV. It would thus relieve ITV of its regional news commitments (as it had been requesting for the better part of a decade) and fulfill Ofcom's desire to promote broadband in the delivery of local news and information. Great enthusiasm gathered behind this idea, with Ofcom, DCMS, the government, and the press all in support. IFNCs were even included in the government's Digital Economy Bill. With this widespread support, DCMS announced the creation of three pilot projects for January 2010 in Wales, Scotland, and Tyne Tees.

Despite this political enthusiasm, ITV refused to support the consortia, declaring that any ITV journalists who wished to take part would have to quit their current positions and be rehired by the IFNC. The plan also failed to receive cross-party support in parliament. Jeremy Hunt, then-Conservative shadow secretary for culture and sport, vehemently opposed the plan, particularly the idea that it would be partially funded by taxpayers. Instead, Hunt preferred the deregulation of cross-media ownership, and the creation of a commercial local digital television service.

Local terrestrial television had of course been considered by Ofcom in Digital Local, and earlier, but the INFCs seemed to be the best of many worlds: OTA and broadband, public and private, and most important, local. Nevertheless, Hunt feared that it would inhibit "new, local media models" (qtd. in UK, 2010a, par. 129). Certain public interest groups, such as United for Local Television, joined Hunt in his advocacy for local television. Local DTT also received support from parliamentarians, many of whom signed an "early day motion" in 2008 to "congratulate Ofcom in finding a means to deliver local television to every household across the UK . . ." (UK, 2008). An empty section of the 2003 Communications Act (§244) even allowed for the creation of local digital television.

Ofcom remained skeptical despite the new groundswell of support, reporting results of a 2009 economic analysis that concluded that only the largest markets (London and Manchester) could support local television (2009b; see Oliver & Ohlbaum, 2009). The regulator suggested that more study was needed before any conclusions should be reached. Such caution was not heeded by government.

2010: JEREMY HUNT, DCMS, AND THE BIG SOCIETY

When the Conservative/Liberal Democrat coalition government came to power in May 2010, Hunt became secretary of state for culture, media, and sport (the minister responsible for DCMS). No sooner had this happened than he began to aggressively campaign for his vision of local television. The groundwork had been laid the year before, when Hunt released plans to create eighty city-based stations rather than support the Labour government's IFNC project (Sabbagh, 2009). The original plan was for stations to mimic Canadian community media—low-budget programming and volunteers—rather than the more polished local stations found in the United States. The brainchild of this early plan was former chairman of Johnston

Press, Roger Perry, who strongly believed that local stations could cover "four fifths of the country after 2012" (Sabbagh, 2009). Perry believed that the era of YouTube had changed (lowered) expectations for quality local television, and that programming could therefore run on as little as £500 per hour (Sabbagh, 2009).

By 2010 Hunt's plan had shifted from doing localism on the cheap, to a professional service. His first steps were to terminate the IFNC project and push for the deregulation of cross-media ownership, thereby laying the legislative foundations for local television. In a speech to London's Hospital Club in June 2010, Hunt called the lack of local television in the UK a "missed opportunity," arguing that "I have long believed that the lack of high quality local TV is one of the biggest gaps in British broadcasting. . . . Why? Because, ironically, in an age of globalism people feel the need for stronger not weaker connections to the communities in which they live" (np). It was also in this speech that Hunt offered the now infamous comparison between Birmingham, England, and Birmingham, Alabama: "Birmingham Alabama . . . has 8 local TV stations—despite being a quarter the size of our Birmingham that . . . doesn't even have one" (np). As many would come to argue, this comparison demonstrated Hunt's alleged inability to grasp the intricacies of television, given the massive market for local advertising in the United States, and the dearth of any such market in the UK (e.g., Hewlett, 2011). Nonetheless, the point had been made: the UK did not have local television, and this was a problem.

Hunt's vision for local television is accurately described as his contribution to the "Big Society" (see Midgley, 2010, 2011). A product of the Conservative Party, the Big Society refers to a vision for the decentralization ("devolution") of the federal state through the distribution of powers to municipalities. To make good on this promise of increased municipal power, for instance, the government planned for mayoral elections in communities outside London (which already had a mayor) (see DCLG, 2011). Grounded in rhetoric of greater personal responsibility and faith in the private sector, the Big Society, according to some, is a thinly veiled attempt to deconstruct what is left of the welfare state (Westwood, 2011; North, 2011). Hunt's local television service fit squarely within this new vision of British politics, as the privately owned-and-operated stations would act as counterweights to these devolved powers. As he argued, "How can we devolve power to locally elected politicians if we don't have a properly developed local broadcasting sector to help hold them to account?" (qtd. in Midgley, 2010). The first step toward this neoliberal vision was to assess the economic viability of local television. Therefore, in the same speech as the Birmingham anecdote, Hunt announced the creation of a steering committee headed by investment banker Nicholas Shott to investigate the commercial viability of local television.[7]

2010: THE "SHOTT REPORT"

Five months later Shott delivered his final report. Much, we can presume, to the chagrin of Hunt, Shott was not optimistic about the viability of local television. Consistent with the findings of Ofcom, the report concluded that local digital terrestrial television would only be viable in the largest cities. It would be particularly unsustainable in the smallest areas. The report advocated that IPTV was the most realistic and viable medium for local television across the entire country. Acknowledging, however, that universal broadband was a while off, Shott conceded that ten to twelve local television services might be commercially sustainable in the largest centers, as long as certain conditions were met. Government support, for instance, would be essential. Even with this support, Shott envisioned a frugal venture, with programming costs around £1,500/hour. Shott further recommended that ownership be local and encouraged "the participation of local media groups and local enterprise[s]" (p. 6). This would require the deregulation of cross-media ownership, which prohibited newspapers from owning television stations.

In terms of technical deliverability, Geographic Interleaved (GI) spectrum (the white spaces between occupied frequencies) would be the most feasible, and importantly, the most affordable. Coverage, however, would not include the entire country because "DTT does not . . . naturally lend itself to local TV purposes" (p. 19). This again reinforced Shott's commitment to IPTV over DTT. Just as spectrum could not cover all localities, neither could programming be entirely local. Shott recommended a network-affiliated model, with a minimum of two hours per day of "reasonably low cost but high quality" local content (p. 37). User-generated content (UGC) was discouraged, since quality was a major concern. Shott also recommended that licenses be awarded through a "beauty contest" rather than an auction, and that all stations be given electronic program guide (EPG) preference, meaning low channel assignments on digital guides to assure discoverability. The report ultimately stressed the importance of keeping an eye toward IPTV, rather than a full commitment to conventional local television.

Echoing Shott's reticence, the press voiced concern with Hunt's vision, focusing on its lack of specificity and economic sustainability. One notable critic was *The Guardian's* Steve Hewlett, who quipped that "it is hard not to admire Hunt's vision and commitment to the idea of much more decentralized, localized TV services. When it comes to practicalities, however, the whole project is beginning to look pretty flaky" (2010a). Even the more conservative *Times* observed that while Hunt cited examples of local television around Europe, Germany's RTL was refusing to invest in local television (Boyle, 2010). By December 2010, it seemed neither the press, nor Shott, nor Ofcom were prepared to endorse Hunt's plan.

2011: THE FRAMEWORK FOR LOCAL TELEVISION

Despite this lackluster support, DCMS released the proposed framework for what was now being called the local digital television programme service (L-DTPS) in July 2011. DCMS clearly favored a market-based approach to local television. As a member of DCMS mentioned, "[W]e wanted to see the market deliver linear style, local TV. And by local TV, we meant in broadcast form, accessible to the majority of the population in that area" (D. Lake, personal communication, 9/21/12). Added the respondent, "Ultimately, it's down to the market. It's a market force that's perhaps the greatest risk to this.... It's now for the market to make it happen." Not only would local television be an economic driver, it would also be essential for the Big Society: "Local TV brings with it numerous economic, social, cultural and democratic benefits. It will be important in the wider localism agenda, holding institutions to account and increasing civic engagement at a local level" (DCMS, 2011a, p. 11).

In the framework itself, DCMS decided that GI spectrum space would be designated for the stations. The spectrum would be managed by a separate entity—a licensed multiplex company ("MuxCo")—rather than the stations themselves. This was justified by the assumption that stations would not have the technical expertise, or the economic ability, to manage the spectrum properly. The MuxCo would distribute the signals of the individual stations and would also have the capacity to distribute two additional national channels of its choosing. As predicted, the spectrum would not cover every community, and those outside the coverage areas would have to wait until another phase of the plan, which would incorporate the Shott report's recommendation of IPTV.[8]

Four legislative initiatives were necessary to secure the framework for the L-DTPS. First, a bill to activate section 244 of the 2003 Communications Act, which allows for the creation of local digital television. Second, a change to the Wireless Telegraphy Act of 2006 to reserve spectrum for the multiplex. Third, a change to Section 310 of the Communications Act to "secure EPG prominence" (DCMS, 2011a, p. 33). Fourth, the deregulation of cross-media ownership rules to allow newspapers to hold a television license (see UK, 2011b). The most crucial of these, the Local Digital Television Programme Service Order, was approved early in 2012, thus paving the way for Ofcom to draft regulation. DCMS was confident that the first services would launch by the middle of 2013. To meet this goal, sixty-five locations were designated as technically suitable to host a local television service, and Ofcom began inquiring into potential applicants.

By the time DCMS (2011b) released its final policy framework in December 2011, the sixty-five initial locations had been whittled down to twenty-one based on population size and business interest. The selection of cities proved challenging from a number of perspectives, no less from the technological side. As one respondent noted, ". . . spectrum doesn't recognize cities. It just exists, and that's that" (D. Lake, personal communication, 09/21/12). As a result, DCMS acknowledged that the service would not be universal across the UK. The twenty-one locations represented the first phase of the television rollout and included larger cities like London, Manchester, Belfast, Bristol, and Glasgow, and smaller towns such as Preston, Brighton and Hove, and Grimsby (see table 5.2). The second phase would include another twenty-four towns, such as Aberdeen, Bedford, Cambridge, and Luton. The goal was for forty-four stations to be on the air within the next few years.

It was made abundantly clear that the L-DTPS would be a market-driven project, with economic sustainability the priority. In line with this market fundamentalism, there would be no restrictions on the ownership of stations, no restrictions on networking, and no restrictions on the number of stations one company could own. While there would also be no discrimination against nonprofit or community-based applicants, there would be no provisions to support them. Surprisingly, there would be no local content requirements, only a vague expectation of at least one hour of local news per day. In fact, the only content regulation proposed was a prohibition on adult content and "premium rate advertising services"—in other words, no porn and no psychics (p. 16). Stations would be encouraged but not required to broadcast local civic-affairs programming. DCMS had conflicting views on the issue: "whilst we haven't mandated it very strongly in regulation . . . we do expect to set out in the legislation that there has to be sufficient programming of interest, relevance to the local population" (D. Lake, personal communication, 09/21/12).[9]

Echoing this light-touch approach, no protections or requirements were suggested for minority-language programming. This goes against the long-term commitment within the UK media system to cater to national language groups, particularly Welsh. It was left to the local market and to the licensees themselves to make these commitments. The lack of content regulation was permitted partly because these stations would be exempt from any precedent-taking EU regulations, notably the Audiovisual Media Services Directive (AVMS), so long as they did not transmit outside the country. Another salient factor was that, contrary to the other terrestrial broadcasters, L-DTPS stations would not be considered traditional public-service broadcasters, which exempted them from many public-interest requirements.

The stations and the MuxCo would each be licensed for twelve years, with one license awarded per community. DCMS, however, failed to provide guidelines for license renewal, suggesting a lack of clarity over the long-term future of these services. Complementing this hands-off approach, DCMS declared the MuxCo free to do as it pleased with the two unused channels the spectrum allocation permitted. In essence, this decision permitted it to profit directly from government-awarded spectrum and, as such, operate as a de facto monopoly in local spectrum management. To support these new services, both the MuxCo and the stations would benefit from BBC assistance during the first three years. This included £25 million dedicated to the MuxCo for infrastructure development, and £15 million to purchase news stories from the local stations, thus guaranteeing a stable source of income.

2011: OFCOM AND THE REGULATION OF LOCAL TELEVISION

In concert with DCMS's final statement, Ofcom released a consultation document on how it would exercise its newly awarded powers (2012b). While agreeing with DCMS's framework, Ofcom made clear that this was a government-directed policy and not one originating from the regulator. The crux of the consultation document was to propose guidelines for applicants for the MuxCo and station licenses.

The stations would be licensed for twelve years, but like DCMS, Ofcom did not mention license renewal, suggesting a short-term solution to a long-term democratic deficit. Despite declaring the utmost importance of local news, Ofcom also agreed with DCMS and *recommended* only one hour per day of local news, with no staunch quantitative requirements. By omitting content quotas, which, like language provisions, had been a longtime staple of the regulatory landscape, this decision belies the public-service role of local television. That said, applicants were required to provide the number of hours per day or week of local programming, first-run local programming, and locally produced programming they intended to air (Ofcom, 2012c).

Ofcom balked, however, at any overly prescriptive models for local content and like so much of the L-DTPS framework, left programming commitments to the applicants. Contrasting the relaxed approach to programming, Ofcom did propose a "Localness Requirement," where, like the American "Main Studio Rule," stations would be required to be physically located within the community of license so as to encourage local production. Last, Ofcom suggested that the MuxCo be given the latitude to select the second round of station locations, rather than itself or DCMS. Planners thought that the MuxCo would know best which areas it could serve. In concert with DCMS, then, Ofcom proposed to instill the MuxCo with a tremendous degree of autonomy.

Ofcom received a total of seventy-two responses to its consultation. On the whole, respondents were supportive of the local services, with many noting the "hunger for local news" in their communities, and the dearth of such a service at present (Watson & Howell, 2011; Channel 7, 2011). Critics focused on the vagueness of many of the provisions, particularly the concepts of "localness" and local news (Archant, 2011; Channel 6, 2011; Channel 8 North East, 2011). City Broadcasting (2011), for instance, argued against the Localness Requirement, noting that simply having a station in the community does not demonstrate a commitment to localism. This was echoed by Solent Television (2011), which argued that applicants should have to explain how their programming would reflect a more general "local sensibility" (p. 3). Astra, a satellite operator, questioned whether Ofcom was violating its statutory duties by inappropriately favoring terrestrial television (Ofcom, 2012b). Enders Analysis (2011) voiced confusion over whether DCMS preferred commercial or community stations, adding that the "ambiguity is likely to frustrate organizations that are weighing up a bid for one of the licenses" (p. 3). Inverness Community Media (2011) and First Broadcasting (2011) both questioned Ofcom's decision to permit the MuxCo to decide on the second round of stations. The Institute for Local Television (2011), though, offered the most scathing critique: "In moving slowly Ofcom has become the hand-maiden of incumbent broadcasting and by negligence and lack of foresight the regulator looks set to ensure that local TV is at best a half hearted venture lacking the security of audience on which to secure investment and public confidence" (p. 1). In spite of these critiques, Ofcom's final *Statement on Licensing Local Television* (2012d) released on May 10, 2012, saw few changes from the consultation document. The regulator held fast to its Localness Requirement, arguing that it was the best way "to ensure locally produced programming *without constraining commercial viability, or limiting the range of business models, more than necessary"* (2012d, p. 54, emphasis added). It also continued to support the lack of requirements for local news, stating instead that an expectation of seven hours per week was not overly burdensome. Any programming commitments would be self-drafted by the stations and written into the individual licenses. There is a disparity here between this light-touch approach and the desire for local news. How local can a local service be with only one hour of local programming a day? The definition of a local program, moreover, was only loosely spelled out. In supporting documentation, for instance, Ofcom acknowledged (but did not explicate) the difference between local programming and locally produced programming. It counseled applicants to be clear in their applications about what was to be locally produced and what was to be local program material (Ofcom, 2012d). Nevertheless, there remains significant ambiguity on how to consider programming that is produced elsewhere but may be considered of relevance to the local population. Finally, stations were expected to be on the air within a year of being awarded a license, and the logical channel numbers (LCN) were assigned as Channel 8 in England and Northern Ireland and Channel 45 in Scotland and Wales.

2013: LOCAL TELEVISION IN THE UK

When the license application window closed in August 2012, Ofcom had received fifty-seven applications for nineteen of the twenty-one licenses advertised. Two locations, Swansea and Plymouth, failed to receive any bids, while Brighton, Bristol, and Grimsby had only one applicant each, which promptly won the license. As expected, the London license was the most contested, receiving a total of five bids. By December 2015, thirty-four licenses had been awarded, including the original nineteen plus fifteen from the second phase (Aberdeen, Ayr, Basingstoke, Cambridge, Carlisle, Dundee, Guildford, Maidstone, Middlesbrough, Mold, Reading, Salisbury, Scarborough, Swansea, and York).[10]

As predicted, several companies were awarded multiple licenses (Made TV, for instance, has four), although it remains to be seen if they will take advantage of economies of scope and scale and network the stations. The MuxCo license was awarded to Canis Media through a nonprofit subsidiary called Comux UK. As determined by DCMS and Ofcom, Comux controls two national channel slots in addition to the local station spectrum. It promised that any profit derived from leasing the additional channels (each valued at approximately £3m/year) would be invested back into the infrastructure for the local stations.

Table 5.2: Original 19 L-DTPS Licenses, Programming Commitments, and Launch (Ofcom, nd)

Location (number of households)	Company	Expected launch (m/d/y)	First-run local programming (hrs/wk) - year	Business model (m/d/y)	Community participation	Actual launch
Belfast (190,000)	NvTv	9/9/13	10 - yr 1 11 - yr 2 13 - yr 3	Advertising	UGC, training, citizen input	9/29/14
Birmingham (1,000,000)	City TV/ Kaleidoscope d/b/a Big Centre TV[1]	April–June 2013	41 - yr 1 55 - yr 2 68 - yr 3	Advertising	Training	2/28/15
Brighton & Hove (140,000)	Latest TV	Sept. 2013	10 - yr 1 12 - yr 2 12.5 - yr 3	Advertising	Training, citizen input	8/28/14
Bristol (370,000)	Made in Bristol	3/1/13	14 - yr 1 21 - yr 2 28 - yr 3	Advertising	Student productions	10/8/14
Cardiff (480,000)	Made in Cardiff	3/1/13	14 - yr 1 21 - yr 2 28 - yr 3	Advertising	Citizen journalism, student productions	10/15/14
Edinburgh (590,000)	STV d/b/a ETV	10/1/13	21 - yr 1–3	Advertising	Student productions, some UGC, citizen input	1/12/15
Glasgow (800,000)	STV d/b/a GTV	10/1/13	28 - yr 1–3	Advertising	Student training and productions, UGC, citizen input	6/2/14
Grimsby (250,000)	Lincolnshire Living n/k/a Estuary TV	9/2/13	3 - yr 1 7.5 - yr 2 10 - yr 3	Advertising	Training, citizen journalism, UGC	11/26/13
Leeds (980,000)	Made in Leeds	3/1/13	14 - yr 1 21 - yr 2 28 - yr 3	Advertising	Citizen journalism, student training and production	10/6/14

Location (population)	Station	Launch date	License fee (£m)	Revenue model	Content focus	Expiry date
Liverpool (900,000)	BayTV	9/2/13	17.5 - yr 1 23.75 - yr 2 41.5 - yr 3	Advertising	Training, some public participation, student productions	12/4/14
London (4,500,000)	ESTV d/b/a London Live	9/30/13	56 - yr 1 63 - yr 2 70 - yr 3	Advertising	Training, community contributions	3/31/14
Manchester (1,100,000)	YourTV Manchester	10/1/13	94 - yr 1–3	Advertising	Public participation, training, citizen journalism	5/31/15
Newcastle (980,000)	Made in Tyne and Wear	3/1/13	14 - yr 1 21 - yr 2 28 - yr 3	Advertising	Citizen journalism, UGC, student productions	11/12/14
Norwich (150,000)	Mustard TV	10/1/13	11.25 - yr 1–3	Advertising	Student productions and training	3/24/14
Nottingham (270,000)	Notts TV	4/1/14	17.5 - yr 1 20 - yr 2–3	Advertising	Some student productions	5/27/14
Oxford (100,000)	That's Oxford	1/1/14	35 - yr 1–3	Advertising	Citizen journalism	4/17/2015
Preston (370,000)	YourTV/That's Lancashire[2]	10/1/13	3 - yr 1 6 - yr 2 9 - yr 3	Advertising	UGC, citizen journalism, citizen input, training	1/5/15
Sheffield (180,000)	SLTV/Sheffield Live	10/1/13	5 - yr 1 6 - yr 2–3	Mixed	UGC, student productions, training	1/23/14
Southampton (440,000)	That's Solent	1/1/14	51 - yr 1–3	Advertising	Citizen journalism, training, student productions	11/26/14

1. CityTV won the original license for Birmingham but went into administration before it could launch. The station launched in 2015 with new owner, Kaleidoscope, under the name "Big Centre TV."
2. YourTV won the original license for Preston, but ownership was transferred to That's TV.

As table 5.2 illustrates, only SLTV indicated that it would operate as a charitable organization (the "mixed" model). NvTv, a former community television station (see chapter 3) will operate as a non-shareholder company, reinvesting profits back into the organization. On the whole, license documents reflect a clear preference for commercial operations, although many noted a plan for training programs and a certain amount of user-generated content (UGC), both of which are hallmarks of nonprofit media (Howley, 2005). Three have committed to heavy UGC usage (Belfast, Grimsby, and Sheffield), two of which—NvTv and Estuary TV—have previous experience as community broadcasters (see chapter 3). Most stations indicated they will take advantage of some UGC and most will have volunteer positions. Solent, for instance, promises to rely heavily on citizen journalists. Some licensees have also promised huge commitments to local programming, which may be unsustainable, particularly for those that have pledged more than fifty hours per week of first-run local programming. No station in the United States or Canada offers that much local programming.

By the summer of 2015, all of the original stations had launched. The first was Estuary TV, which launched on November 26, 2013, with a newscast and sports program. London Live, which launched in March 2014, boasts the largest annual budget. Bankrolled by newspaper moguls Alexander and Evgeny Lebedev (owners of the *Evening Standard*), London Live has budgeted an astounding £20,000 per hour for programming. In comparison, most stations estimate £1,500 per hour. Made TV has even claimed that it will run ads for as little as £10 and believes it can break even on revenues of less than £1 million per year (Sweney, 2013). Unfortunately, in its first three weeks on air, London Live's lavish expenses did not translate into viewers, with programs garnering scant measurable audiences (Midgley, 2014).

Questions continue to linger about economic sustainability and station visibility. Halfway through the licensing process, Jeremy Hunt left his portfolio as secretary of state for culture, media, and sport and was replaced by Maria Miller. While Hunt continues to voice his support for the L-DTPS service, concerns have risen about whether Miller demonstrates the same amount of "zeal" toward local television as Hunt (Greenslade, 2012, 2014). Though the launch of the first stations represents an historic moment for UK broadcasting, some critics have been unable to suppress their skepticism: "Within a year," one blogger for *The Guardian* wrote after the launch of Estuary TV, "who knows, there might even be talk of a golden age of local broadcasting. Or a golden age of mockery. Either way, we will be entertained" (Benedictus,

2013). If the London ratings are any indication, the future of UK local television may not be as certain as some may have hoped or expected.

Conclusion: The Market for Localism

In this chapter I documented three regulatory attempts to address what has been called the "localism problem" in North Atlantic media systems. These efforts each began as interventionist attempts to understand and protect local media, be it through a taskforce, a subsidy, or an entirely new sector. The end result in all three instances, however, was withdrawal to a status quo reliance on the market, and a fallback to default localism. Regulators seem overly comfortable letting the market speak for local communities through designated marketed areas in the United States, succumbing to industry pressure in Canada, and advancing conservative political ideologies in the UK.

Despite these neoliberal outcomes, we did see alternative recommendations that could benefit both the commercial and public-interest sectors, such as the Brennan Center's proposal in the United States, the IFNCs in the UK, and the LPIF in Canada. What is apparent, however, is that these alternative conversations are occurring on the periphery of regulatory discourse—in public comments and hearings—rather than being debated within primary regulatory documents. Regulators seem keen to ask questions in preliminary consultations, but have been less sanguine in final reports. As we have witnessed, a discursive impasse has built up within regulatory proceedings. A fresh approach is therefore needed if localism is to remain a central component of media regulation in the public interest *and* an economically sustainable business practice.

PART III

Fixing Localism

6

The Political Economy of Localism
Critical Regionalism and the Policies of Place

> Localism is an expensive value.
> —US H. Rep, 1996, qtd. in FCC, 2003a

The Place and Space of Media Localism

At the end of his voluminous history of British broadcasting, Lord Asa Briggs described a 1960 debate about the introduction of local commercial radio to the UK. C.O. Stanley, a supporter of the plan, quipped that local services are needed because "nobody in Cambridge is interested in the traffic jams in Bedford" (1995, p. 631). Continued Mr. Stanley: "The Cambridge housewife has not the slightest interest in what is selling in Bedford shops, though they are only 25 miles away" (p. 631). The Cambridge housewife, we are led to believe, requires a local radio station that caters only to the Cambridge market.

This anecdote emphasizes the primary challenges of media localism in the twenty-first century, namely that it is misunderstood, ill-defined, and taken for granted. It also gives us a fertile starting point to reflect on the relationship between communities of place, communities of interest, and media regulation. That it occurred some fifty-five years ago is equally significant because it places my research in historical context. The emergence of a media localism agenda is neither new nor unique for the CRTC, FCC, or Ofcom. Quite the opposite, localism has been an area of contention since the origins of broadcasting (Scannell & Cardiff, 1991; Raboy, 1990; Napoli, 2001a). Regulatory interest in media localism ebbs and flows with changes in technology, ideologies, markets, and social relationships. This book thus focuses on one specific incident of a recurring trend in the history of North Atlantic media systems: how to localize the ether.

Recent debates of media localism stand apart from earlier considerations because they developed alongside the hegemony of global neoliberalism, the changing role of the nation-state within the context of globalization, changing attitudes toward broadcasting and media consumption in light of digital communication technologies, and changing approaches to social relationships amid what Appadurai (1996) calls the "scapes" of Western modernity. This makes it both a dynamic and exciting moment to study what it means to be local within media policy, and what it means to be local in the digital age.

Historically, there was never a need to regulate the discursive or geographical boundaries of daily newspapers. Free-speech laws generally prohibited much intervention, and local interest took care of the rest—how well would the *Saskatoon Star Phoenix* fare in Winnipeg, anyway? The Internet is a different story, and though physical infrastructures remain tethered to place, content has remained largely placeless. Most consumers (at least in North America) turn to broadcasting or word of mouth for their local news and information (Hindman, 2011; Pew, 2011). Increasingly, however, mobile apps and hyperlocal Web sites are emerging that encourage us to reconsider the placelessness of the Internet, and challenge us to think about it as a local environment (Farman, 2012). Still, it will be a while before these platforms reach maturity. In the meantime, we need to figure out what to do with local broadcasting, that uncertain medium that we would like to be as geographically sacrosanct as newspapers, but transcends place and space like the Internet.

With the aim of clarifying the tangled mess that is media localism in contemporary communication regulation, this chapter revisits the case studies covered in previous chapters through the lens of the overarching theories of critical regionalism, critical political economy, and critical discourse analysis. These methodological approaches share grounding in Marxism and neo-Marxism, meaning they are concerned with the exertion of power and control in the form of lived materiality but that they also may fuse Marxism with other disciplines (like geography and psychoanalysis).[1] Important for our purposes, these approaches bring attention to how actors discursively mobilize "the local" to their own advantages.

A conceptual approach based on critical regionalism encourages us to look for and examine alternative ways for regulators to think about and report on localism. Additionally, critical regionalism focuses on the construction of places with the understanding that regions, communities, and localities are created out of an intersecting relationship of geography, history, context, and discourse (Powell, 2007; Herr, 1996). The local is not synonymous with a market, nor is it synonymous with a singular community of place or a community of interest. It is "not just the 'where' of something; it is the location plus everything that occupies that location seen as an integrated and meaningful phenomenon" (Relph qtd. in Wilken, 2011, p. 62). The questions we need to be asking are how have we, and how do we, translate something so mercurial into policy?

The introduction and chapter 1 identified a dichotomy between the spatial and social dimensions that have come to define media localism. I called these, respectively, communities of place and communities of interest. I argue that the discursive positioning of these two communities as antagonistic prevents alternative conceptualizations of regulation from gaining recognition. Critical regionalism, however, eschews dichotomy and embraces complexity with ". . . great potential for producing a unified but highly adaptable analysis of international flows of capital and resistance to the negative effects of those flows at the local-regional level, toward the end of a more heterogeneous and tolerant future. Critical regionalism marks less a space-and-place opposition than one that allows for understanding places seeking some form of relation beyond that woven by capital" (Herr, 1996, p. 18). A critical regionalist approach to policy has allowed me to examine the seam between spatial and social localism, and to locate those stakeholders and interventions that seek common ground. I have found examples that bridge this artificial divide, suggesting that media localism is not a hermitically sealed concept but rather hegemonically constructed and reconstructed by powerful media corporations and media regulators themselves, and then challenged by peripheral actors like community media groups. Even with these challenges, however, regulators will not always be looking for alternatives in the discourses of localism. For localism to surpass the spatial/social dichotomy and move away from neoliberal policy, we need to observe where regulators encounter alternatives, and understand the obstacles that prevent these alternatives from being considered.

The previous four chapters demonstrated that a political economy of localism permeates regulatory discourse in the United States, United Kingdom, and Canada. This system of political and commercial pressures works to stifle or obfuscate alternative regulatory proposals vis-à-vis the local from entering into concrete policy decisions. Examples include political pressure to favor local commercial broadcasting (as in the UK), the ownership of community cable channels by cable companies (as in Canada), and the association of localism with Designated Market Areas (as in the United States). These political economic forces assure the status quo of neoliberalism and light-touch regulatory approaches as the mainstays of broadcast policy. This argument is perfectly summarized in the epigraph to this chapter—"localism is an expensive value." Here, the market is at the center of this value system, and we are instructed to *buy* local rather than *be* local.

While the status quo is largely maintained, there exist what I call "moments" of critical regionalism within regulatory discourse. Put differently, regulatory discourse is not fully captured by corporate and political power. Suggestions and innovative strategies are being proposed by stakeholders, but only on the periphery of policy discussions. This observation suggests that regulators have had opportunities (or "moments") to think productively across the spatial and social divide of localism, but have largely failed to take coherent and sustained regulatory action. In order to unpack these observations, I return to the key conceptual themes identified in part I: place, default localism, political economy, and critical regionalism.

Local Media as Place Media

At their core, regulatory discussions of media localism have been grounded in the association between local media and geographically defined places—what we can call "place media." Local broadcasters are first and foremost meant to serve the local communities to which they are licensed, particularly through the provision of local news. As described in the American Local Community Radio Act of 2005, localism means a commitment to "local operations, local research, local management, locally originated programming, local artists, and local news and events" (§3 qtd. in Dunbar-Hester, 2015, p. 142). Normative commitments to what former FCC Commissioner Jonathan Adelstein calls "local self-expression" (FCC, 2004c, p. 7) are also found at the core of community media practices, which advocates emphasize to demonstrate the relationship between communities of place and media that does not exist with platforms where users can simply upload content. "Community programming relies not only on programming outlets," the FCC heard from Lewisboro Community Television (2010), "but [also] on programming centers. Even in the digital age, there continues to be a strong need for public places where consumers can both receive and create appropriate local information that can be easily found." As the Alliance for Community Media (ACM) phrased it, community television "is a physical, publicly-accessible place where individuals of different politics, religions, colors, native origins, physical abilities, languages, educational level and economic status are able to meet, interact and become familiar with each other" (2010, p. 11). Local media as place media means first and foremost media produced by and for members of a specific geographic community, be it for commercial (e.g., NBC29 6:00 P.M. News—Charlottesville), public (e.g., CBC Winnipeg), or community purposes (e.g., PhillyCam, Philadelphia's Public Access Station).

What these factors attest to is the relationship between the local and communities of place and between local media and place-based communities. In spite of the rhetoric and interest in the network society, we continue to live in specific places and to require news and information about those places (Howley, 2010; Aldridge, 2007). "Local media may lack glamour, but their importance is beyond doubt," writes Aldridge (2007, p. 160). Put bluntly, place still matters. Ofcom goes furthest in boldly asserting this connection, investigating not only what the local means for the regulation of broadcasting, but also what it means for a changing UK society: "Although different services may target communities of different sizes, we define 'local' services as any targeted at geographic communities ranging from a neighbourhood of a few hundred or thousand households, to a major metropolitan area with a million or more inhabitants. This includes services that are intended to meet the needs of particular population sub-groups (such as minority ethnic audiences) who may be dispersed over larger areas, but still have some element of geographic concentration" (Ofcom, 2006, p. 11). Even with the recognition of socio-linguistic groups, Ofcom adheres to a definition of the local based on a "targeted geographic community."

To foster a sense of communities of place, regulators have enacted regulatory actions such as quotas for local news, community advisory boards, and studio location. None of these have proven particularly successful. The problem with place-media, and even community media, is how big the local area is meant to be. Is it a city, like Winnipeg or Manchester? Is it a region, like ITV's Borders or CTV's northern Ontario? Is it a province like Prince Edward Island, a state like Texas, or a market that encompasses numerous cities, like the DMA of Philadelphia? Or is it simply an undefined geographic boundary where a socio-linguistic group is concentrated, as noted in the Ofcom statement above? Without such distinctions, the local has become an empty signifier, a term bandied about without concrete footing in the worlds of broadcasting or regulation.

To be sure, there is nothing wrong with the association between the local and communities of place. Indeed, why should those in Victoria, a separate political and cultural space from Vancouver, not have outlets for local expression? Various scholars and studies have attested to the seminal link between place and the human condition, between the local and the democratic, and the role that local media play in fostering a sense of local community. Friedland (2001) calls these links "communicatively integrated communities," which form the basis of local deliberative democracies. Local communication, both mass and interpersonal, lies at the heart of Habermas's (1987) "lifeworld," Friedland's (2001) "communicatively integrated community," Dewey's (1927) "Great Community," and Williams's (1973) "knowable community." Normatively speaking, these communicative actions form the basis of a healthy democracy and serve the information needs of communities through local media ecologies.

The problem is when these definitions, associations, and discursive constructions rest on uncritical and unreflexive rationales rather than on considered or empirical approaches—in other words, when alternatives are left unconsidered and the status quo upheld for ease and convenience. Given the precarious nature of local broadcasting in an era of the Internet, it is more important than ever for regulators to assess critically the relationship between local media and place, and to open the conversation to multiple stakeholders about what it means to be local in the digital age. As previous chapters have shown, this has not been the case, with regulators preferring to rely on default localism.

Default Localism

Default localism occurs when a regulator takes the local for granted, gives little or no indication that alternatives have been considered, or positions communities of place and communities of interest as antagonistic. In others words, this occurs when the epistemological question of the local goes undiscussed, or when definitions go unexplained. This leads to ambiguity within regulation (e.g., what counts as a local broadcaster or local news), which can have serious consequences when it comes to the provision, quality, and quantity of local news. To this end, the three categories of default localism are reintroduced here: The local as taken for granted, the local as geographic, and the local as tautological. Each connotes a market-based definition of the local. Recall the UK's L-DTPS (chapter 5), which had the opportunity to ascribe local character and local voices into the regulatory system, but chose instead a market-based approach that allowed for massive levels of corporate concentration and a lack of bright line local news regulations. Additionally, consider fee-for-carriage in Canada (chapter 2), the end result of which favored cable companies in the fight for local newscasts and permitted BDUs to engage in tactics of regulatory ransom (also observed in the UK). Of all the examples of default localism it is the

FCC's reliance on DMAs (chapter 2) to define the parameters of the local where we find the quintessential example of default localism. Here, the FCC takes the local for granted, assumes a geographic enclave, and defines the local in terms of markets. Indeed, the FCC allows a private corporation to make this decision that the Commission itself should be making as the appointed regulator of American media.

These selective examples are used to better explicate the meaning of default localism, and they should not be read as occurring in each and every regulatory instance. To the contrary, I argue that peripheral conversations, documents, and actors do seriously address the epistemology of the local in deliberate and considerate fashions. Nonetheless, as previous chapters have demonstrated, reliance on default localism is pervasive among the three regulators. Its consistent usage leads to some troubling consequences. It demonstrates how regulatory agencies often fail to take into account the heterogeneous composition of local communities regardless of size or population. This represents a nod toward the essentialist tendencies of the local—reducing the local to a homogenous population, and quite often, a homogeneous market. Reliance on default localism stifles opportunities for a definition of the local to grow and develop, or to include alternative and peripheral voices and opinions. Indeed, it heightens the previously identified rift between the "spatial" and "social" elements of localism, wherein the "spatial" element is privileged at the expense of nuance. When the local goes unconsidered or unchallenged, it becomes difficult (if not impossible) to get at underlying power structures and inequities. As Joseph (2008) observes, "Fetishizing community only makes us blind to the ways we might intervene in the enactment of domination and exploitation" (p. ix). Drawing on Joseph's point, it is difficult to debate the inclusion of minority groups, ethnic media, or language communities into broader definitions of media localism if the local is *a priori* taken to be a hermetically sealed unit whose contours are presumed out of bounds for policymakers.

There are also immediate policy implications when regulators rely on default localism. One concern that we have seen repeatedly is the definition of local news and information programming. As the flag bearer of localism, local news is what broadcasters and regulators use to underscore its importance in the media system. What counts as local news, however, is often left undefined. Is it news about the immediate geographic locality? Is it news of interest to the local population? Is it news produced within the locality? Or is it something else or a combination therein? As I contend elsewhere, "These questions are far from trivial, as definitions of local news have consequences for regulations through license renewals, quotas, and diversity of voices" (Ali, 2016b).

If the regulator does not, or is prevented from, opining on the epistemological question of the local, then it is important that we ask, "Who does?" In the absence of regulation, it is often the market, and more specifically, commercial enterprises. This is what happened when the FCC opted to use Nielsen's DMA definition to stand as the de facto definition of what constitutes a local community. This is certainly problematic, not least because a federal agency is allowing a commercial company to determine what is local for the purposes of regulation (see chapter 2). It reduces a community to a homogeneous market, but also often lumps several municipalities together for the purposes of ratings and regulation (Goldfarb, 2005). Similarly in Britain, Ofcom's decision to give the MuxCo the ability to opine on the next round of local stations places the local in the hands of a private company that is in no way beholden to the public interest (see chapter 5).

The Political Economy of Media Localism

The examples of default localism mentioned in this chapter and noted throughout this book point to a larger structural concern within contemporary media regulation: a political economy of localism. Regardless of the romantic associations of the local espoused by regulators (e.g., "a building block of the community"), there are embedded power structures and ideological interests at work. In short, there is a political economy of localism within the discourse of communications regulation that succeeds in stifling alternative conceptualizations of the local, local news, and local programming. This is not some nefarious conspiracy among regulators and corporate interests, but rather it indicates how commercial actors successfully mobilize discourses of the local to meet their ideological and business interests. At its broadest, political economy refers to the "study of control and survival in social life" (Mosco, 2009, p. 26). More narrowly tailored, the political economy of communication "is the study of the social relations, particularly the power relations, that mutually constitute the production, distribution, and consumption of resources" (p. 25). The power to control the discursive agenda of media regulation and thereby set the parameters of what is and is not acceptable discourse is part and parcel of this political economy.

Canada's Local Programming Improvement Fund (LPIF) speaks directly to this "media power" (Freedman, 2014) and the ability of media corporations to control the discursive agenda. Here, cable companies succeeded in convincing the CRTC that not only are their community stations successfully replacing local commercial stations as providers of local news, but also that the LPIF is a drain on consumers. I have used the term *regulatory ransom* to describe a similar tactic of large media conglomerates, whereby companies such as Bell Media in Canada and ITV in the UK use the local as a bargaining chip during negotiations with regulators.

A second example of media power and control of regulatory discourse comes from the UK. In chapter 5 we learned that Ofcom favored public intervention for local digital media, and encouraged experimentation with IPTV and universal broadband. In contrast, the system that eventually emerged dismantled public interest provisions to ease the entry of commercial local television at the behest of political powers (e.g., Jeremy Hunt) and favoring incumbent media organizations (e.g., the *Evening Standard*). That the multiplex operator (MuxCo) will control the spectrum for local television and holds sway over the next round of local stations further illuminates how the political economy functions as it ranks for-profit organizations above other stakeholders such as community groups and municipalities. This has serious implications for who will receive local news because Ofcom will select the next round of local stations based on the recommendations of the MuxCo (Dowell, 2013).

The present discussion is not intended to demonize the earnest attempts of regulators, who at times have sought alternatives, expressed awareness of local news and information as public goods, and voiced concerns for the local. Still, questions implicit in the critical regionalism approach, such as definitions and market alternatives, remain unanswered, unresolved, and more often than not, unasked. Not to be dissuaded, critical theory reminds us to seek out moments of opposition and resistance to the status quo (Hall, 1980; Kraidy, 2005). In this regard, critical regionalism focuses on alternatives to taken-for-granted understandings of the local and underscores a belief in moral economies, praxis, social justice, and collective rights, which are also the hallmarks of critical political economy. Through these complementary lenses, unpacking the local within broadcast regulation is less about cementing definitions and more about identifying and promoting discourses that seek alternatives to the status quo.

Solutions are about encouraging regulators and policymakers to take holistic perspectives on these important questions—questions that have come to define communications regulation in the digital age. We can now turn our attention to those instances where alternatives and negotiations vis-à-vis the spatial and social dichotomy have taken place within communications regulation over the past decade.

The Ambiguity of Local Media

The strongest alternative readings of the local come when definitional boundaries are challenged. Ofcom has been the most prolific actor in this regard, with several notable attempts to understand the local in regulation, the media system, and UK society. The 2006 *Digital Local* report represents the acme of progressive localism thought because it interrogates the local from multiple vantage points. At one point, for instance, Ofcom questions whether a place-based definition of the local is the appropriate target for regulatory intervention, or if communities of interest would be better suited:

> It has been argued . . . that information and communication technologies have weakened people's ties to shared localities, by providing access to global information and media, enabling larger and more dispersed groups to communicate and facilitating the development of services to niche communities that are not bound by geographical location or proximity to the service provider. . . . We may have as much in common with somebody at the end of a telephone line in a different continent, as we do with our nextdoor neighbour, if not more. (p. 10)

Acknowledging the rise of social localism, Ofcom was not content to rely on taken-for-granted assumptions of communities of interest or communities of place. Instead, the regulator engaged in an epistemological debate. While eventually settling on the belief that "'[geographically] local' still does matter," Ofcom acknowledged the complexity of defining the local for regulatory purposes: "In practice, 'locality' is a multilayered concept, which means different things in different places, and to the same person at different times" (p. 22)

Despite Ofcom's acknowledgment of the contextual nature of the local, media localism must still be narrowed down to avoid regulatory ambiguity. While raising the issue for different ideological reasons (i.e., for greater deregulation), this was the position of American commercial broadcasters who frequently argued that ambiguity in terms like "local" and "local news" only serve to weaken and confuse the regulatory landscape. Argued the NAB: "The lack of a workable and consistent definition for 'local' . . . undermines the entire regulatory regime that the Commission is attempting to implement. The uncertainty created by this failure will leave the agency, the public and broadcasters mired in regulatory uncertainty for years" (2008, pp. 9–10). While it is of course in broadcasters' interests for the FCC to refrain from proposing more stringent regulations and definitions, the NAB raises the important point that regulators cannot simply deploy these terms without a more concrete discussion about their meaning and impact.

A Canadian example echoes the importance of reducing ambiguity in localism regulation. As detailed in chapter 4, the Lincoln Report recognized how complex it is to define community, local, and regional for Canadians and the CRTC alike. At one point in its voluminous nine hundred pages, it poignantly observed, "one person's regional can be someone else's local, regional or provincial; and, depending on one's location, it can be all three" (Canada, 2003, p. 356). The ambiguity of regulatory definitions of the local has significant implications for the regulation of local broadcasting, and the CRTC was chastised for failing to take this into account when drafting what the Lincoln Report considered its poorly considered, yet overly complex regulation of these important issues.

While clarifying definitions are important, part of the solution to the challenge of media localism also lies in the realization that previous taken-for-granted assumptions of the local are insufficient. The FCC, CRTC, and Ofcom have each been confronted with questions, either from within or by outside commentators, about definitions of the local, particularly with regard to local news. The very act of asking these questions exemplifies alternatives to the status quo. The FCC, for instance, has asked on a handful of occasions if its approach to localism requires revisiting in light of changes in technology and social behavior (see FCC, 2008, 2010). Early on, Ofcom contemplated "what geographical units would make most sense . . . if we were starting to develop regional programming from scratch?" (2004e, p. 48). The CRTC has also contemplated what it means to be local. As Commissioner Elizabeth Duncan asked during a hearing: "Do you think that the definition of local news is specific enough, narrow enough, precise enough to allow us to be able to analyze all across the country and compare the results or do you think we need to fine tune that?" (CRTC 2012b, par. 1564). In asking these broad questions, regulators invite responses from numerous stakeholders, rather than just those who have commercial or regulatory interests in a given proceeding. They make available the possibility of alternatives to long-standing and outmoded assumptions of the local. Part of the challenge for scholars is to get regulators to follow up on these questions, pay more attention to the peripheral conversations (such as community media), and integrate them into localism regulation.

Moments of Critical Regionalism

The aforementioned examples represent what I call "moments of critical regionalism." Thinking about critical regionalism as a series of moments adds nuance in three ways. First, it demonstrates that this is not merely an academic exercise but rather a pragmatic approach that emphasizes alternatives to static and reductive definitions of the local within regulatory discourse. Second, it demonstrates that alternatives to the spatial/social divide exist within regulatory discourse. Third, it reminds us that media policymaking is an imperfect process (Freedman, 2008, 2014). Critical policy research should not be about determining if policy decisions are critically regionalist or not, but rather should place policy and critical regionalism on a spectrum. Following Lowrey et al.'s (2008) assessment of community journalism in mainstream news, critical regionalism should be thought of as a "continuing effort rather than a static goal" when it comes to identifying moments within media policy (p. 288). With this in mind, two instances may be regarded as templates for critical regional moments. The first is when regulators think about communities of interest *within* communities of place. The second is when regulators consider more inclusive definitions, such as the alignment of localism and language.

The first example is community media. Though situated on the periphery of regulatory discourse, community media advocates frequently attest that place still matters in the production of media content, despite the growth of disembodied online platforms (Howley, 2010). The "community media center" has become a focal point in these arguments, described as a place for gathering, community building, and skill development (Ali, 2014). Bringing community media into conversations about localism adds complexity to these positions, and serves to illustrate "the definitional ambiguities and inconsistencies inherent in the existing uses of the terms community, local and regional" (Canada, 2003, p. 362). The UK has again been the trendsetter in these discussions, passing legislation that directly acknowledges the complex and heterogeneous nature of the local. As the 2004 Community Radio Order proclaimed, a community can consist of:

> (a) the persons who live or work or undergo education or training in a particular area or locality, or
> (b) persons who (whether or not they fall within paragraph [a]) have one or more interest or characteristics in common. (UK, 2004, §2[1])

This definition recognizes both communities of *interest* and communities of *place*, and communities of interest *within* communities of place. With ease it bridges the spatial/social divide that has stymied other regulators. It also recognizes the mobility inherent in these communities, and engenders the inescapable truism that human beings continue to live their lives around and within places (Casey, 1998; Entrikin, 1991). Outside policymakers and regulators would do well to study the applicability of the Community Radio Order because it recognizes that the local is both geographically determined in terms of scope and socially determined in terms of depth, a true moment of critical regionalism.

Canada and the United States have at times demonstrated such consideration. In the United States, the Congressional Research Service discussed the difficulties of defining local communities based on commercial markets (e.g., DMAs), rather than political or cultural communities (Goldfarb, 2005). Similarly, the Brennan Center for Social Justice (2004) proposed a definition of localism that took into account both the salience of place and the need to understand that communities of place are not homogeneous markets, but rather heterogeneous social ecosystems. It noted, "The [FCC] has long equated localism with broadcast markets. But as these markets expand through increased power levels and other technological advances, the needs of local communities get lost" (pp. 9–10). To address this liberalization, it suggested "Assign[ing] more broadcast licenses to nonprofit, independent media that serve the needs and interests of diverse social, economic, ethnic, and racial groups within local communities" (p. v). This recognizes both the salience of place-based communities (predicated upon political or cultural markers rather than market parameters) and that diversity exists below the surface of the local.

Paralleling the Brennan Center, Canada's Lincoln Report recommended the creation of a unified local media policy that would take into account such elements as ethnic media and minority-language broadcasting (Canada, 2003). Similarly, a 2009 Canadian House of Commons report on local television recommended that any public funding initiative to support local media should include "private and public broadcasters, including CBC/Radio-Canada, Aboriginal broadcasters, educational broadcasters, community television, and small broadcasters representing official language minority communities" (p. 31).

The Canadian example anticipates the second template for critical regionalism—the inclusion of ethno-linguistic groups. These groups have mobilized the discourse of the local to argue that they too should be included in its definition. Francophone and Aboriginal producers have been particularly vocal in wanting to be labeled "local broadcasters." As Stanley James of Northern Native Broadcasting noted in testimony to the House of Commons: "We believe the federal government must continue to assist local aboriginal broadcasters and to assist in meeting the cost of digital transmission. . . . The role of the cultural development fund to ensure the survival of local broadcasting should be strengthened and have the involvement of local broadcasting in the terms of reference. Oftentimes, non-profit societies such as Northern Native Broadcasting . . . find themselves ineligible" (Canada, 2009e, p. 26). Such discursive tactics invite regulators to think beyond taken-for-granted definitions, and contemplate whether these groups belong in the category of the local. As the Lincoln Report noted, such contemplation, particularly regarding the role of indigenous media, "is further evidence of how the boundaries between community, local and regional programming can blur" (Canada, 2003, p. 378). What media fall into the categories of local, community, and regional need to be considered, but heretofore have not been debated in Canada, or elsewhere.

In highlighting these examples, we must be cognizant that policies and regulations are themselves discursive constructions, and as such contain their own embedded power dynamics (Lentz, 2011). The examples I provided in this chapter illustrate how different actors mobilize the discourse of the local to their advantage. Nevertheless, they are significant discursive acts, and regulators should pay attention to actors that seek to call themselves local. It is therefore the *conversation* among multiple stakeholders that is important at this early juncture in localism's rejuvenation.

Conclusion: In Defense of Media Localism

The primary goals of this chapter were to interrogate the dichotomy between spatial and social localism through my case studies and conceptual frameworks and to demonstrate the application of critical regionalism to media policy studies. In doing so, I argue that a more dynamic approach is needed to reimagine localism in the twenty-first century. Escobar (2003) asks, "Is it possible to envision a defense of place without naturalizing, feminizing, or essentializing it, one in which place does not become the source of trivial processes or regressive forces?" (p. 40). I respond affirmatively because critical regionalism allows for this possibility. Unfortunately, the moments of critical regionalism that expand on Escobar's defense of place remain largely confined to the peripheries of regulatory discourse in the form of forgotten proposals, neglected reports, or buried recommendations. Regulators have yet to heed their important calls.

If the local is to continue as a normative ideal in media regulation—as the FCC, CRTC, and Ofcom each attest—the moments I have discussed in this chapter and throughout this book need to enter into mainstream regulatory discourse. In particular, a regulatory system is required that recognizes the heterogeneous composition of local communities, rather than one that flattens out the nuances of place, community, and localism. Critical regionalism is a useful approach by which to analyze localism in media policy because it circumvents the artificial dichotomy between spatial and social conceptualizations. This is not a zero-sum game of local or not, place-based or not, community or not, but rather a process where both the spatial and the social contribute to the construction of the local (Dirlik, 1999; Soja, 1995). A critical regionalist approach has the potential to lead us to a more progressive theory of localism policy, and at the very least, expand the conversations that inform regulatory and legislative discourse by highlighting alternatives to the status quo.

What might a definition of localism look like through the lens of critical regionalism? While not wanting to be overly prescriptive, we can be sure that any such definition for media policy and regulation would have to be technologically neutral (i.e., not exclusively about broadcasting). The need for such a broad technological stance was made evident by the ecosystems reports of chapter 4, which went to great lengths to describe media practices beyond those residing under the jurisdiction of media regulators. The definition would also have to be "community neutral," meaning that it must incorporate communities of place and (to a limited extent) communities of interest. This does not mean all communities of interest, mind you, but at the very least those referenced in the UK's Community Radio Order described in chapter 3 and that I argue could be a template for local media regulation. This is akin to what Hess (2013) and Hess and Waller (2014) call "geo-social news"—news that is rooted in a "sense of place" but not incumbent upon consumers living in that place. Last, any definition of localism should be holistic, meaning that it cannot be tethered exclusively to place, interest, or capital. This is based on the findings from critical geography detailed in chapter 1, which remind us that places are both geographically and socially constructed.

Having said this, the immediate future of media localism and its definitional, conceptual, and operational boundaries should not be about cementing definitions. Rather, its future lies in the conversation. "'Senses' of place and region are not so much essential qualities . . ." Powell (2007) writes, "as they are ongoing debates and discourses that coalesce around particular geographical spaces" (p. 14). At this moment, the debate is needed more than the short-term fix. A spirited discussion is required if localism is to survive as a governing principle of media regulation, particularly when it comes to local news. The ultimate goal is simply put but herculean in practice: develop media policies that embrace the local as a site of dynamism and heterogeneity. Critical regionalism is a framework to encourage such conversations. Powell (2007) continues, "the path that the practice of critical regionalism draws across this intellectual landscape is designed to lead toward a view of the best possible version of the region from among all the versions that are out there (whether or not it actually gets there)" (p. 7). This should be the goal of regulators and scholars of localism—to locate and theorize the "best possible version" of the local within Western media systems. The following chapter outlines my contributions to this conversation.

7

Interventions in Localism
From Public Goods to Merit Goods

> It may be that the sewer, street light,
> school bond substance of local politics
> is too boring to ever excite much literary
> or scholarly attention.
> But people need to install sewers,
> fix street lights, and pass school bond measures.
> This is where civic life begins.
> —Michael Schudson (1999)

Plus ça change . . .

The bulk of primary research for this book took place between 2009 and 2013, and the scope of the book spans roughly from 2000 to 2012. The present chapter was written in 2015, two full years after the original research was conducted. Much has changed on the media landscape in these short twenty-four months. We already know, for instance, that we live in a world of Netflix and streaming, rather than broadcasting, and of *The Daily Show* and *Last Week Tonight* rather than the 6 P.M. news. Now, we are learning about how new platforms such as geospatial Web mapping, mobile locative technologies, and community wi-fi initiatives work to insert place-based narratives into an erstwhile global medium (Farman, 2012; Powell & Shade, 2012; Powell, 2012). Hyperlocal Web sites, meanwhile, spring up in droves and disappear almost as quickly. AOL's Patch network of hyperlocal news sites had to be gutted in 2013 after running losses upward of $300 million (Carr, 2013). From the perspective of both media consumption habits and media policy discourse, local television has been displaced by the emergence of the digital. This discursive displacement, however, blinds us to the fact that the majority still turn to television for local news and information (Pew, 2011).

184 · FIXING LOCALISM

Media localism cannot be neglected within media policy regulation, but that is exactly what has happened. The underlying issues described throughout this book—ambiguity, default localism, and market fundamentalism—continue to define the regulation of media localism. *Plus ça change, plus c'est la meme chose* (the more things change, the more they stay the same).

In Canada, the CRTC recently completed a two-year public inquiry called "Let'sTalkTV"—a campaign designed to get Canadians talking about the state of Canadian television. Hearing from thousands of Canadians through written comments, testimony, and interactive questionnaire, the Commission noted that despite 91.2 percent of Canadians subscribing to pay television (cable, satellite), "over-the-air reception plays an important role in the Canadian broadcasting system . . . particularly with respect to the local and Canadian programming offered by conventional television stations" (CRTC, 2014, par. 14). Agreeing for the moment at least that local stations "continue to play a significant role in the lives of Canadians," the CRTC decided to prohibit stations from shutting off their over-the-air transmitters, less they forfeit privileges such as mandatory cable carriage and simultaneous substation. Paradoxically, while acknowledging the importance of local television and the dire financial conditions of stations, the Commission declined to intervene through levies or subsidies. Instead, it argued: "there is currently sufficient funding within the system to ensure the creation of locally relevant and reflective programming" (par. 26). In sum, the CRTC recognizes the importance of local programming, acknowledges that Canadians value local news, admits the market failure of this public good, but refuses to intervene, opting instead to study the matter further in 2015–2016.

In the United States, a 2014 Supreme Court Case, *American Broadcasting Company v. Aereo,* had the potential to rewrite rules for the distribution of local television (SCOTUS, 2014). Aereo was a subscription-based online streaming service that allowed users to watch live programming in (almost) real-time. Each subscriber was assigned an individual micro-antenna that was stored in a warehouse. Once a program was selected, the antenna tunes to the local station's signal and the subscriber could stream it through any number of devices. The program was also stored for later viewing. The service cost approximately $8/month. This distribution system challenged the conventional model in three separate ways. First, Aereo was effectively mimicking a cable service in the distribution of local channels. Second, it was distributing the signals of local channels without paying retransmission fees (as cable systems are required to do). Third, Aereo was violating the copyright agreements that local stations have on programming by refusing to get broadcasters' permission for retransmission.

Broadcasters sued Aereo in 2013, but the New York Second Circuit Court ruled in favor of the company. However the Tenth Circuit in Utah, along with district courts in California and Washington, D.C., issued injunctions, forcing the issue to the Supreme Court. Aereo argued it was not equivalent to a cable service but rather an equipment provider because it was simply retransmitting over-the-air signals that any individual could pick up using a household antenna. Broadcasters focused their arguments on copyright infringement, arguing that Aereo was illegally conducting a "public performance,"[1] to which they (the broadcasters) had exclusive rights. Aereo denied the claim, countering that it was not conducting public performances, but rather hundreds of private performances (because each subscriber was assigned an individual micro-antenna). While the Supreme Court recognized the difference between Aereo and conventional cable systems (because Aereo only transmitted upon subscriber request whereas cable systems transmitted constantly), it ultimately ruled in favor of broadcasters, declaring that Aereo was in violation of the Copyright Act. The Court may have been in the right with regard to this decision, but the ruling nevertheless had digital optimists nervous. Indeed, despite the Court's assurance that "this decision will [not] disrupt the emergence or use of different kinds of technologies," dissenters argued that the decision would stymie innovation in cloud storage for everything from YouTube to Dropbox (Rogowsky, 2014).[2] Had the Court ruled the other way, we would have seen the emergence of a radically new local television distribution system that would have (for better or worse) required immediate regulatory action from the FCC.[3]

Across the North Atlantic, the United Kingdom has experienced its own setbacks as the new local television service continues to struggle. Joining the financial difficulties of London Live discussed in chapter 5, Birmingham's City TV went bankrupt in August 2014, and was placed into administration by its creditors, all before broadcasting a single program. Through the autumn, the administrators were seeking a buyer for the license, which was found in the form of Kaleidoscope TV. Now called Big Centre TV, the station launched in February 2015, with the new owners committing to "live news coverage and to the delivery of hyper-local news involving local partnerships and arrangements with local studios" (Johnston, 2014). Even with several stations now on the air, Ofcom is skeptical of success, admitting that "it is 'very unlikely' that all local TV stations it is licensing will succeed" (qtd. in Reynolds, 2014).

Despite these changing consumption patterns, regulators continue to remind us of the importance of local television, local news, and media localism, while consumers consistently vocalize their support for these institutions. A recent Canadian survey (CRTC, 2014) found that 81 percent of respondents valued local television news, while in Britain 77 percent of respondents in a 2014 survey said they consult local television at least weekly, and 40 percent said "regional and local news on television was considered to be the most important type of local media" (Ofcom, 2013a). Local television is apparently valued by both regulators and consumers, but is challenged technologically and economically. How can we reconcile these contrasting discursive and experiential practices?

I argue in this book for a move toward a more inclusive definition of the local—one that recognizes our seminal relationship to place, but that eschews reductivism, essentialism, and market fundamentalism. This means embracing the complexities and nuances of the local by incorporating communities of interest within discussions of localism, local media, local news, and local media ecosystems. A robust, plural, and diverse local media system is necessary for a robust, plural and diverse democratic system. So, how do we make this happen?

Former FCC Commissioner Michael Copps says that new regulatory initiatives need to embrace creative thinking to solve the challenges inherent within our media system. Similarly, a Canadian respondent argued that part of the goal for Canadian regulation needs to be to get people "excited about CanCon [Canadian Content]," which, of course, includes *local* Canadian content. The common point is the need to develop innovative ways to think about the local in the digital age, to think across spatial and social divides, and to think about inclusiveness rather than exclusivity. In this spirit, I offer two policy interventions. The first—local media policy frameworks—draws on my four case studies and the moments of critical regionalism discussed in chapter 6. My second recommendation draws on critical political economy, normative theory, and my research into local media ecosystems to argue for a semantic and purposive shift away from thinking about local news as a "public good" and framing it instead as a "merit good."

Local Media Policy Frameworks

Victor Pickard (2014) uses the term "policy failure" to describe "existing policy mechanisms' insufficiency in dealing with significant social problems including market failure" (p. 216). Des Freedman (2010, 2014) coined the term "policy silence" to describe the conditions of "non-decision making." Accordingly, "Policy silences... refer to the options that are *not* considered, to the questions are [sic] kept *off* the policy agenda, to the players who are *not* invited to the policy table, and to the values that are seen as unrealistic or undesirable by those best able to mobilize their policymaking powers" (p. 74). The lack of a coherent local media policy framework in Canada, the United States, and the United Kingdom represents both of these conditions, and was acknowledged as far back as 2003 when the Lincoln Report recommended the creation of a coherent and comprehensive local media policy for Canada. Similarly, the CPRN report discussed in chapter 4 argued that the United States would be wise to "capture the increasingly complex functioning of local media systems in ways that fully account for the role played by *all* relevant stakeholders, the interconnections and interdependencies that exist among media platforms that embed the analysis of media systems within the analysis of the ways different kinds of local communities actually function, and the extent to which local community information needs are being effectively served" (2012, p. 10). The FCC, Ofcom, and the CRTC should be encouraged to develop such comprehensive and holistic local media policy frameworks. Ideally, these frameworks should move away from the technologically siloed approach to media policy currently employed (Bar & Sandvig, 2003; Shade & Lithgow, 2009), and think instead in terms of ecosystems and "communicatively integrated communities" (Friedland, 2001). This would of course include community media as well as platforms not under the regulators' immediate jurisdiction, but that contribute to the ecosystem: blogs, citizen journalism, hyperlocal sites, and mobile platforms. As discussed in chapter 3, a number of proposals regarding media localism have been made in community media circles, particularly in the United Kingdom, where Ofcom is directed by the Community Radio Order to consider communities of place *and* communities of interest that exist within particular communities of place. This is echoed by the CPRN (2012), which recommended "researchers ... take into account variations within communities and specific populations in identifying and designing responses to critical information needs" (p. xi). These local media policy frameworks must account for all media technologies, communities, platforms, and most important, stakeholders.

This book is as much about the "ideal" of localism as it is about the real-world policies of localism. Local television remains the primary medium of localism and represents the anchor of the local media ecosystem, at least for the time being. Still, local television and the policies that govern it have failed to live up to their potential for public communication. Local newscasts remain wedded to murder and mayhem, while local education, local health, and local politics are often waylaid. But, as Rasmus Kleis Nielsen (2015) puts it, "local journalism may well be frequently terrible and yet also terribly important" (p. 1). It is for this precise reason that regulators must think holistically about localism. Television may still follow the lamentable credo, "if it bleeds, it leads," but if placed in an ecosystem alongside local radio covering local fundraising efforts, community television covering city council meetings and minor league hockey (decidedly *not* murder and mayhem), the daily newspaper covering local politics, hyperlocal blogs and citizen journalists covering local events, and new journalistic platforms such as apps and maps covering local storytelling, a more complete picture may indeed be possible to glean.

Regulators constantly point to the need for pluralism and diversity in the media system but do not follow their own advice when drafting policies. Input into regulatory debates comes mainly from lobby groups and major industry stakeholders such as the National Association of Broadcasters, Comcast, NBC, Fox, and Clear Channel in the United States, the BBC and ITV in the UK, and the CBC, CTV, Global, Bell, Shaw, Rogers, and Quebecor in Canada. These regulated industries are not only engaged in regulatory capture but also in a process of "discursive capture" by dominating regulatory proceedings (Pickard, 2014). This discursive capture overshadows the contributions made by public interest organizations, religious broadcasters, and community media groups, and serves to foster the political economy of localism outlined in chapter 6 by demonstrating the power of media corporations to mobilize regulatory discourse to suit their agendas. If the goal of media regulation is to create the most robust local media ecosystem possible, a comprehensive local media policy framework accounting for a diversity of intervening voices is not only "warranted, but necessary" (Ali, 2016b).

Last, these policy frameworks need to account for the various funding models at work within local media ecosystems. While clearly favoring market forces, regulators need to acknowledge that media is funded privately, publicly, and philanthropically. It is hardly the case that "government is not the key player in this drama" as is claimed in the Waldman Report. Instead, as Pickard reminds us, "the government is always involved in markets" (p. 218).[4] Regulators should investigate ways in which subsidies can help bolster local media ecosystems. Greater investment in public media is warranted across jurisdictions, and tax incentives, particularly in the United States, would go a long way toward creating a sustainable future for nonprofit local journalism (see Pickard, 2014). Another option is cross-media subsidies: diverting revenues from one part of the media industry, like cable, to another, like broadcasting. In Canada, for instance, the Local Programming Improvement Fund and the Small Market Local Programming Fund diverted revenue from broadcast distribution undertakings to local broadcasters in an attempt to bolster local news production. In the United States, the Universal Service Fund, supported with contributions from telecommunication companies, subsidizes rural telephone infrastructure and service. Similar proposals are now being heard to support universal broadband (FCC, 2010a). In a 2009 report on local news and information, Downie Jr. and Schudson recommended a similar path in the creation of a "national Fund for Local News . . . created with money the Federal Communications Commission now collects from or could impose on telecom users, television and radio broadcast licensees, or Internet service providers and which would be administered in open competition through state Local News Fund Councils" (p. 36). Given the neoliberal climate in which we operate, cross-media subsidies are a realistic compromise between public and private funding of local media.

From Public Goods to Merit Goods

My recommendations for regulatory intervention represent what Victor Pickard (2013, 2014) calls a "social democratic perspective" of media policy. It is a move away from the myopic neoliberal or "corporate libertarian" model of media governance and a move toward a system that recognizes multiple stakeholders, including the federal government. "A social democratic perspective assesses the value of a media system by how it benefits society as a whole, rather than the criteria of individual freedoms, private property rights, and profit for a relative few" (2013, p. 342). In order to encourage such an approach to media localism within the current neoliberal climate, however, we need to do some additional justificatory work to reconcile this social democratic intervention strategy with the current (de-)regulatory system in place in the North Atlantic triangle. The language of neoclassical economics helps us bridge this gap.

Throughout this book, I have commented on ways in which many have sought to classify news and information as a public good to align journalistic practices with the essential requirements of democracy (Pickard, 2013, 2014; McChesney & Nichols, 2010; Baker, 2002; Starr, 2011). As recalled in the introduction, the discourse of public goods derives from neoclassical economics and is used to describe how local news and information is nonrivalrous, nonexcludable, and containing of numerous social and democratic benefits (known as positive externalities). Public goods are those that cannot be deprived and that benefit those who do not pay (the "free riders"). Classic examples include national defense and public health (McChesney & Nichols, 2010).

By definition, however, public goods are expensive to produce, provide little financial return, and are therefore underproduced by the private market. "Market failure" is the term given to the underproduction of public goods, and government intervention is necessary to remedy the situation (Pickard, 2013, 2014; Bator, 1959; Baker, 2002; Stiglitz, 1989; see also generally Ver Eecke, 2007a). Again, turning to the example of national defense, it is inconceivable for the private market to sustain such an expensive enterprise. Journalism, particularly local investigative journalism, is another specific example of the market failure of a public good.

Public goods and market failures exemplify the push and pull of the "theory of public finance" (Musgrave, 1959). I argue, however, that the discourse of public goods is insufficient to fully capture the social democratic importance of local news and information. In place of public goods theory, I call for a rhetorical and purposive shift toward thinking about media localism and local news as what Richard A. Musgrave (1959) called a "merit good." Allan Pulsipher (1971/2007), a supporter of merit goods, argues that if we are to "use merit goods theory . . . to recommend policy, it is important and legitimate that this theory be stated explicitly and as clearly and consistently as possible" (p. 173). In this spirit, I use the following pages to explain merit goods and the theory's applicability to media localism.

WHAT IS A MERIT GOOD?

The idea of a merit good was first proposed by Richard Musgrave in 1959 to designate those goods (or "wants") that are so socially valuable ("meritorious") that they should be provided "through the public budget over and above what is provided for through the market and paid for by private buyers" (p. 13). A merit good is thus something that is underproduced by industry and underinvested in by consumers, but should nonetheless be provided. For this to happen, government intervention and funding through the public budget is necessary. Examples of merit goods include free school lunches, education, and vaccinations (Musgrave, 1959), higher education (Koch, 2008), museums (Fullerton, 1991), and even organic foods (Mann, 2013).

Though merit goods rest on the same normative foundations as public goods—correcting market failure—two factors delineate the concepts. First, the discourse of public goods is often misrepresented. Indeed, public goods, as a set of specific economic principles, are often conflated with "*the* public good"—a more general philosophical and moralistic idea. Colloquially, we often refer to the "common good," the "social good," and "the public interest" in the same breath as public goods. Rooted in Aristotelian philosophy, these connote notions of community and collectivity—a shared existence, or *koinonoi* (Kane, 1998). In the strictest reading, however, public goods as a group of economic concepts are more about the provision of goods and services requested by consumers and underproduced by the market than they are about the normative common good.

To be sure, many scholars use the term "public goods" deliberately as both a reference to economics and as a reference to the broader public good. Many also use "public good" to describe exactly what Musgrave is getting at with merit goods, especially because "merit goods" have yet to gain strong traction in economic theory. They are not wrong to do so. My argument here, however, is about pragmatics and not nomenclature. The fact that policymakers themselves have started to use the term "merit goods" to describe journalism, and have subsequently begun to ask the questions typical of merit goods thinking, signals that it is time to have a larger conversation about placing merit goods at the center of political economic justifications for local journalism.

Second, the theory of public goods is bound by respect for consumers, consumer choice, and consumer sovereignty. Public goods are "goods which the government provides with the intention of respecting the wishes of consumers" (Ver Eecke, 1998, p. 5). If individuals do not consume public goods to some degree, they should not be provided. In contrast, merit goods are based on a normative assumption that the good should be provided regardless of consumption habits. They represent those goods "which the government provides by a method or at a level which disregards the wishes of consumers" (Ver Eecke, 1989, p. 5). Merit goods, by definition, violate the principle of consumer sovereignty in order to provide a good deemed essential by society. There is a strong normative value system inherent within the discourse of merit goods, which assumes that individuals should have access to certain goods regardless of their consumer behavior.

Musgrave stressed that one of the reasons consumers may not understand the value of certain goods is because of erroneous information. As Head (1966) describes, merit goods are "those of which, due to imperfect knowledge, individuals would choose to consume too little" (qtd. in Pulsipher, 1971/2007, p. 156). Both Head and Musgrave (1959) label this the "preference distortion problem." Here it is understood that "information is costly to acquire; and as a result, the preferences of a rational individual will rarely if ever be based upon complete and accurate information" (Pulsipher, 1971/2007, p. 157). Put another way, consumers may not always directly express their wishes, know the societal benefits of certain goods, or even be aware that the option exists. The market does not take these intangibilities into account. Koch (2008) uses the example of diphtheria shots in that "one individual is helped by another individual's diphtheria shot even if he isn't aware of that fact" (p. 369). For our purposes, I suggest that consumers do not recognize the larger values engendered within local news. It is certainly true that I benefit from local news even if I do not consume it. For instance, those who do consume local news may share information about local politics with me. At the very least, then, I would be a better-informed voter. If I do consume local news, I benefit even more (Oberholzer-Gee & Waldfogel, 2009).

Echoing this moral philosophy, Ellen Goodman (2006) calls the underproduction of public interest programming a "broad market failure" that necessitates public intervention. It is worth quoting Goodman at length to understand the relationship between merit goods and local news (which I am equating here with public-interest programming):

> But perhaps the diversity deficit has another source, namely the failure of consumers to demand the range of expressive goods that democracy requires. . . . *In this case, if there is a market failure, it is a broad failure of markets to do what markets are not designed to do: produce goods for which there is insufficient consumer demand, but important civic value. The appropriate policy response to this kind of market failure is proactive, in that it seeks to expose people to content that they do not, at least initially demand.* (p. 366, emphasis added)

Goodman suggests here that (1) consumers cannot demand what they do not know exists; (2) the market is incapable of providing goods that consumers do not demand, and; (3) that public interest programming *ought* to be available. In sum: a merit good. Drawing from Goodman's idea that individuals are not consuming democratically important media services despite their benefits, our next question should be: What are the implications of categorizing localism and local news not as public goods, but as merit goods?

Stakeholders recognize that local news is vital to the democratic health of a nation and the everyday lives of citizens, but also note its decline in production and consumption. Recognizing local news as a merit good would require a substantial overhaul of the way in which regulators approach the local within their respective media systems. Legislators and regulators would have to ensure that local news is universally accessible through a variety of platforms, and not just broadcasting. Regulators would have to enter into a serious conversation with multiple stakeholders about how to define regulatory elements such as "local," "local news," and "local programming," something we know they have been reluctant to do. It would also change the way we finance local news, and would necessitate increased public support to deliver on the promise of universal accessibility. This last point might even require regulatory requirements for cross-media subsidies, as described above. Thinking about local news and information through the lens of merit goods suggests they are more than commodities, or even goods, but closer to what we might remember Babe (1995) calling an "essence." There is an argument to be made that we have a *right* to local news and information. As Babe (1995) contemplates: "Information/knowledge therefore historically have been treated as public goods and as community resources, not as mere commodity: folklore, public education, libraries, museums, access to information, legislation, sponsorship of the arts, public broadcasting, freedom of the press and of speech—all these exemplify this non-market tradition of information as community resources and as public good, as well as fundamental human right" (p. 205). Aligning local news and information with merit goods also provides another layer of rationalization for increased public funding on local media in addition to the arguments supplied by political economists (see Downie Jr. & Schudson, 2011; McChesney & Nichols, 2010; Graham & Davies, 1997). Last, local news as merit good does not eschew the public/private mixed media systems incumbent in the UK and Canada (and to a limited extent in the United States), but rather would seek to realign the balance of these economic models. Public, private, community, and citizens' media all have a role to play in ensuring the universal accessibility of local news and information.

It is true that Musgrave himself was ambiguous about his idea of merit goods, concerned with how much intervention is necessary, the authoritarian potentialities of the concept, and what goods qualify for merit good status (*meritorisieren*)[5] (Ver Eecke, 2007b; Pulsipher, 1971/2007; Head, 1988/2007). Subsequent scholars, most notably Wilfred Ver Eecke, Allan Pulsipher, John G. Head, and Norbert Andel (all in Ver Eecke, 2007a), however, have expanded and clarified the idea of merit goods as a theory to correct for market failure. All agree (as do I) that the theory provides a sound justification for market intervention.

This is not just a hypothesis posed for the sake of academic curiosity. To the contrary, regulators and researchers have already contemplated this question. The Waldman Report (2011), for instance, asked: "what happens if consumers don't demand something they essentially need?" (p. 125). Similarly, Ofcom's (2004a) first PSB review noted: "individuals themselves can get more value from a programming, for example, in terms of news and information than they realize" (p. 72). Both suggest that local news and information is a good that is socially desirable, possessing of positive externalities, and contains values not presently recognized by the consumer. In essence, a merit good.

Critical media policy scholars have also, on occasion, invoked the discourse of merit goods. Des Freedman (2008), for instance, notes that media products *writ large* are "merit goods, products or services of significant social value but in which individual consumers are likely to under-invest" (p. 9). This is particularly true, he writes, of investigative journalism and current-affairs programs. The most direct connection between media localism and merit goods comes from a report on the social role of broadcasting in the UK, written by Andrew Graham and Gavyn Davies in 1997. Here, Graham and Davies argue specifically that broadcasting is a merit good, "analogous to eating sensibly or receiving preventative health care. No matter how much someone tells us in advance that we need it, the evidence is that, in general, we underinvest in it" (p. 20) The consideration of local news and information as merit goods has clearly gained traction in the last decade, and is deserving of increased consideration by regulators and legislators as a political economic strategy for intervention.

Conclusion: The Value(s) of Localism

If cross-media subsidy is the compromise between full regulatory intervention and market fundamentalism, then merit goods represent a full social-democratic articulation of local journalism because its application distances local news from the exclusive purview of the commercial market and demands correction for market failure regardless of consumption habits (a position not incompatible with my recommendation of cross-media subsidy). Nelson (2002/2007), for instance, reminds us that government intervention can take place both in the form of direct funding and in the form of subsidizing "competitive for-profit firms" (p. 540). While more radical political economists of communication (e.g., Smythe, 1981) might envision a new paradigm to replace the current capitalist system, my proposal seeks instead to alter the status quo from within (hence the reason I argue that my two recommendations are commensurate). Framing media localism as a merit good lends economic justification for cross-media subsidy and for increased public support through regulation and public expenditure. As Musgrave

(1959/2007) himself wrote, "there may . . . be a special case for interference with consumer (or voter) choice in the provision of social goods at the local level" (p. 43).

The obvious critique of local news as a merit good is that it is paternalistic, in that for something to be deemed a merit good, some*one* needs to label it as such. Consequently, it is vulnerable to the same critiques as public-service broadcasting (especially in the United States) (see Ouellette, 2002). Musgrave seems to channel Walter Lippman (1927) here in his willingness to surrender democratic decision-making power to an "informed group" (p. 110).[6] A multi-stakeholder approach to local media policy frameworks functions in this context both to mitigate concerns of paternalism and to acknowledge that relying solely on political elites is undesirable (Head, 1988/2007). It should also be noted that we already rely on expert agencies—communication regulators—to ensure the public interest is upheld in the media industries. In many countries, public-service broadcasting is also esteemed for its contribution to information and entertainment. Media localism, and in particular local news and information, is necessary for a healthy democracy and should be assured, regardless of the market: "If all television is elicited by the market," write Graham and Davies (1997) "there is a very real danger that consumers will under-invest in the *development* of their *own* tastes, their *own* experiences and their *own* capacity to comprehend. This is not because consumers are stupid but because it is only in retrospect that the benefits of such investment become apparent" (p. 20). Civic life begins at the site of the local (however we might define it), as the excerpt by Michael Schudson (1999) that began this chapter argues. To fully embrace this vision, we need to provide the communicatory and informational tools to community members, and these tools need to be available through a plethora of platforms and outlets.

We can no longer repeat the mantra that "local news still matters" and expect something to change. Regulatory and discursive intervention—what Freedman (2008) calls "corrective surgery"—based on merit good theory and articulated through local media policy frameworks are necessary "if the range of individual and collective benefits that the media may potentially offer is to be guaranteed" (p. 9). This is how we can foster the positive externalities within local news, media localism, and public policy.

Conclusion
The Right to be Local?

> It seems to me that Canadian sensibility has been profoundly disturbed, not so much by our famous problem of identity, important as that is, as by a series of paradoxes in what confronts that identity. It is less perplexed by the question "Who am I?" than by some such riddle as "Where is here?"
> —Northrop Frye (1995)

Localism and Infrastructure

The next chapters in the history of media localism will be written by the digital and not the analogue. Indeed, they will most likely not be written by broadcasting at all, at least not conventional broadcasting. While we wait for emergent platforms to deliver robust and universally accessible local content, local reflection, and local production—such as hyperlocal Web sites, mobile storytelling apps, and community wi-fi initiatives—we need mechanisms in place to ensure the survival of localism both as a policy principle and as a component of our media ecosystems.

Through a comparative analysis of local broadcasting policies, regulations, and laws in the United States, United Kingdom, and Canada, I have come to four conclusions about media localism in the North Atlantic triangle. First, regulators tend to fall back on default localism through their refusal or inability to speak to what it means to be local in the digital age. Second, the political economy of localism mobilizes the discourse of default localism to stymy alternatives in favor of the status quo. Third, critical regionalism can push through the dichotomy between spatial and social localism to bridge the gap between communities of place and communities of interest as discursively constructed in regulation. Fourth, moments of critical regionalism can push back on both the complacency of default localism and the political economy of localism. From these conclusions, I developed two policy interventions: local media policy frameworks and the reframing of local news and information as merit goods.

If localism is to survive as a governing principle in media policymaking in North Atlantic countries, doing nothing is no longer an option, as our traditional avenues for media localism are disappearing and our conceptualizations of the local are quickly changing. To do nothing would continue to allow for default localism and the political economy of localism to hold sway over regulatory discourse—a tyranny of the status quo. Critical regionalism provides us with the conceptual tools to address these challenges, and the moments of critical regionalism demonstrate that there have been instances where ideological and practical alternatives have already been voiced. The issue comes down, as so many political economic questions do, to that of power and control (Freedman, 2014). This struggle is articulated in terms of control over the regulatory discourse and policymaking process, and in terms of the control of content and means of access to local media.

In the early months of 2015 these discursive and regulatory debates of power and control came to a head in the United States over the issue of municipal broadband. This emergent policy debate pushes the discussion of media localism beyond the realm of broadcasting and toward that of infrastructure, access, and interconnection. Indeed, as much as local news and information should be available to all, availability means nothing without access. "The future Town Square will likely be paved with broadband bricks," says former FCC Commissioner Michael Copps, "and we need to make sure that every community, every group, and every individual in this country has access to that Town Square" (qtd. in FCC, 2010d, p. 14). As we transition from broadcasting to broadband in the delivery of local content, access to the bricks represents the next challenge for local media policy.

This conclusion is intended to guide future research in media localism. To that end, I aim to accomplish two things. First, I discuss the case of municipal broadband as an indicator of the policy struggles that lie ahead for media localism. Second, and drawing on the promising literature on communication rights and the right to city, I conclude with a "thought experiment" on the nature of the local for us to consider.

The Case of Municipal Broadband

On the morning of February 26, 2015, the same morning that the FCC made the historic ruling to reclassify Internet service providers (ISPs) within Title

II of the 1996 Telecommunications Act and therein legally protect network neutrality, a second ruling was made that has the potential to reshape the telecommunications landscape of the United States. This has to do with municipal broadband and the rights of municipalities in Tennessee and North Carolina to compete as ISPs against incumbents like Comcast, AT&T, and Time Warner Cable.

The issue had been brewing for years, during which time dozens of municipalities, fed up with the inadequate service by ISPs and concerned with high prices and subpar speeds, began launching their own fiber-to-the-home (FTTH) broadband services, allowing residents to bypass the traditional telecommunication companies, pay less for their broadband connections, and receive speeds as much as one hundred times faster than cable broadband providers could offer (Whitehouse, 2015).[1] Paralleling the trajectory taken during the statewide franchising debates (see chapter 3), telecommunication companies, most notably AT&T, took to lobbying state governments to limit the expansion of municipal broadband. Currently twenty states have passed laws that either ban or limit the development of municipal broadband services under the rationale that local government involvement in Internet provision distorts the free market (FCC, 2015). These impediments range anywhere from prohibitive legal requirements, such as in North Carolina, to outright bans, such as in Pennsylvania (Muninetworks, nd; FCC, 2015; Dunne, 2007).

In 2014, the city of Wilson, North Carolina, and the Electric Power Board of Chattanooga, Tennessee, petitioned the FCC to preempt certain language in their respective states' laws that prohibit or disenfranchise the growth of municipal broadband. The FCC ruled in favor of the plaintiffs, invoking the power invested in it by Section 706 of the 1996 Telecommunications Act to argue that the laws in Tennessee and North Carolina caused barriers to investment and competition.

The issue of American municipal broadband gives us a glimpse into the future for media localism where the struggles are for infrastructure as much as for information. In the specific incident of the case cited above, we see clear examples of how the political economy of media localism has carried over into this discursive and regulatory battle, with telecommunication companies stressing adherence to the status quo of their stranglehold on the broadband market. Equally, we see the emergence of moments of critical regionalism, with the FCC arguing that not only will municipal broadband help the economic viability of the municipality and improve access, but that it will also serve numerous community benefits above and beyond "the bottom line," such as broadband deployment in libraries and schools and infrastructure investment.

Moving away from the specifics of this case, municipal broadband continues our trajectory of thinking holistically about media localism. Municipal broadband permits the formation of alternative networks such as community wi-fi groups and community mesh networks by untethering broadband from the unwieldy demands of the market. To be sure, the municipality derives profit from these activities (as they should), but their actions serve to reinsert communities of place into digital technologies and inspire communities of interest to form through digital infrastructure. Early in the development of community wi-fi, Christian Sandvig (2004) highlighted its cooperative and noncommercial roots. In particular, he describes the community of Warchalkers in London, who would mark buildings with a chalk symbol to indicate an open wireless access point. This is also done digitally through Web-based geographic information systems (the so-called "geo-web").

A decade later, Alison Powell (2012) used a case study of Montreal's Ilesans-fils to offer an example of how communities of interest are formed within the community of place that is Montreal, and around the existence of a wi-fi network in the downtown core. Powell, we may remember from chapter 1, calls this a "community public." She profiled a civic organization dedicated to creating freely available community wireless networks and sees "local community Wi-Fi experiments [as] attempts to reestablish the community as an appropriate site for political and social action" (p. 203). The network of wireless community activists is thus an attempt to create new democratically organized online publics that are located within a certain geographic proximity—a moment of critical regionalism.

Back in the United States, community media groups are positioning themselves as "anchor institutions" within community information ecosystems and alongside schools and libraries to provide a backbone for community mesh networks that serve to digitally enable tightly delineated places, such as a neighborhood. According to a recent study by the New America Foundation, public, educational, and government (PEG) access stations must now distinguish themselves from YouTube and other user-generated content platforms by investing in local broadband infrastructure and inserting localism in the design of the network itself: "This struggle to localize communications infrastructure is the single feature of community media that distinguishes it, by and large, from the individuals and institutions that began their participation in the media with broadband access" (Breitbart et al., 2011, p. 27). Just like municipal broadband in Chattanooga, or community wi-fi in Montreal, community media ushers in a new dimension of media localism through an investment in broadband network technology.

Thinking about municipal broadband as an example of the future of media localism brings us back to the central problematics of this book: What does it mean to be local in the digital age, and how do regulators address this issue? With the inclusion of infrastructure into this problematic comes the need for new language to describe these political economic issues. If it is indeed the case that information is "an essence" and a basic human right (Babe, 1995), that local news and information represents a merit good beyond the purview of the market, *and* that broadband represents a vital utility that is universally warranted, what language can we apply to the local in the digital age? Might it be time to ask ourselves if we have the *right* to be local?

The Right to be Local

I conclude my book with a thought experiment about media localism: Do we have the right to be local? What would the right imply for media localism? What would the right mean for information and infrastructure?

The right to be local is both an individual and collective right. It is individual in that it recognizes, as critical regionalism does, the subjective and contextual meaning of the local: everyone's local is different. There is not "one local" but an array of meanings, experiences, and discourses. It is also collective, in the sense of information, media, and infrastructure. Recall Lew Friedland's (2001) "communicative integrated community," where we require certain communicatory and informational tools to prosper in the lifeworld of the local.

A right to be local underscores the shifting ground on which definitions of the local are found. It suggests that the experience of localism is both individual and collective, spatially and socially constructed, and therein recognizes the contextuality and discursive construction of the local. Importantly, it moves us away from the commercialized and commodified construction of community and information, and asks us to be local rather than to buy local. Moreover, it holds implications beyond the parameters of my book—media policy in the North Atlantic triangle—to larger issues of media governance both nationally and supranationally. Two international rights–based discourses have also danced around this question: communication rights and the right to the city.

COMMUNICATION RIGHTS AND THE RIGHT TO COMMUNICATE

The idea for communication rights (CR) and the right to communicate (R2C) find their genesis in the creation of the 1948 Universal Declaration of Human Rights, and the adjacent 1966 International Covenant on Civil and Political Rights, and the International Covenant on Economic, Social and Cultural Rights (Raboy & Shtern, 2010a). Article 19 of both the UDHR and the ICCPR grants everyone: "the right to freedom of opinion and expression; this right includes freedom to hold opinions without interference and to seek, receive and impart information and ideas through any media and regardless of frontiers" (UN, 2013). In short, these declarations articulate the right to free expression and the right to information for individuals around the world

Falling silent for several decades, CR and R2C found resurgence in the 1980s with the New World Information and Communication Order (NWICO). It would not be until the mid-2000s, however, that policymakers began to pay more attention to this set of normative, collective, and positive rights that seek to expand the purview of the right to free expression and the right to information. CR advocates argue that these dual rights do not do justice to the technologies and political economies of contemporary communication and that a new and expansive set of rights needs to be enacted. In addition to the right to freedom of expression and the right to information, communication rights and the right to communicate "ensure that all people are able to seek and receive information, generate thoughts and opinions, have others hear, understand, learn from, and create on the basis for freely expressed ideas, and share with and respond to the ideas of others" (Raboy & Shtern, 2010a, p. 14).

Akin to the philosophy behind community media, CR/2RC invoke the rights to be heard, understood, learn, enhance and create, and respond and share (Raboy & Shtern, 2010a). CR/R2C therefore requires a holistic approach to media ecosystems. Indeed, the right to expression and the right to information as enumerated in founding documents of the United Nations are diminished without access to the media of expression and information, an argument underscored by both communication rights and the right to communicate.

THE RIGHT TO THE CITY

If communication rights and the right to communicate invoke the "essence" qualities of media localism—information, communication, social relationships—in other words, social localism, the right to the city deals with the physical, the infrastructural, and the spatial. First proposed by Henri Lefebvre in a series of articles and books in the 1960s (see Lefebvre, 1996), and taken up by David Harvey in 2013, the right to the city begins with the premise that neoliberal capitalism has unevenly shaped and reshaped geography to the detriment of the working class. Capitalism is dependent upon built urban environments for the absorption of surplus capital. We need cities like New York, Toronto, and London as much to house people as to absorb the staggering amount of capital that is globally accumulated. This means, however, that cities have been constructed and reconstructed to suit the interests of capital. Harvey (2013) points to Paris under Napoleon III, who razed the city and displaced thousands, and to New York in the 1970s, which destroyed several long-standing minority neighborhoods, particularly in the Bronx. We might also look to the massive levels of inequality in emergent centers like Mexico City, Mumbai, Seoul, and Chongqing as examples of the displacement and uneven geographic development of neoliberal capitalism.

The right to the city seeks to reappropriate the urban environment for residents and citizens rather than for capital. Because the urban milieu is so crucial (with now more than half of the world's population living in cities), a right to the city can translate into more democratic control over the means of production and surplus capital. It seeks to reinsert public elements into the city, like parks, adequate and affordable housing, a greater role for workers' rights, and an emphasis on social well-being. This intimates a right to public space—an idea that can be exported and applicable to rural communities and small towns as much as to cosmopolitan urban spaces. Though Lefevbre and Harvey speak of urban centers, we should not lose sight of the important roles played by smaller communities of place. These places are the driving factors in policy debates over rural broadband and universal service, which are in turn the future policy challenges of media localism. Accordingly,

> The right to the city, complemented by the right to difference and the right to information, should modify, concretize and make more practical the rights of the citizen as an urban dweller (*citadin*) and user of multiple services. It would affirm, on the one hand, the right of users to make known their ideas on the space and time of their activities in the urban area; it would also cover the right to the use of the centre, a privileged place, instead of being dispersed and stuck into ghettos (for workers, immigrants, the "marginal" and even for the "privileged"). (Lefebvre, 1996, p. 34)

It is important that Lefebvre connects the right to the city, as a place-based construct, with the right to information and the right to difference, two aspects exalted by communication rights advocates. The right to the city, then, also assumes the right to information about the city. It encourages us to consider the role of place in our lives, alongside the roles of capital, labor, and infrastructure. While Harvey and Lefebvre focus more on the city as a built environment, given Lefevbre's description above, it would not be too far a stretch to consider communication technologies and infrastructure as essential qualities in the right to the city and the right to a community of place.

Conclusion: A Thought Experiment

The right to be local brings communication rights and the right to the city together by allowing us to consider the roles of both information and infrastructure and of physical places and social relationships. It furthermore incorporates my recommendations of merit goods and local media policy frameworks drawn from this research and inspired by critical regionalism. Still, this is just a thought experiment, a proposition about how the language of localism can extend from the peripheries of media policy to larger discourses of the global, the urban, the rural, and the digital.

Unlike Harvey and Lefevbre, I see the right to the local as more about reform than about revolution. This mirrors the trajectory of the right to communicate, wherein its latest iteration seeks to frame it "as an informal rallying cry . . . [and] . . . embracing the notion's conceptual fluidity" so as to garner the attention of policymakers (Raboy & Shtern, 2010b, p. 40). I therefore argue that the right to be local falls in line with reform efforts: media reform, information reform, infrastructure reform, communication reform, and localism reform.

David Harvey (2013) says that the right to the city is an empty signifier where "everything depends on who gets to fill it with meaning" (p. xv). He expresses concern that more often than not, it is the capitalists and financiers who have shaped its meaning and messages. But, he contends, the opportunity is not lost for reformers. Inspired by this statement, I suggested in the previous chapter that the local, too, is an empty signifier. Information and infrastructure are crucial in filling this discursive space, and the right to be local permits us to imagine greater access both to the information we require as citizens, consumers, and human beings, and to the infrastructure that we require to live in the twenty-first century. This is the right to be local and this is the future of media localism.

Appendix
An Essay on Method

It is a rare opportunity to have space in a monograph to expand on one's methodological decisions. This is particularly the case for media and communication policy scholars, who tend not to go beyond nominal listing of methods (e.g., interviews, document analysis) and methodology (e.g., textual analysis). This may diminish the impact of media policy scholarship, both by reducing its replicability and by hampering attempts to gain purchase with regulators and policymakers who already overprivilege economic and legal analyses over qualitative studies. "It is jarring," note Just and Puppis (2012)—two of the few scholars who reflect on method in policy studies—"that methodological approaches to communication policy studies are seldom explicated" (p. 24).

In a recent article, Christian Herzog and I (Herzog & Ali, 2015) address this paucity by encouraging a spirited discussion about methods and methodology in media and communications policy studies. In particular, we encourage the use of ethnographic methods (specifically elite interviews) and the self-reflexivity that accompanies ethnography for media policy scholars. It is in this spirit of methodological reflexivity that I expand on three aspects of my research design: selection of sources, access to sources, and analysis of sources. I hope to continue the discussion encouraged by Herzog and Ali and join the group of scholars calling for greater methodological reflexivity, transparency, and discussion in media and communication policy studies (Just & Puppis, 2012; Reinhard & Ortiz, 2005).

Selection and Access

As noted in the introduction, I relied on two primary methods to operationalize my research agenda: document analysis and in-depth interviews. This multimethod approach is one familiar to media-policy scholars (see Freedman, 2008; Lunt & Livingstone, 2011; Taylor, 2013; Just & Puppis, 2012). For the former, I relied on the document selection process found in Franklin's (2001) study of British media policy and Taylor's (2013) study of Canadian media policy, and focused my attention on retrieving government acts and bills, regulatory undertakings and policy decisions, white papers, committee and task force reports, comments filed by interest groups and broadcasters, hearing testimony, news releases, and press articles. The comments to regulatory consultations proved particularly salient, as they underscored my arguments that important conversations are occurring on the periphery of media policymaking *and* that media policy resides within a larger social totality. This engenders the shift from media policy to media governance and recognizes that policies are constructed by a variety of actors, not just the regulator or parliament (Lunt & Livingstone, 2011). In terms of document retrieval, since this is a study of *contemporary* practices and discourse (2000–2012), materials were all indexed online and did not require archival research.

Interview respondent selection, write Herzog and Ali (2015), is "perhaps the most challenging, yet most important aspect of research design.... This challenge only increases when one seeks to engage in comparative research ... as greater care needs to be given to selecting comparable respondents to satisfy methodological rigour" (p. 42). Sensitive to these challenges, my initial interview respondents were identified through a search of the online directory of the respective regulators and federal departments. Particular attention was paid to those who were involved in licensing, policy creation, and who held positions of leadership (e.g., commissioners). This follows standard interview selection techniques, where "it is ... important to gain access to people who can best inform the researcher about the problem under examination" (Löblich & Pfaff-Rüdiger, 2012, p. 208).

A snowball method was also used to broaden the respondent pool, and several respondents were identified through this technique (see Sender, 2004). In particular, I made sure to ask respondents: "Is there anyone else whom you would recommend that I speak to about issues of localism in media policy?" This is consistent with recent studies that sought to combine interviews with policy analysis. Potschka (2012), for instanced, recognized that "who is actually interviewed in elite-based research is unpredictable and often emerges as part of the fieldwork" (p. 8).

In total, fourteen respondents were formally interviewed: four from Canada, four from the United States, and six from the United Kingdom. Interviews were conducted in person or through Skype or phone, with each lasting at least one hour and some as many as three hours. Interviews were then transcribed using a transcription service and subsequently analyzed (see below for more on analysis). It should be noted that several respondents asked to remain anonymous, and as such they are referenced as "anonymous, personal communication." To further assure anonymity and to adhere to ethics protocols, the location and date of the interview is omitted from the in-text citation. This is consistent with Potschka (2012), who finds, "not all informants wished to be mentioned and some of the quotes used in the book must remain undisclosed" (p. 9).

I employed an open-ended or "non-directive" interview technique. Here, the interview protocol is not a static list of questions but rather a dynamic, "living" document. This "allows interviewees to move in a direction of their own choosing, and to impose their own definitions and frameworks of interpretation upon the subject under discussion" (Lewis, 1991, p. 84). As Lewis (1991) continues, "one of the main advantages of the qualitative interview is the freedom it allows the respondent to set the agenda, and the scope it allows the interview to probe into potentially interesting areas" (p. 83). In addition to encouraging spontaneity, another advantage of this approach is that it often reduces the need to ask delicate questions because responses may emerge naturally from the conversation (Herzog & Ali, 2015).

Because of their elite positions, my interviews represented examples of "studying up" and "ethnography among elite" (Nadar, 1974; Radway, 1989; Dornfeld, 1998). As a result, the researcher needs to be sensitive to the power dynamic when conversing with those who hold greater cultural, economic, social, or political capital (Herzog & Ali, 2015). Radway (1989), for instance, cautions researchers to avoid "self-indulgent narcissism" (p. 10)—that is to say, steering the conversation solely toward what the interviewer and interviewee have in common. A second concern is "nonjudgmental relativism." Dornfeld (1998) calls this "over-indeptedness" while Hammersley and Atkinson (1995) prefer "over-rapport." Whatever label it is given, the result is the same: "compromising [one's] willingness and ability to critique the practices of that elite" (Radway, 1989, p. 10). This happens because we feel so privileged to have been granted access that we lose our critical mindset. Cognizant of the pitfalls of studying up, I found inspiration in Dornfeld (1998), who deliberately included longer interview excerpts to allow respondents' own voices to come forth.

Despite being familiar with the challenges of studying up, access was an unexpected issue in my research (Nadar, 1974; Dornfeld, 1998). I initially assumed that issues of access would be tempered by previous relationships with gatekeepers at the FCC and Ofcom, and with potential contacts at the CRTC. Though this was true for Canadian and British respondents, potential interlocutors from the FCC and the American policymaking community more broadly were less than willing to take part in this study. As such, a number of conversations took place with individuals who did not wish to be acknowledged, named, cited, or even counted. What I take from this is that stronger relationships need to be created and sustained between the policymaking and policy-studying communities. What Paddy Scannell (2014) calls a "hermeneutics of trust" is therefore missing in the relationship between academics and certain policy stakeholders.

Analysis

Both sources—document and interview—were analyzed using the methodological framework of critical discourse analysis (CDA). The usefulness of CDA for media policy studies is well documented, and I discuss the advantages of CDA in the introduction. I take CDA to be an analytical "approach" more than a "method" *per se,* in that there are no hard and fast rules or steps to follow. As such, primary sources were approached with what Glaser and Strauss (1967) call "sensitizing concepts," and an eye toward the following keywords: "local," "community," "region," "place," and "market." From here, analytical categories and themes were established and texts subsequently coded and categories refined and tailored. This methodological progression draws on the "grounded theory" approach developed by Glaser and Strauss (1967). Grounded theory is interpretive, generative, and inductive, meaning that theory is derived *from* data, rather than using data to *prove* theory. It is also a comparative method, where theories are built from the ground up through a comparison of individual instances. This creates a pyramidal structure of increasing abstraction, where relationships are clarified and then moved up a level. The initial incidents are the small units of meaningful data, which are then grouped into more abstract properties. These properties are then refined and tailored and grouped in to categories. This requires constant comparison among levels and within levels. The ultimate goal is theory generation, which I accomplish through my theories of the political economy of media localism and the moments of critical regionalism.

Conclusion

Methodology is not only about what one did, but also requires an explanation of *how* one did it, and *why* it was the best choice. Communication policy scholars tend to forget to address the questions of "how" and "why," content to list methods and move on to conceptual and empirical discussions. Robust reflection and explanation of method are important components of any research program, but even more so in a field that laments its lack of "real-world" impact (Noam, 1993).

Notes

Introduction

1. There are important differences between the public interest as a regulatory concept and the public good as an economic concept. The public interest, as used here, refers to the term found in legislation, most notably the 1934 Communications Act (US), the 1991 Canadian Broadcasting Act, and the 2003 Communications Act (UK). This highly ambiguous term has gravitated from loosely connoting society's interest to now being synonymous with the interests of the market (Aufderheide, 1999). "Public good" is a term found in neoclassical economics to designate goods that are nonrivalrous and nonexcludable (see chapter 7).

2. The Localism Act transferred select federal powers to municipalities. The government also planned for mayoral elections in cities outside London (which already has a municipal council and mayor) (Westwood, 2011).

3. Ofcom was created through the merger of five regulators: the Independent Television Commission (ITC), the Radio Authority (RA), the Office of Telecommunications (Oftel), the Broadcasting Standards Commission (BSC), and the Radiocommunications Agency (Radio Com).

4. For more on critical theory, see Babe (2010) and Kellner (1989).

5. For more discussion of method and methodology, see the appendix.

6. I am indebted to Dr. Bruce Williams, who reminded me that "status quo" might differ between North America and the UK, where it might mean public service broadcasting rather than market fundamentalism. I contend that given the UK's shift from a welfare to a neoliberal state, the development of the "Big Society," the rise in commercial media, and a dedication to light-touch regulation, the status quo in the UK today represents the aforementioned attachment to deregulation and neoliberalism.

Chapter 1. Mapping the Local

Parts of this chapter appear in "Critical Regionalism and the Policies of Place" (Ali, 2016a) in *Communication Theory*.

1. This is not the case for "space," as in the *Gundrisse* Marx intimates a dialectical relationship between time and space and between the social and spatial (Soja, 1989).

Chapter 2. The Policies of Localism

1. Grade B contours represent the signal strength of a station's transmitter.
2. The national ownership cap was removed from FCC authority by Congress in 2004.
3. The FCC would eventually restrict sharing agreements, but not until 2014 (see FCC, 2014a).
4. In 2007 Bellglobemedia was rebranded as CTVglobemedia to reflect its full acquisition of the CTV television network. In 2010 CTVglobemedia sold its majority stake in the *Globe and Mail* newspaper. CTVglobemedia was rebranded as Bell Media in 2011 (CCF, nd).
5. The difference between fee-for-carriage and value-for-signal is that FFC represented a systemwide standard fee, whereas VFS assessed the value for each individual station's signal
6. An Order-in-Council is a directive from the cabinet of the federal government (Canada, 2015).
7. The CBC also faced a 2011 budget cut of $115 million, which jeopardized its plan to revitalize its commitment to localism through the launch of new digital services, such as a radio service for Hamilton, ON (CBC, 2011).
8. This occurred again in 2012 when Bell threatened to close small-market stations if the CRTC did not approve its takeover of Astral Media.
9. Sub-regional news, or local opt-outs, refers to the news segments targeting "sub-regions" within a larger ITV region (Ofcom, 2008a, par. 9.20).

Chapter 3. The Communities of Localism

1. Appropriately, the title of this section is the opening line from Maddin's, *The Saddest Music in the World*.
2. Though I use "community media" and "community television" interchangeably, it should be noted that community media encompass practices and media beyond television (see Howley, 2005; Rennie, 2006).
3. Low-power television (LPTV) is an over-the-air station whose signal reaches less than twelve kilometers and whose power output is less than fifty watts. These stations are now referred to as "community-based low-power television undertakings" (CRTC, 2002).
4. A video-on-demand system does not require a formal studio because programming can be uploaded onto a server through file-transfer-protocols, in the same way that YouTube operates.

Chapter 4. The Ecosystems of Localism

1. I served as an intern with the FCC working on this report.

2. Not unlike with the word "local," both regulators take these terms for granted, failing to define them, trace their etymology, or reflect on their origins or larger meanings.

3. It is necessary to differentiate a local media ecosystem approach as described by Friedland from the subfield of media studies known as "media ecology." Popularized by prolific writer and public intellectual Neil Postman, media ecology is based on the theories of the Toronto School of Communication and the work of Marshall McLuhan and Harold Innis (Scolari, 2012; Stephens, 2014). Media ecology takes a technologically determinist approach to social analysis, believing that media technologies determine social behavior, and analyzing the roles that "media force us to play, how media structure what we are seeing or thinking, and why media make us feel and act as we do" (Scolari, 2012, p. 205). Though a local media ecosystem approach differs from media ecology in refusing to recognize a technologically determinist epistemology, both share a commitment to thinking about media holistically.

4. The John S. and James L. Knight Foundation is a nonprofit philanthropic foundation dedicated to journalism.

5. *Ex parte* means when a document or oral presentation "is not served on all parties to the proceeding . . . [or] . . . is made without giving all the parties to the proceeding advance notice and an opportunity to be present" (FCC, nd).

6. Noted the Association of Public Television Stations (2008): "Public Television Stations are in many cases the last locally owned and operated television stations in their areas, and their success—indeed, their survival—depends on their ability to connect with their communities and serve local needs through on-air programming and other initiatives" (p. i).

7. Known as the "free rider" problem.

8. The fairness doctrine came into effect in 1949 and required that a reasonable percentage of airtime be devoted to the discussion of public issues and that broadcasters had the duty to present contrasting views in the case of controversial topics.

9. One of my respondents did suggest that the CRTC does take note of media outside its jurisdiction, but not on a systematic basis: "There's a significant chunk of [the] Communications Monitoring Report that looks at unregulated Internet sources of telecommunications and broadcasting. Without an indication that it's time to regulate it . . . they're monitoring it. But they've said very explicitly . . . it is too early to intervene as a result of these being in the marketplace" (anonymous, personal communication).

10. The Department of Canadian Heritage is the federal department responsible for, among other things, promoting Canadian culture, communication, and official languages.

Chapter 5. The Solutions of Localism

1. "Blue Book" is the colloquial name for the FCC's progressive report *Public Service Responsibility of Broadcast Licensees,* which recommended greater public interest requirements for broadcasters (Pickard, 2014).

2. In 1986 the FCC ruled that local programming did not have to be locally originated (see FCC, 2004a).

3. "Class-A" is a category of low-power television that was created in 1999 to supplement traditional low-power television stations (LPTV). Unlike LPTV, Class-A stations are given frequency protection in return for public-interest requirements such as broadcasting three hours of locally originated content a week and locating their studio within the community of license (FCC, 2000).

4. Multicasting refers to the multiple program streams that come with the digital spectrum given to broadcasters after switching from analogue. This new spectrum allows broadcasters to program up to six different channels where previously there was only space for one (Siklos, 2006)

5. This excludes Vancouver, Calgary, Edmonton, Toronto, Anglophone Ottawa-Gatineau, and Montreal.

6. Morin was referring to the license renewal of Quebec broadcaster TQS wherein the Commission allowed the station to broadcast more general local programming rather than local news (see CRTC 2008c).

7. It is notable that Hunt did not ask Ofcom to conduct this study, indicating perhaps an attempt by DCMS to gain greater control over media policy (see Potschka, 2012).

8. The government has yet to release any details of this phase.

9. According to DCMS: "Content that is broadcast by the local TV services will need to be of relevance and interest to audiences in the licensed area and cater to their tastes and needs. The order [Sec. 244] requires that local digital television programme services provide a range of programmes including those which contribute to civic understanding and debate through coverage of news and current affairs" (2011b, p. 15).

10. Stations are also planned for Bangor, Barnstaple, Bedford, Bromsgrove, Derry/Londonderry, Hereford, Inverness, Kidderminster, Limavady, Luton, Malvern, Plymouth, Stoke-on-Trent, Stratford-upon-Avon, and Tonbridge.

Chapter 6. The Political Economy of Localism

1. The tenets of Marxism are centered on a commitment to the study of social reality and social change as based in material interests and dialectical materialism as a method of analysis. In classic Marxism, class struggles and hierarchies are the products of how individuals/groups are positioned in relation to the means of production. Neo-Marxist approaches have, to various extents, moved away from "vulgar Marxism," or economic determinism, to address issues of ideology and power that

are not (per neo-Marxists) reducible to material relations alone (Foster-Carter, 1973; Mosco, 2009). Neo-Marxists thus tend to place greater emphasis on consciousness and communication, ideology, and even psychoanalytic approaches, and are not exclusively focused on class. This allows them to broaden the conversation to include race, gender, sexuality, culture, and geography. Critical geography, for instance, draws our attention to how capitalism has unevenly reshaped geography through the accumulation of wealth in specific spaces and places (Harvey, 2013, Soja, 1989).

Chapter 7. Interventions in Localism

1. According to the Copyright Act (United States, 1976): "To perform or display a work 'publicly' means—(1) to perform or display it at a place open to the public or at any place where a substantial number of persons outside of a normal circle of a family and its social acquaintances is gathered" (Sec. 101).

2. Aereo filed for bankruptcy not long after the Supreme Court decision (Roberts, 2014).

3. The FCC did launch a Notice of Proposed Rulemaking in December 2014 to update the definition of a Multichannel Video Programming Distributor (MVPD) to make it technologically neutral (and thereby include streaming services) (FCC, 2014c).

4. For example, postal subsidies for newspapers, funding for public broadcasting, and universal service funds for telephony (Pickard, 2014).

5. Musgrave was a German immigrant, and the concept of merit goods is significantly more nuanced in German. For instance, "*meritorisieren* . . . means 'making something a merit good'" while "*meritorisierung* . . . means 'the act by which a good is treated as a merit good'" and *meritorisiert* means "declared a merit good" (Ver Eecke, 2007b, p. 3).

6. Musgrave was more convinced that government should provide public goods, and less clear about who should provide merit goods (Wildvasky, 1987/2007).

Conclusion

1. In 2015, the FCC declared that minimum broadband standards were to be 25mpbs download, and 3mbps upload. This was a dramatic increase from the previous standard of 4Mbps/1Mbps, but still pales in comparison to Chattanooga's 1Gbps download speed (FCC, 2015b).

References

Aldridge, M. (2007). *Understanding the local media*. Berkshire, U.K.: Open University Press.
Ali, C. (2010, October 27). "The evolution of WHYY's NewsWorks website." *Future of public media*. Center for Social Media, American University, Washington, D.C. Available at: http://www.centerforsocialmedia.org/future-public-media/public-media-showcase/evolution-whyy%E2%80%99s-newsworks-website-0.
———. (2012a). "A broadcast system in whose interest? Tracing the origins of broadcast localism in Canadian and Australian television policy, 1950–1963." *International Communication Gazette* 74 (3): 277–97.
———. (2012b). "Of logos, owners, and cultural intermediaries: Defining an elite discourse in re-branding practices at three private Canadian television stations." *Canadian Journal of Communication* 37 (2): 259–79.
———. (2012c). "Media at the margins: Policy and practice in American, Canadian, and British Community Television." *International Journal of Communication* 6: 1119–38.
———. (2014). "The last PEG or community media 2.0? Negotiating place and placelessness at PhillyCAM." *Media, Culture & Society* 36 (1): 69–86.
———. (2016a). "Critical regionalism and the policies of place: Revisiting localism for the digital age." *Communication Theory*. DOI: 10.1111/comt.12091.
———. (2016b). "Understanding Canadian 'local media ecosystems': An international comparative approach." In M. Gasher, C. Brin, C. Crowther, G. King, E. Salamon, and S. Thibault (eds.), *Journalism in crisis: Bridging theory and practice for democratic media strategies in Canada*. Toronto: University of Toronto Press.
Ali, C., and D. Conrad. (2015). "A community of communities? Emerging dynamics in the community media paradigm." *Global Media and Communication* 11 (1): 2–23.

REFERENCES

Alkon, A. H., and J. Agyeman. (2011). "Introduction: The food movement as policy-culture." In A. H. Alkon and J. Agyeman, eds., *Cultivating food justice: Race, class, and sustainability* (pp. 1–20). Boston: MIT Press.

Alliance for Community Media (ACM) (2010). *Comments of the Alliance for Community Media. Examination of the future of media and information needs of communities in a digital age (GN Docket. No. 10–25)*. Available at: http://www.fcc.gov/.

American Community Television (ACT) (n.d.). Trouble in the states. Available at: http://acommunitytv.org/act-now/trouble-in-the-states/.

Anderson, B. (1983/1991). *Imagined communities: Reflections on the origin and spread of nationalism*. London: Verso

Anderson, M. (1988). *The American census: A social history*. New Haven, Conn.: Yale University Press.

Anderson, C., and M. Curtin (1999). "Mapping the ethereal city: Chicago Television, the FCC, and the politics of place." *Quarterly Review of Film and Video* 16 (3–4): 289–305.

Appadurai, A. (1996). *Modernity at large: Cultural dimensions of globalization*. Minneapolis: University of Minnesota Press.

Archant Ltd. (2011). "Response to Ofcom's local TV licensing consultation." Available at: http://licensing.ofcom.org.uk/tv-broadcast-licences/local/.

Armstrong, R. (2010). *Canadian broadcasting policy*. Toronto: University of Toronto Press.

Association of Free Community Papers et al. (2012). *Comments of the Association of Free Community Papers, Mid-Atlantic Community Papers Association, and the Free Community Paper Industry: In the matter of: 2010 quadrennial regulatory review (MB Docket No. 09-182)*. Available at: http://www.fcc.gov/.

Association of Public Television Stations (APTS) (2008). *Comments of the Association of Public Television Stations and the Public Broadcasting Service in the matter of broadcast localism*. Available at: http://www.fcc.gov/.

AT&T (2009). *Comments of AT&T opposing petitions for declaratory ruling (MB Docket No. 09-13)*. Available at: http://www.fcc.gov.

Atton, C. (2002). *Alternative media*. Thousand Oaks, Calif.: SAGE.

Aufderheide, P. (1999). *Communications policy and the public interest: The Telecommunications Act of 1996*. New York: Guilford Press.

Babe, R. (1995). *Communication and the transformation of economics: Essays in information, public policy, and political economy*. Boulder, Colo.: Westview Press.

———. (2010). *Cultural studies and political economy: Toward a new integration*. Landham: Lexington Books.

Baker, C. E. (2002). *Media, markets and democracy*. Cambridge, U.K.: Cambridge University Press.

Barney, D. (2005). *Communications technology*. Vancouver: UBC Press.

Barr, F., and C. Sandvig. (2008). "US communication policy after convergence." *Media, Culture & Society* 30 (4): 531–50.

Bator, F. (1958). "The anatomy of market failure." *Quarterly Journal of Economics* 72 (3): 351–79.

Baym, N. K. (2010). *Personal connection in the digital age.* Cambridge, U.K.: Polity.

BBC (2002, November 18). "BBC launches drama and news on demand in Hull" [News Release]. Available at: http://www.bbc.co.uk/pressoffice/pressreleases/stories/2002/10_october/18/bbci_hull.shtml.

BBC Trust (2009). *Local video: Public value test final conclusions.* Available at: http://www.bbc.co.uk/bbctrust/.

Bell, C. (2008, March 25). "Local broadcasters deserve a fair share." *National Post*, A14.

Bell Aliant. (2010). *Submission of Bell Aliant: Broadcasting notice of consultation CRTC 2009-661, Review of community television policy framework* (BNC 2009-661). Available at: www.crtc.gc.ca.

Belo Corp. (2010). *Comments of Belo Corp. In the matter of future of media and information needs of communities in a digital age (GN Docket No. 10-25).* Available at: http://www.fcc.gov.

Benedictus, L. (2013, November 26). "Grimsby's Estuary TV makes television history." *The Guardian.* Retrieved from: http://www.theguardian.com/media/shortcuts/2013/nov/26/grimsby-estuary-tv-local-television.

Blackwell, R. (November 28, 2008). "CTV cuts 105 positions." *Global and Mail* (Toronto), B3.

Blanchard, S. (2001). *A third tier of television? The growth of 'Restrictive Service Licence' in the UK—Trends and Prospects.* AHRB Centre for British Film and Television Studies, Sheffield Hallam University. Available at: http://www.bftv.ac.uk/projects/thirdtier.htm.

Boyle, C. (2010, September 30). "Not quite as popular as we thought." *Times* (London), 52.

Braman, S. (2007). "The ideal vs. the real in media localism: Regulatory implications." *Communication Law and Policy* 12: 231–78.

Breitbart, J., T. Glaisyer, B. Ninan, and J. Losey, (2011) *Full spectrum community media: Expanding public access to communications infrastructure.* New America Foundation. Available at: http://www.newamerica.net/publications/policy/full_spectrum_community_media.

Brennan Center for Justice (2004). *Comments of the Brennan Center for Justice, et al. in the matter of broadcast localism.* Available at: http://www.fcc.gov/.

Briffault, R. (1990a). "Our localism: Part I—The structure of local government law." *Columbia Law Review* 90 (1): 1–115.

———. (1990b). "Our localism: Part II—Localism and legal theory." *Columbia Law Review* 90 (2): 346–454.

Briggs, A. (1995). *The history of broadcasting in the United Kingdom: Volume V—Competition.* London: Oxford University Press.

Brodie, J. (1990). *The political economy of Canadian regionalism.* Toronto: Harcourt Brace Jovanovich.

Brown, S. (2001, October). "The renaissance of regional nations." *Admap*, 421. Available at: http://www.warc.com.

Buchanan, C. (2009). "Sense of place in the daily newspaper." *Aether: The journal of media geography* 4: 62–84.

———. (2014). "A more national representation of place in Canadian daily newspapers." *Canadian Geographer* 58 (4): 517–30.

Burgess, M. (June 14, 2011). "Canadian broadcasters can take lessons from FCC report on local news, critics say." *The Wire Report*. Available At: http://www.thewirereport.ca/reports/content/12571-canadian_broadcasters_can_take_lessons_from_fcc_report_on_local_news_critics_say.

Calabrese, A. (2001). "Why localism? Communication technology and the shifting scale of political community." In G. Shepherd and E. Rothenbuhler, eds., *Communication and Community*, pp. 235–50. Mahwah, N.J.: Lawrence Erlbaum Associates.

Canada. (1991). *The Canadian broadcasting act (1991)*. Statues of Canada. C.11. Ottawa: Public Works and Government Services Canada.

———. (2003a). *Our cultural sovereignty: The second century of Canadian broadcasting*. Standing Committee on Canadian Heritage. Available at: http://www.parl.gc.ca/HousePublications/Publication.aspx?DocId=1032284&Language=E&Mode=1&Parl=37&Ses=2.

———. (2003b). *The Government of Canada's response to the report of the standing committee on Canadian heritage,* Our Cultural Sovereignty: The Second Century of Canadian Broadcasting. Available at: http://www.parl.gc.ca/HousePublications/Publication.aspx?DocId=1726418&Language=E&Mode=1.

———. (2005). *Reinforcing our cultural sovereignty—Setting priorities for the Canadian broadcasting system: Second response to the report of the standing committee on Canadian Heritage*. Available at: http://publications.gc.ca/site/eng/271589/publication.html.

———. (2009a). *Issues and challenges related to local television*. Standing Committee on Canadian Heritage. Available at: http://publications.gc.ca/.

———. (2009b). Transcripts of the House Standing Committee Standing Committee on Canadian Heritage Mtg. 18, 2nd Session, 40th Parl. Monday, May 4, 2009. Available at: http://www.parl.gc.ca/CommitteeBusiness/CommitteeHome.aspx?Cmte=CHPC&Parl=40&Ses=3.

———. (2009c). Transcripts of the House Standing Committee Standing Committee on Canadian Heritage Mtg. 14, 2nd Session, 40th Parl. Monday, April 20, 2009. Available at: http://www.parl.gc.ca/CommitteeBusiness/CommitteeHome.aspx?Cmte=CHPC&Parl=40&Ses=3.

———. (2009d). Transcripts of the House Standing Committee Standing Committee on Canadian Heritage Mtg. 15, 2nd Session, 40th Parl. Wednesday, April 22, 2009. Available at: http://www.parl.gc.ca/CommitteeBusiness/CommitteeHome.aspx?Cmte=CHPC&Parl=40&Ses=3.

———. (2009e). Transcripts of the House Standing Committee Standing Committee on Canadian Heritage Mtg. 22, 2nd Session, 40th Parl. Monday, May 25, 2009. Available at: http://www.parl.gc.ca/CommitteeBusiness/CommitteeHome.aspx?Cmte=CHPC&Parl=40&Ses=3.

———. (2012). *Reference re broadcasting regulatory policy CRTC 2010-167 and broadcasting order CRTC 2010-168.* Supreme Court of Canada. 2012 SCC 68.

———. (2015). Order-in-Council. Available at: http://www.bac-lac.gc.ca/eng/discover/politics-government/orders-council/Pages/orders-in-council.aspx).

Canadian Association of Community Television Users and Stations (CACTUS). (2010). *Putting communities back into community programming. Review of community television policy framework, broadcasting Notice of Consultation CRTC 2009-661.* Available at: www.crtc.gc.ca.

———. (2015). Preliminary comments and background by the Canadian Association of Community Television Users and Stations (CACTUS) for the CRTC's Review of Local and Community TV Policy CRTC 2015–421. Available at: www.crtc.gc.ca.

Canadian Association of Broadcasters (CAB). (2013). *Small market local programming fund—2011-2012 Annual Report.* Available at: http://crtc.gc.ca/eng/BCASTING/ann_rep/cab_m9.pdf.

Canadian Communications Foundtion (CCF). (nd). Radio/Television Station Group History: Bell Media Inc. Available at: www.broadcasting-history.ca.

Canadian Radio Television Commission (CRTC) (1971). *Canadian broadcasting "a single system": Policy statement on cable television.* Ottawa: Queen's Printer.

Canadian Radio-television and Telecommunications Commission. (CRTC) (1990). *Public Notice CRTC 1990-57: Community channel policy review.* Available at: http://www.crtc.gc.ca/eng/archive/1990/PB90-57.HTM.

———. (1999). *Public Notice 1999-97: Building on success—A policy framework for Canadian television.* Available at: www.crtc.gc.ca.

———. (2001a). *Public Notice CRTC 2001-19: Review of community channel policy and low-power radio broadcasting policy.* Available at: www.crtc.gc.ca.

———. (2001b). *Public Notice 2001-129: Proposed policy framework for community-based media.* Available at: www.crtc.gc.ca.

———. (2002). *CRTC 2002-61: Policy framework for community-based media.* Available at: http://www.crtc.gc.ca.

———. (2003a). *Broadcasting public notice CRTC 2003-37: Direct-to-home (DTH) broadcasting distribution undertakings—simultaneous and non-simultaneous program deletion and the carriage of local television signals in smaller markets.* Available at: www.crtc.gc.ca.

———. (2007a). *Broadcasting public notice CRTC 2007-53: Determinations regarding certain aspects of the regulatory framework for over-the-air television.* Available at: www.crtc.gc.ca.

———. (2007b). *Broadcasting notice of public hearing CRTC 2007-10-3: Review of the regulatory framework for broadcasting distribution undertakings and discretionary programming services: Expansion of scope, extension of filing deadlines and revised hearing date.* Available at: www.crtc.gc.ca.

———. (2007c). *Broadcasting decision CRTC 2007-86: Licence amendments related to the funding and provision of an outlet for local expression.* Available at: www.crtc.gc.ca.

———. (2008a). *Broadcasting public notice CRTC 2008-4: Diversity of voices.* Available at: www.crtc.gc.ca.

———. (2008b). *Broadcasting public notice CRTC 2008-100: Regulatory frameworks for broadcasting distribution undertakings and discretionary programming services.* Available at: www.crtc.gc.ca.

———. (2008c). *Broadcasting decision CRTC 2008-129: Change in the effective control of TQS inc. and licence renewals of the television programming undertakings CFJP-TV Montréal, CFJP-DT Montréal, CFAP-TV Québec, CFKM-TV Trois-Rivières, CFKS-TV Sherbrooke, CFRS-TV Saguenay and of the TQS network.* Available at: www.crtc.gc.ca.

———. (2009a). *Broadcasting notice of consultation CRTC 2009-70-1: Clarification of Scope.* Available at: http://www.crtc.gc.ca/eng/archive/2009/2009-70-1.htm.

———. (2009b). *Broadcasting regulatory policy CRTC 2009-406: Policy determinations resulting from the 27 April 2009 public hearing.* Available at: www.crtc.gc.ca.

———. (2009c). *Broadcasting notice of consultation CRTC 2009-411-3: Clarification on the scope of the proceeding—negotiated fair value for conventional television signals.* Available at: http://www.crtc.gc.ca/eng/archive/2009/2009-411-3.htm.

———. (2009d). *Broadcasting notice of consultation CRTC 2009-614: Notice of hearing: Call for comments following a request by the Governor in Council to prepare a report on the implications and advisability of implementing a compensation regime for the value of local television signals.* Available at: www.crtc.gc.ca.

———. (2009e). *Broadcasting notice of consultation CRTC 2009-70: Scope of licence renewal hearings for private conventional television stations.* Available at: www.crtc.gc.ca.

———. (2010a). *The implications and advisability of implementing a compensation regime for the value of local television signals.* Available at: http://www.crtc.gc.ca/eng/publications/reports/rp100323.htm.

———. (2010b). *Broadcasting regulatory policy CRTC 2010-622: Community television policy.* Available at: www.crtc.gc.ca.

———. (2011a). *Broadcasting notice of consultation CRTC 2011-788: Review of the local programming improvement fund.* Available at: www.crtc.gc.ca.

———. (2011b). *Broadcasting notice of consultation CRTC 2011-788-2: Review of the local programming improvement fund: Additional information added to the public file: weekly local programming averages* Available at: www.crtc.gc.ca.

———. (2012a). *Communications monitoring report.* Available at: www.crtc.gc.ca.

———. (2012b). *Transcription of proceedings before the Canadian Radio-television and Telecommunications Commission: Subject: Review of the local programming improvement fund—Broadcasting notice of consultation CRTC 2011-799, 2011-788-1 and*

2011-788-2. Gatineau, QC. Available at: http://www.crtc.gc.ca/eng/transcripts/2012/tb0416.html.

———. (2012c). *Broadcasting regulatory policy CRTC 2012-385: Review of the local programming improvement fund.* Available at: www.crtc.gc.ca.

———. (2012d, July 18). Consumer cable bills to be adjusted with phase out of fund [News Release]. Available at: http://www.crtc.gc.ca/eng/com100/2012/r120718.htm.

———. (2013). *Communications monitoring report 2013.* Available at: www.crtc.gc.ca.

———. (2014). *Let's talk TV: Quantitative research report.* Available at: http://www.crtc.gc.ca/eng/publications/reports/rp140424.htm.

———. (2015). *Communications monitoring report 2015.* Available at: www.crtc.gc.ca.

Carpentier, N. (2008). "Translocalism, community media and the city." Working Paper, Center for Media Sociology. Available at: http://libra.msra.cn/Publication/14042843/translocalism-community-media-and-the-city.

Carr, D. (2013, December 15). "AOL chief's white whale finally slips his grasp." *New York Times.* Available at: http://www.nytimes.com/2013/12/16/business/media/aol-chiefs-white-whale-finally-slips-his-grasp.html?_r=1.

Carroll, D. (2009). "The cable song." Available at: https://www.youtube.com/watch?v=uKLS6sNKRGU (accessed May 5, 2015).

Casey, E. (1998). *The fate of place: A philosophical history.* Berkeley: University of California Press.

Castells, M. (1996) *The rise of the network society.* Oxford, U.K.: Blackwell Publishers.

———. (2000). "Grassrooting the space of flows." In J. Wheeler, Y. Aoyama, and B. Warf, eds. *Cities in the Telecommunications Age: The Fracturing of Geographies,* pp.18–30. New York: Routledge.

Canadian Broadcasting Corporation (CBC) (2011). *Everyone.Everyway: CBC/Radio-Canada's five-year strategic plan.* Available at: http://www.cbc.radio-canada.ca/strategy2015/.

CBC Arts. (2008, January 25). CRTC hearing submissions on fee-for-carriage. Available at: http://www.cbc.ca/news/arts/crtc-hearing-submissions-on-fee-for-carriage-1.697491.

Channel 6 (2011). Channel 6 response to Ofcom's local TV licensing consultation. Available at: http://licensing.ofcom.org.uk/tv-broadcast-licences/local/.

Channel 7 CIC (2011). Response to Ofcom's local TV licensing consultation. Available at: http://licensing.ofcom.org.uk/tv-broadcast-licences/local/.

Channel 8 North East (2011). Response to Ofcom's local TV licensing consultation. Available at: http://licensing.ofcom.org.uk/tv-broadcast-licences/local/.

Charland, M. (1986). "Technological nationalism." *Canadian Journal of Political and Social Theory* 10 (1): 196–220.

Charney, M. (2009). "Society of the quarter: Foodroutes network and the local food movement." *Journal of Agriculture & Food Information* 10: 173–81.

Christians, C. G., T. L. Glasser, D. McQuail, K. Nordenstreng, and R. White. (2009). *Normative theories of the media: Journalism in democratic societies.* Urbana: University of Illinois Press.

City Broadcasting Ltd. (2011). Response to Ofcom's local TV licensing consultation. Available at: http://licensing.ofcom.org.uk/tv-broadcast-licences/local/.
Clear Channel (2008). Comments of Clear Channel Communications, Inc. in the matter of broadcast localism. Available at: http://www.fcc.gov/.
Clement, W. (1983). "Regionalism as uneven development: Class and region in Canada." In W. Westfall, ed., *Perspectives on regions and regionalism in Canada, Canadian Issues/Themes Canadiens* 5: 68–80.
Cole, H., and P. Murck. (2007). "The myth of the localism mandate: A historical survey of how the FCC's actions belie the existence of a governmental obligation to provide local programming." *CommLaw Conspectus* 15 (2): 339–71.
Collins, R. (1990). *Culture, communication and national identity: The case of Canadian television*. Toronto: University of Toronto Press.
Comcast. (2007). *Comments of Comcast Corporation: In the matter of implementation of Section 621(a)(1) of the Cable Communications Policy Act of 1984 as amended by the Cable Television Consumer Protection and Competition Act of 1992 (MB Docket No. 05-311)*. Available at: http://www.fcc.gov/.
Communications Policy Research Network (CPRN) (2012). *Review of the literature regarding critical information needs of the American public*. Available at: http://www.fcc.gov.
Community Broadcasters Association. (2004). *Comments of the Community Broadcasters Association in the matter of broadcast localism*. Available at: http://www.fcc.gov/.
Copps, M. (2003a). Statement of Commissioner Michael J. Copps. Dissenting. Available at: http://www.turnoffyourtv.com/networks/coppsstatement.html.
———. (2003b, August 20). Copps criticizes willingness to let media consolidation continue [News Release]. Available at: http://www.fcc.gov.
———. (2011, June 9). Statement of Commissioner Michael J. Copps on release of FCC staff report "The Technology and Information Needs of Communities." Federal Communications Commission. Available at: http://transition.fcc.gov/Document_Indexes/Miscellaneous/2011_index_OCMJC_Statement.html.
Cowling, P. (2005). "An earthly enigma: The role of localism in political, cultural and economic dimensions of media ownership regulation." *Hastings Communication and Entertainment Law Journal* 27: 257–358.
Cox Broadcasting. (2008). Comments of Cox Broadcasting, Inc. and Cox Radio, Inc. in the matter of broadcast localism. Available at: http://www.fcc.gov/.
Crisell, A. (1997). *An introductory history of British broadcasting*. London: Routledge.
Crisell, A., and G. Starkey. (2006). "News on local radio." In B. Franklin, ed., *Local journalism and local media: Making the local news*, pp. 16–26. London: Routledge.
Curran, J., and J. Seaton. (2010). *Power without responsibility: Press, broadcasting and the internet in Britain*. London: Routledge.
Curtin, M. (2000). "Connections and differences: Spatial dimensions of television history." *Film & History* 30(1): 50–61.

Curtin, M. (2007). *Playing to the world's biggest audience: The globalization of Chinese film and TV.* Berkeley: University of California Press.
Davidson, S. (2004, January 5). "Report? What report? Critics warn that media concentration is threatening debate and broadcast reform." *Playback.* Available at: http://www.friends.ca/news-item/552.
Davies, I. (2004, May 10). "Regional papers want the BBC to get its tanks off their lawn". *The Guardian,* 11.
de Certeau, M. (1984). *The practice of everyday life.* Trans: S. Rendal. Berkeley: University of California Press.
de Tocqueville, A. (1835/1945). *Democracy in America.* New York: Knopf.
Department for Communities and Local Government (DCLG) (2011). *A plain English guide to the Localism Act.* Available at: http://www.communities.gov.uk/publications/localgovernment/localismplainenglishupdate.
Department for Culture, Media and Sport (DCMS) (2009). *Digital Britain.* Available at: http://www.culture.gov.uk/.
———. (2011a). *A new framework for local TV in the UK.* Available at: http://www.culture.gov.uk/consultations/8298.aspx.
———. (2011b). *Local TV: Making the vision happen: Government response to the consultations on the Local TV Framework and pioneer locations and final policy position.* Available at: http://www.culture.gov.uk/publications/8706.aspx.
Depew, D., and J. D. Peters. (2001). "Community and communication: The conceptual background." In G. J. Shepherd and E. W. Rothebuhler, eds., *Communication and community,* pp. 3–20. Mahwah, N.J.: Lawrence Erlbaum Associates.
Dewey, J. (1927). *The public and its problems.* New York: Henry Holt.
Dirlik, A. (1996). "The global in the local." In R. Wilson and W. Dissanayake, eds., *Global/Local: Cultural production and the transnational imaginary,* pp.21–45. Durham, N.C.: Duke University Press.
———. (2001). "Place-based imagination: Globalism and the politics of place." In R. Prazniak and A. Dirlik, eds., *Place and politics in an age of globalization,* pp. 15–52. Lanham, Md.: Rowman and Littlefield.
Dornfeld, B. (1998). *Producing public television, producing public culture.* Princeton, N.J.: Princeton University Press.
Dowell, B. (2012, November 23). "Ofcom delays local TV licence decision." *The Guardian.* Available at: www.guardian.co.uk/media/2012/nov/23/ofcom-delays-local-tv-licence-decision.
Downie, L., Jr., and M. Schudson. (2009). "The reconstruction of American Journalism." *Columbia Journalism Review.* Available at: http://www.cjr.org/reconstruction/the_reconstruction_of_american.php.
Downing, J. (2001). *Radical media: Rebellious communication and social movements.* Thousand Oaks, Calif.: SAGE.
Dunbar-Hester, C. (2013). "What's local? Localism as a discursive boundary object in low-power radio policymaking." *Communication, Culture & Critique* 6(4): 502–24.

———. (2015). *Low power to the people: Pirates, protest, and politics in FM radio activism.* Cambridge, Mass.: MIT Press.

Dunne, M. (2007). "Notes: Let my people go (online): The power of the FCC to preempt state laws that prohibit municipal broadband." *Columbia Law Review* 107: 1126–63.

Durkin, J., and T. Glaisyer. (2011). *An information community case study: Scranton: An industrial city with a media ecosystem yet to take advantage of digital opportunities.* New America Foundation. Available at: http://mediapolicy.newamerica.net/home.

Drucker, S., and G. Gumpert. (2009). "Freedom of expression in communicative cities." *Free Speech Yearbook* 44 (1): 65–84.

Enders Analysis (2011). "Licensing local television—Enders Analysis." Available at: http://licensing.ofcom.org.uk/tv-broadcast-licences/local/.

Entrikin, J. N. (1991). *The betweenness of place: Towards a geography of modernity.* Baltimore: John Hopkins University Press.

Escobar, A. (2003). "Place, nature, and culture in discourses of globalization." In A. Mirsepassi, A. Basu, and F. Weaver, eds., *Localizing knowledge in a globalizing world: Recasting the area studies debate*, pp. 37–59. Syracuse, N.Y.: Syracuse University Press.

Essential Research (2008). *Assessing the likely impact of ITV's regional news proposals.* Available at: http://stakeholders.ofcom.org.uk/consultations/psb2_1/.

Everitt, A. (2003). *New voices: An evaluation of 15 access radio projects.* Available at: http://www.ofcom.org.uk/static/archive/rau/newsroom/news-release/03/pr044.htm.

Ewart, J. (2000). "Capturing the heart of the region—how regional media define a community." *Transformations* 1: 1–13.

Folami, A. (2010) "Deliberative democracy on the air: Reinvigorate localism—resuscitate radio's subversive past." *Federal Communications Law Journal* 63: 141–92.

Farman, J. (2012). *Mobile interface theory: Embodied space and locative media.* New York: Routledge.

Fealing, K. H., N. Sakaimbo, M. Henry, D. McFarlane, and S. Kelley. (2009). *Statewide video franchising legislation: A comparative study of outcomes in Texas, California and Michigan.* University of Minnesota. Available at: http://heartland.org/policy-documents/statewide-video-franchising-legislation-comparative-study-outcomes-texas-california.

Federal Communications Commission v. Midwest Video Corp (1979). 440 U.S. 689.

Federal Communications Commission (FCC) (1971). In the matter of: Primer on ascertainment of community problems by broadcast applicants, 27 FCC2d 650.

———. (1973). *In the matter of: Amendment of part 0 of the commission's rules, commission organization, with respect to delegations of authority to the chief broadcast bureau* 43 FCC 2d 638, 640.

———. (1976). *Amendment of Section 0.281 of the commission's rules: Delegations of authority to the chief, Broadcast Bureau* 59 FCC 2d 491.

———. (1998). *Review of the commission's rules regarding the main studio and local public inspection files of broadcast television and radio stations, report and order.* Available at: http://www.fcc.gov/encyclopedia/main-studio-rules.

———. (2000). *In the matter of: Establishment of a Class A television service (MM Docket No.: 00-10).* Available at: http://www.fcc.gov/.

———. (2001). Roundtable discussion on media ownership policies transcript (MM Docket No. 01-235). Available at: http://www.fcc.gov/.

———. (2002). *In the matter of: 2002 biennial regulatory review: Notice of proposed rulemaking (MB Docket No. 02-277).* Available at: http://www.fcc.gov/.

———. (2003a). *In the matter of: 2002 biennial regulatory review: Report and order and notice of proposed rulemaking (MB Docket No. 02-27).* Available at: http://www.fcc.gov/.

———. (2003b, April 14). Transcript. Field Hearing, Broadcasting ownership en banc, Richmond, Virginia. Available at: http://www.fcc.gov/.

———. (2003c, August 20). FCC Chairman Powell launches 'localism in broadcasting' initiative [News Release]. Available At: http://www.fcc.gov.

———. (2003d, October 22). Transcript. Field Hearing, Broadcast localism hearing, Charlotte, North Carolina. Available at: http://www.fcc.gov/.

———. (2004a). *In the matter of: Broadcast localism: Notice of inquiry (MB Docket No. 04-233).* Available at: http://www.fcc.gov/.

———. (2004b, January 28). Transcript. Field Hearing: Broadcast localism hearing: San Antonio, Texas. Available at: http://www.fcc.gov/.

———. (2004c, May 26). Transcript. Field Hearing: Broadcast localism hearing: Rapid City, South Dakota. Available at: http://www.fcc.gov.

———. (2004d, July 21). Transcript. Field Hearing: Broadcast localism hearing: Monterey, California. Available at: http://www.fcc.gov.

———. (2005). *Notice of proposed rulemaking: In the matter of implementation of section 621(a)(1) of the Cable Communications Policy Act of 1984 as amended by the Cable Television Consumer Protection and Competition Act of 1992 (MB Docket No. 05-311).* Available at: http://www.fcc.gov/.

———. (2006). *2006 quadrennial regulatory review: Further notice of proposed rulemaking (MB Docket No. 06-121).* Available at: http://www.fcc.gov/.

———. (2007a). *In the matter of implementation of section 621(a)(I) of the Cable Communications Policy Act of 1984 as amended by the Cable Television Consumer Protection ad Competition Act of 1992, report and order and further notice of proposed rulemaking.* Available at: http://www.fcc.gov.

———. (2007b). *In the matter of implementation of section 621(a)(I) of the Cable Communications Policy Act of 1984 as amended by the Cable Television Consumer Protection ad Competition Act of 1992, second report and order.* Available at: http://www.fcc.gov.

———. (2007c). Transcript: Field Hearing: Broadcast localism hearing: Washington, D.C. Available at: http://www.fcc.gov.

———. (2008a). *In the matter of: Broadcast localism: Report on broadcast localism and notice of proposed rulemaking (MB Docket No. 04-233)*. Available at: http://www.fcc.gov/.

———. (2008b). *In the matter of petition for declaratory ruling regarding primary jurisdiction referral in City of Dearborn et al. v. Comcast of Michigan III, Inc. et al. (MB Docket 09-13)*. Available at: http://www.fcc.gov/.

———. (2008c). *In the matter of: 2006 quadrennial regulatory review: Report and order and order on reconsideration*. Available at: http://www.fcc.gov.

———. (2009a). *In the matter of: Petition for declaratory ruling on requirements for a basic service tier and for PEG channel capacity under sections 543(b)(7), 531(a) and the commissioner's ancillary jurisdiction under Title I: Petition for declaratory ruling: City of Lansing, Michigan (MB Docket No. 09-13)* Available at: http://www.fcc.gov/.

———. (2009b). *In the matter of: Petition for a declaratory ruling that AT&T's method of delivering public, educational and government access channels over its U-verse system is contrary to the Communications Act of 1934, as amended, and applicable commission rules (MB Docket. No. 09-13)*. Available at: http://www.fcc.gov.

———. (2010a). *Connecting America: The national broadband plan*. Available at: http://www.fcc.gov.

———. (2010b). *In the matter of: 2010 quadrennial regulatory review: Notice of inquiry (MB Docket No. 09–182)*. Available at: http://www.fcc.gov.

———. (2010c). *FCC launches examination of the Future of Media and information needs of communities in a digital age: GN Docket No. 10-25*. Available at: http://www.fcc.gov.

———. (2010d). Transcript: The future of media and information needs of communities: Serving the public interest. March 4, 2010, Washington, D.C. Available at: http://www.fcc.gov/events/serving-public-interest-digital-era-0.

———. (2010e). Transcript: Public and other noncommercial media in the digital era. April 30 2010, Washington, D.C. Available at: http://www.fcc.gov/events/public-and-other-noncommercial-media-digital-era.

———. (2011a). *In the matter of: 2010 quadrennial regulatory review: Notice of proposed rulemaking (MB Docket No. 09-182)*. Available at: http://www.fcc.gov.

———. (2012). *An RFQ for a study examining the critical information needs of the American public*. Available at: http://www.fcc.gov/encyclopedia/rfq-study-examining-critical-information-needs-american-public.

———. (2014a). FCC adopts JSA rules and begins 2014 media ownership quadrennial review [News Release]. Available at: https://www.fcc.gov/document/fcc-adopts-jsa-rule-and-begins-2014-media-ownership-quadrennial-review.

———. (2014b). Small entity compliance guide: 2014 quadrennial regulatory review (DA 14–1817). Available at: https://www.fcc.gov/document/2014-quadrennial-regulatory-review-1.

———. (2014c). *In the matter of promoting innovation and competition in the provision of multichannel video programming distribution services (MB Docket No. 14-261*.

Notice of Proposed Rulemaking. Available at: https://apps.fcc.gov/edocs_public/attachmatch/FCC-14-210A1.pdf.

———. (2015a). Broadcast station totals as of September 30, 2015. Available at: https://apps.fcc.gov/edocs_public/Query.do?docTitleDesc=Broadcast+Station+Totals&parm=all.

———. (2015b). *In the matter of: City of Wilson, North Carolina petition for preemption of North Carolina general statute section 160A-340 . . . The Electric Power Board of Chattanooga, Tennessee petition for preemption of a portion of Tennessee code annotated section 7-52-601. Memorandum Opinion and Order.* Available at: https://www.fcc.gov.

———. (nd). Ex Parte Resources. Available at https://www.fcc.gov/proceedings-actions/ex-parte/general/ex-parte-resources.

Ferrier, M. (2014). The media deserts project: Monitoring community news and information needs using geographic information system technologies. Paper presented at the AEJMC Midwinter Conference, University of Oklahoma. Available at: https://www.academia.edu/11469030/The_Media_Deserts_Project_Monitoring_Community_News_and_Information_Needs_Using_Geographic_Information_System_Technologies.

First Broadcasting (2011). Response to Ofcom's local TV licensing consultation. Available at: http://licensing.ofcom.org.uk/tv-broadcast-licences/local/.

Fitzsimmons, C. (2009, February 17). Seventeen regions into nine. *The Guardian*. Available at: http://www.theguardian.com/media/organgrinder/2009/feb/16/seventeen-regions-into-nine-itv-news.

Foster-Carter, A. (1973). "Neo-Marxist approaches to development and underdevelopment." *Journal of Contemporary Asia* 3 (1), 7–33.

Frampton, K. (1983/1985). "Toward a critical regionalism: Six points for an architecture of resistance." In H. Foster, ed., *The anti-aesthetic: Essays on postmodern culture,* pp. 316–30. Seattle: Bay Press. Republished in H. Foster, ed., *Postmodern culture,* pp. 16–30. London: Pluto.

Franklin, B., ed. (2001). *British television policy: A reader.* London: Routledge.

Franklin, B., and D. Murphy. (1996). "Changing times: Local newspapers, technology and markets." In B. Franklin and D. Murphy, eds., *Making the local news,* pp. 7–23. London: Routledge.

Fraser, G. (2001, May 11). Broadcasting review on the way. *Toronto Star,* n.p.

Frau-Meigs, D. (2011). *Media matters in the cultural contradictions of the "information society"—Towards a human rights-based governance.* Strasbourg: Council of Europe Publishing.

Free Press. (2012). *Comments of Free Press. In the matter of: 2010 quadrennial review (MB Docket No. 09-182).* Available at: http://www.fcc.gov.

Freedman, D. (2008). *The politics of media policy.* Cambridge, U.K.: Polity Press.

———. (2010). Making Policy Silences: The hidden face of communications decision making. *International Journal of Press/Politics* 15 (3): 344–61.

———. (2014). *The contradictions of media power.* London: Bloomsbury.

Friedland, L. (2001). "Communication, community, and democracy: Toward a theory of the communicatively integrated community." *Communication Research* 28 (4): 358–91.
Friesen, G. (2001). "The evolving meanings of region in Canada." *Canadian Historical Review* 82: 520–45.
Fry, N. (1995). *The bush garden: Essays on the Canadian imagination.* Concord, Ont.: House of Anansi Press.
Fuentes-Bautista, M. (2009) *Beyond television: The digital transition of public access.* Available at: http://mediaresearchhub.ssrc.org/news/beyond-television-the-digital-transition-of-public-access/.
Fullerton, D. (1991). "On justification for public support of the arts." *Journal of Cultural Economics* 15 (2): 67–82.
Geertz, C. (1973). *The interpretation of cultures: selected essays.* New York: Basic Books.
Giddens, A. (1990). *The consequences of modernity.* Stanford, Calif.: Stanford University Press.
Glaser, B., and A. Strauss. (1967/2010). *Discovery of grounded theory: Strategies for qualitative research.* New York: Aldine de Gruyter.
Goldfarb, C. B. (2005). *"Localism": Statues and rules affecting local programming on broadcast, cable, and satellite television.* Congressional Research Service. Available at: http://congressionalresearch.com/RL32641/document.php?study=Localism+Statutes+and+Rules+Affecting+Local+Programming+on+Broadcast+Cable+and+Satellite+Television.
———. (2008). *Public, educational, and governmental (PEG) access cable television channels: Issues for congress.* Congressional Research Service. Retrieved from http://opencrs.com/document/RL34649/2008-09-05/.
Goodman, E. (2006). Proactive media policy in an age of content abundance. In P. Napoli, ed., *Media Diversity and Localism: Meaning and Metrics*, pp. 363–82. Mahwah, N.J.: Taylor & Frances.
Graham, A., and G. Davies. (1997). *Broadcasting, society and policy in the multimedia age.* Luton, U.K.: University of Luton Press.
Greenslade, R. (2012). "Will Maria sing the same local TV song as Hunt?" *The Guardian.* Retrieved from: http://www.guardian.co.uk/media/greenslade/2012/sep/06/local-tv-maria-miller.
———. (2014, June 18). "Jeremy Hunt reaffirms his faith in local TV despite low viewing ratings." *The Guardian.* Retrieved from: http://www.theguardian.com/media/greenslade/2014/jun/18/local-tv-jeremy-hunt.
Habermas, J. (1962/1989). *The structural transformation of the public sphere: An inquiry into a category of bourgeois society,* trans. Thomas Burger. Cambridge, Mass.: MIT Press.
———. (1987). *The theory of communicative action: Vol. 2. Lifeworld and system: A Critique of Functionalist Reason.* Boston: Beacon Press.
Hall, S. (1980). Encoding/Decoding. In S. During, ed., *The cultural studies reader*, pp. 507–17. New York, Routledge.

——. (1986). "Gramsci's relevance for the study of race and ethnicity." *Journal of communication inquiry* 10: 5–27.

Hallin, D., and P. Mancini. (2004). *Comparing media systems: Three models of media and politics.* Cambridge, U.K.: Cambridge University Press.

Harvey, D. (1989). *The condition of postmodernity: An enquiry into the origins of cultural change.* Hoboken, N.J.: Wiley-Blackwell.

——. (1993). "From space to place and back again: Reflections on the condition of postmodernity." In J. Bird, B. Curtis, T. Putnam, G. Robertson, and L. Tickner, eds., *Mapping the futures,* pp. 3–29. London: Routledge.

——. (2005). *A brief history of neoliberalism.* London: Verso

——. (2010). *A companion to Marx's capital.* Oxford, U.K.: Oxford University Press.

——. (2013). *Rebel cities: From the right to the city to the urban revolution.* London: Verso.

Head, S. (1988/2007). "On merit wants: Reflections on the evolution, normative status and policy relevance of a controversial public finance concept." In W. Ver Eecke, ed., *An anthology regarding merit goods: The unfinished ethical revolution in economic theory,* pp. 114–51. West Lafayette, Ind.: Purdue University Press.

Herr, C. (1996). *Critical regionalism and cultural studies: From Ireland to the American Midwest.* Gainesville: University Press of Florida.

Herzog, C., and C. Ali. (2015). "Elite interviewing in media and communication policy research." *International Journal of Media and Cultural Politics* 11 (1): 37–54.

Hess, K. (2013). "Breaking boundaries: Recasting the 'local' newspaper as 'geo-social' news." *Digital Journalism* 1 (1): 48–60.

Hess, K., and L. Waller. (2014). "Geo-social journalism: Reorienting the study of small commercial newspapers in a digital environment." *Journalism Practice* 8 (2): 121–36.

Hewlett, S. (2010a, October 4). "Media: Opinions: Is Hunt concealing a strategy beneath his smooth exterior?" *The Guardian,* 4.

——. (2011, August 22). "Media: Opinions: Local TV bears no relation to Jeremy Hunt's big vision." *The Guardian,* 4

Hewson, C. (2005). *Local and community television in the United Kingdom: A new beginning?* Community Media Association. Available at: http://www.equal-works.com/resources/contentfiles/1215.pdf.

Hilliard, R., and M. Keith. (2005). *The quieted voice: The rise and demise of localism in American radio.* Carbondale: Southern Illinois University Press.

Hilmes, M. (2012). *Network nations: A transnational history of British and American broadcasting.* New York: Routledge.

Hindman, M. (2009). *The myth of digital democracy.* Princeton, N.J.: Princeton University Press.

——. (2011). *Less of the same: The lack of local news on the internet.* FCC. Available at: https://www.fcc.gov/document/media-ownership-study-6-submitted-study.

Hitchens, L. (2006). *Broadcasting pluralism and diversity: A comparative study of policy and regulation.* Oxford, U.K.: Hart Publishing.

Horwitz, R. (1989) *The irony of regulatory reform: The deregulation of American telecommunications*. New York: Oxford University Press.

Howarth, D. (2000). *Discourse*. Buckingham, U.K.: Open University Press.

Howley, K. (2005). *Community media: People, places, and communication technologies*. Cambridge, U.K.: Cambridge University Press.

———. (2010). Introduction, in K. Howley, ed., *Understanding community media*, pp. 1–14. Thousand Oaks, Calif.: SAGE.

Hunt, J. (2010, June 8). Speech to the Hospital Club, London. Available at: http://www.culture.gov.uk/news/ministers_speeches/7132.aspx.

Hutchins, B. (2004). "Castells, regional news media and the information age." *Continuum: Journal of Media & Cultural Studies* 18 (4): 577–90.

Independent Television Commission (ITC) (2002). *Pride of place: What viewers want from regional television*. Available at: http://www.ofcom.org.uk/static/archive/itc/uploads/PRIDE_OF_PLACE_RESEARCH.pdf.

Institute for Local Television (2011). Response to Ofcom's local TV licensing consultation. Available at: http://licensing.ofcom.org.uk/tv-broadcast-licences/local/.

Inverness Community Media (2011). Inverness Community Media's response to Ofcom's local TV licensing consultation. Available at: http://licensing.ofcom.org.uk/tv-broadcast-licences/local/.

ITV. (2013). *ITV's proposals for nations and regions news for a new channel 3 psb licence*. Available at: http://stakeholders.ofcom.org.uk/binaries/consultations/c3-c5-obligations/annexes/itvs-proposals.pdf.

ITV. (2015, October 19). ITV to acquire UTV's Television business [press release]. Available at: http://www.itv.com/presscentre/press-releases/itv-acquire-utvs-television-business.

Jackson, M. (2002, September. 27). Think local, go broke. *Times* (London), 2, 21.

Jin, D. Y. (2007). "Reinterpretation of cultural imperialism: emerging domestic market vs continuing US dominance." *Media, Culture & Society* 29 (5): 753–71.

Johnson, C., and R. Turnock. (2005b). "From start-up to consolidation: Institutions, regions and regulation over the history of ITV." In. C. Johnson and R. Turnock, eds., *ITV Cultures: Independent Television Over Fifty Years*, pp. 15–35. New York: Open University Press.

Johnston, C. (2014, November 20). "Local TV licence for Birmingham given to Kaleidoscope after City TV collapse." *The Guardian*. Available at: http://www.theguardian.com/media/2014/nov/20/local-tv-licence-birmingham-kaleidoscope-city.

Joseph, M. (2008). *Against the romance of community*. Minneapolis: University of Minnesota Press.

Just, N., and M. Puppis. (2012). "Communication policy research: Looking back, moving forward." In N. Just and M. Puppis, eds., *Trends in Communication Policy Research: New Theories, Methods and Subjects*, pp. 9–29. Bristol, U.K.: Intellect.

Kane, F. (1998). *Neither bests nor gods: Civic life and the public good*. Dallas: Southern Methodist University Press.

Kaniss, P. (1991). *Making local news*. Chicago: University of Chicago Press.

Kellner, D. (1989). *Critical Theory, Marxism, and Modernity*. Baltimore: John Hopkins University Press.
Kentucky (2014). KRS 136.660: Prohibitions—Local franchise fee or tax defined. Available at: http://www.lrc.ky.gov/Statutes/chapter.aspx?id=37644.
Kirkpatrick, B. (2006). *Localism in American media, 1920–1934*. Unpublished doctoral dissertation. Available at: http://www.billkirkpatrick.net/.
Klinenberg, E. (2012). *Going solo: The extraordinary rise and surprising appeal of living alone*. New York: Penguin Press.
Knight Commission on the Information Needs of Communities in a Democracy. (2009). *Informing communities: Sustaining democracy in the digital age*. Available at: http://www.knightcomm.org/read-the-report-and-comment/.
Koch, J. (2008). "The relative decline of a Musgrave 'Merit Good:' The case of public support of flagship public universities." *Journal of Economics and Finance* 32 (4): 368–79.
Kraidy, M. M. (2003). "Glocalization as an international communication framework?" *Journal of International Communication* 9 (2): 29–49.
———. (2005). *Hybridity: Or the cultural logic of globalization*. Philadelphia: Temple University Press.
Laba, M. (1988). "Popular culture as local culture: Regions, limits and Canadianism." In R. Lorimer and D. Wilson, eds., *Communication Canada: Issues in Broadcasting and New Technologies*, pp. 82–101. Toronto: Kagan and Woo.
Labaton, S. (2003a, June 3). "Deregulating the media: the overview." *New York Times*, Business 1.
Laghi, B. (2009, February 27). "The media and the message." *Globe and Mail* (Toronto), A4.
Lefebvre, H. (1991). *Production of space*. Oxford, U.K.: Wiley-Blackwell.
———. (1996). *Writing on cities*, trans. E. Kofman and E. Lebas. Malden, U.K.: Blackwell Publishing.
Lentz, R. (2011). "Regulation as linguistic engineering." In R. Mansell and M. Raboy, eds., *The Handbook of Global Media and Communications Policy*, pp. 432–48. Malden, U.K.: Blackwell.
———. (2013). "Excavating historicity in the U.S. network neutrality debate: An interpretive perspective on policy change." *Communication, Culture & Critique* 6 (4): 568–97.
Lewis, J. (1991). *The ideological octopus: Exploration of television and its audience*. New York: Routledge.
Lewisboro Community Television (2010). *Comments of Lewisboro Community Television in the matter of examination of the future of media and information needs of communities in a digital age GN Docket No. 10–25*. Available at: http://www.fcc.gov/.
Lind, P. (2008, March 25). "The case against fee-for-carriage." *National Post*, A14.
Linder, L. R. (1999). *Public access television: America's electronic soapbox*. Westport, Conn.: Praeger.
Linder, L. R., and G. Kenton, G. (2010) *Comments of the Alliance for Communications Democracy, (GN Docket No. 10–25)*, FCC. Available At: http://www.fcc.gov.
Lippman, W. (1927). *The phantom public*. New Brunswick, N.J.: Transaction.

Livingstone, S., and P. Lunt. (2007). "Representing citizens and consumers in media and communications regulation." *ANNALS of the American Academy of Political and Social Science, 611,* 51–65.

Löblich, M., and S. Pfaff-Rüdiger. (2012). "Qualitative network analysis: An approach to communication policy studies." In N. Just and M. Puppis, eds., *Trends in Communication Policy Research: New Theories, Methods and Subjects,* pp. 177–94. Bristol, U.K.: Intellect.

Lowrey, W., A. Brozana, and J. B. Mackay. (2008). "Toward a measure of community journalism." *Mass Communication and Society* 11 (3): 275–99.

Lunt, P., and S. Livingstone. (2011). *Media regulation: Governance and the interest of citizens and consumers.* Los Angeles: Sage.

MacBride, S. (1980). *One world, many voices: Communication and society today and tomorrow: towards a new more just and more efficient world information and communication order.* Available at: unesdoc.unesco.org/images/0004/000400/040066eb.pdf.

Mair, J. (2013a). "Is there anything to learn from history?" In J. Mair and R. L. Keeble, eds., *What do we mean by local? The rise, fall—and possible rise again—of local journalism,* pp. 21–26. Suffolk, U.K.: Abramis Academic Publishing.

Mair, J. (2013b). "That was then, this is now: From 'Loony TV' to 'Local TV.'" In J. Mair and R. L. Keeble, eds., *What do we mean by local? The rise, fall—and possible rise again—of local journalism,* pp. 278–85. Suffolk, U.K.: Abramis Academic Publishing.

Mann, S. (2003). "Why organic food in Germany is a merit good." *Food Policy* 28 (5–6): 459–69.

Marlow, I. (2009, October 9). "Taking on cable giants." *Toronto Star,* B01.

Martin, N. (2008, June 25). "BBC plans for local news raise web monopoly fears." *Daily Telegraph,* 8.

Marx, K. (1859/1993). *A contribution to the critique of political economy.* Available at: https://www.marxists.org/archive/marx/works/1859/critique-pol-economy/.

Massey, D. (1992). "A place called home?" *New Formations* 17: 3–15.

———. (1993). "Power geometry and a progressive sense of place." In J. Bird, B. Curtis, T. Putnam, G. Robertson, and L. Tickner, eds., *Mapping the Futures: Local Cultures, Global Change,* pp. 59–70. London: Routledge.

———. (1994). *Space, place and gender.* Minneapolis: University of Minnesota Press.

Matei, S., S. J. Ball-Rokeach, and J. L. Qiu. (2001). "Fear and misperception of Los Angeles urban space." *Communication Research* 28 (4): 429–63.

McChesney, R. (1995). *Telecommunications, mass media, and democracy: The battle for the control of U.S. broadcasting, 1928–1935.* Oxford, U.K.: Oxford University Press.

———. (1999). *Rich media, poor democracy: Communication politics in dubious times.* Urbana: University of Illinois Press.

———. (2007). *Communication revolution: Critical junctures and the future of Media.* New York: New Press.

McChesney, R. W., and J. Nichols. (2010). *The death and life of American journalism: The media revolution that will begin the world again.* New York: New Press.

McDowell, R. (2011). Statement of Commissioner Robert McDowell. Re: Information Needs of Communities, GN Docket No. 10–25. Available at: http://www.fcc.gov/.

McEntee, J. C. (2011). "Realizing rural food justice: Divergent locals in the Northeastern United States." In A. H. Alkon and J. Agyeman, eds., *Cultivating food justice: Race, class, and sustainability,* pp. 239–60. Boston: MIT Press.

Meyrowitz, J. (1985). *No sense of place: The impact of electronic media on social behavior.* Oxford, U.K.: Oxford University Press.

Midgley, N. (2010, September 28). "TV stations must cover local news or lose top billing." *Daily Telegraph,* 8.

———. (2011, January 20). "Regional TV news may go when local shows start." *Daily Telegraph,* 15.

———. (2014, April 25). "Local TV plan on the rocks as funding frozen, while London Live head quits." *The Guardian.* Retrieved from: http://www.theguardian.com/media/2014/apr/25/local-tv-london-live-bbc-funding-stefano-hatfield.

Miller, P. (2009). *The business of Canadian OTA television.* Available at: http://www.crtc.gc.ca/eng/publications/reports/miller09.htm.

Miller & Van Eaton P.L.L.C. (2007). "Stable cable franchise laws at a glance." Available at: http://www.millervaneaton.com/content.agent?page_name=LEGISLATIVE%20FEATURE:%20State%20Page.

Morison, O. (2012, July 18). "Consumers' gain is TV stations' loss as CRTC cuts local programming fund." *Globe and Mail.* Available at: http://www.theglobeandmail.com/technology/tech-news/crtc-ruling-to-reduce-cable-satellite-bills/article4424958/.

Morley, D., and K. Robins. (1995). *Spaces of identity: Global media, electronic landscapes and cultural boundaries.* London: Routledge.

Mosco, V. (2009). *The political economy of communication.* Los Angeles: SAGE.

Muninetworks (nd). Fact sheet: Community broadband. Available at: http://muninetworks.org/sites/www.muninetworks.org/files/2page-comty-bb.pdf.

Murray, C. (1999, November). "Flexible regulation: A Can-Con turn-on?" *Policy Options,* 63–69.

Musgrave, R. (1959). *The theory of public finance: A study in public economy.* New York: McGraw-Hill.

———. (1959/2007). *Public finance in theory and practice,* 1st ed. In W. Ver Eecke, ed., *An anthology regarding merit goods: The unfinished ethical revolution in economic theory,* pp. 40–43. West Lafayette, Ind.: Purdue University Press.

Nader, L. (1974). "Up the anthropologist: Perspectives gained from studying up." In D. Hymes, ed., *Reinventing Anthropology,* pp. 284–311. New York: Random House.

Nancy, J. L. (2006). *The inoperative community.* Minneapolis: University of Minnesota Press.

Napoli, P. (2001a). *Foundations of communications policy: Principles and process in the regulation of electronic media.* New York: Hampton Press.

———. (2001b). "The localism principle in communications policymaking and policy analysis: Ambiguity, inconsistency, and empirical neglect." *Policy Studies Journal* 29 (3): 372–87.

Napoli, P., and M. Yan. (2007). "Media ownership regulations and local news programming on broadcast television: An empirical analysis." *Journal of Broadcasting & Electronic Media* 51 (1): 39–57.

National Association of Broadcasters (NAB) (2004). *Comments of the National Association of Broadcasters in the matter of broadcast localism.* Available at: http://www.fcc.gov/.

———. (2010a). *Comments of the National Association of Broadcasters in the matter of: 2010 quadrennial regulatory review.* Available at: http://www.fcc.gov/.

———. (2010b). *Comments of the National Association of Broadcasters in the matter of examination of the future of media and information needs of communities in a digital age.* Available at: http://www.fcc.gov/.

———. (2012). *Comments of the National Association of Broadcasters in the Matter of: 2010 quadrennial regulatory review.* Available at: http://www.fcc.gov.

National Federation of Community Broadcasters (NFCB) (2008). *Comments of Station Resource Group, National Federation of Community Broadcasters, and Public Radio Capital in the matter of broadcast localism.* Available at: http://www.fcc.gov/.

National Organization of Telecommunications Officers and Advisors (NATOA). (2006a). *Comments of the National Association of Telecommunications Officers and Advisors et al. in the matter of implementation of section 621(a)(1) of the Cable Communications Policy Act of 1984 as amended by the Cable Television Consumer Protection and Competition Act of 1992 (MB Docket No. 05-311).* Available at: http://www.fcc.gov/.

———. (2009). *Comments of the National Organization for Telecommunications Officers and Advisors in the matter of: Petition for declaratory ruling that AT&T's method of delivering public, educational and government access channels over its U-Verse system is contrary to the Communications Act of 1934, as amended, and applicable commission rules; MB Docket No., 09.13.* Available at: http://www.fcc.gov/.

———. (2010a). *Comments of the National Association of Telecommunications Officers and Advisors. Comment on applications of Comcast Corporation, General Electric Company and NBC Universal, Inc., to assign and transfer control of FCC licenses (MB Docket No. 10-56).* Available at: http://www.fcc.gov/.

National Public Radio (NPR) (2004). *Comments of National Public Radio in the matter of broadcast localism.* Available at: http://www.fcc.gov/.

———. (2008). *Comments of National Public Radio in the matter of broadcast localism.* Available at: http://www.fcc.gov/.

Native Public Media (2010). *Comments of Native Public Media in the matter of examination of the future of media and information needs of communities in a digital age GN Docket No. 10-25.* Available at: http://www.fcc.gov/.

Nielsen, R. K. (2015). "Introduction: The uncertain future of local journalism." In R. K. Nielsen, ed., *Local journalism: The decline of newspapers and the rise of digital media*, pp. 1–39. London: IB Tauris.

Nelson, R. (2002/2007). "The problem of market bias in modern capitalist economies." In W. Ver Eecke, ed., *An anthology regarding merit goods: The unfinished ethical revolution in economic theory*, pp. 517–57. West Lafayette, Ind.: Purdue University Press.

New America Foundation, et al. (2010). *Joint Comments of . . . Free Press . . . Media Access Project . . . New America Foundation et al. in the matter of examination of the future of media and information needs of communities in a digital age*. GN Docket No. 10-25. Available at: http://www.fcc.gov/.

Nigg, H., and G. Wade. (1980). *Community media: Community communication in the UK: Video, local TV, film, and photography*. Zurich: Regenbogen-Verlag.

Noam, E. (1993). "Reconnecting communications studies with communications policy." *Journal of Communication* 43 (3): 199–206.

Nordicity (2008). *Study of Canadian OTA local news economic and audience trends*. Available at: http://www.crtc.gc.ca/eng/publications/reports/rp090123.htm.

Norris, G. (2006, July 13). "Bell Globemedia bids $1.7B for CHUM." *Calgary Herald* (Canadian Press), E3.

North, P. (2011). "Geographies and utopias of Cameron's big society." *Social & Cultural Geography* 12 (8): 817–27.

Nossek, H. (2003). "Active research as a bridge between theory and practice: A suggested model for playing an active role in organizing community television as a tool of empowerment in the community." *Communications* 28 (3): 305–22.

Oberholzer-Gee, F., and J. Waldfogel. (2009). "Media markets and localism: Does local news en Espanol boost Hispanic voter turnout?" *American Economic Review* 99 (5): 2120–28.

Office of Communications (Ofcom). (2004a). *Ofcom review of public service television broadcasting: Phase 1—Is television special?* Available at: http://stakeholders.ofcom.org.uk/broadcasting/reviews-investigations/public-service-broadcasting/.

———. (2004b). *Ofcom review of public service television broadcasting—Phase 2: Reshaping television for the UK's nations, regions and localities*. Available at: http://stakeholders.ofcom.org.uk/broadcasting/reviews-investigations/public-service-broadcasting/.

———. (2004c). *Licensing community radio: Consultation*. Available at: http://www.ofcom.org.uk/.

———. (2004d). *Licensing community radio: Statement*. Available at: http://www.ofcom.org.uk/.

———. (2004e). *Ofcom review of public service television broadcasting: Summary of phase 1 consultation responses*. Available at: http://stakeholders.ofcom.org.uk/broadcasting/reviews-investigations/public-service-broadcasting/.

———. (2005). *Ofcom review of public service television broadcasting: Phase 3—Competition for Quality*. Available at: http://stakeholders.ofcom.org.uk/broadcasting/reviews-investigations/public-service-broadcasting/.

———. (2006). *Digital local: Options for the future of local video content and interactive services*. At. http://stakeholders.ofcom.org.uk/broadcasting/reviews-investigations/public-service-broadcasting/digital_local/.

———. (2008a). *Ofcom's second public service broadcasting review: Phase one: The digital opportunity*. Available at: http://www.ofcom.org.uk/.

———. (2008b). *Ofcom's second public service broadcasting review: Phase two: Preparing for the digital future*. Available at: http://www.ofcom.org.uk/.

———. (2009a). *Local and regional media in the UK*. Available at: http://stakeholders.ofcom.org.uk/market-data-research/tv-research/lrmuk/.

———. (2009b). *Ofcom's second public service broadcasting review: Putting viewers first*. Available at: http://www.ofcom.org.uk/.

———. (2011a). *Community radio annual report*. Available at: http://www.ofcom.org.uk/.

———. (2012a). *Communications market report 2012*. Available at: http://stakeholders.ofcom.org.uk/market-data-research/market-data/communications-market-reports/cmr12/.

———. (2012b). *Licensing local television: How Ofcom will exercise its new powers and duties to license new local television services: Consultation*. Available at: http://www.ofcom.org.uk/.

———. (2012c). *Invitation to apply for an L-DTPS licence*. http://licensing.ofcom.org.uk/tv-broadcast-licences/local/.

———. (2012d). *Licensing local television: How Ofcom will exercise its new powers and duties to license new local television services: Statement*. Available at: http://www.ofcom.org.uk/.

———. (2013a). *News consumption in the UK: Research report*. Available at: http://stakeholders.ofcom.org.uk/binaries/research/tv-research/news/News_Report_2013_slides.pdf.

———. (2013b). *Ofcom seeks views on ITV, STV, UTV and Channel 5 licences*. Available at: http://media.ofcom.org.uk/2013/02/21/ofcom-seeks-views-on-itv-stv-utv-and-channel-5-licences/.

———. (2013c). *Channel 3 and Channel 5: Statement of programming obligations*. Available at: http://stakeholders.ofcom.org.uk/binaries/consultations/c3-c5-obligations/statement/statement.pdf.

———. (2015). *The communications market report*. Available at: http://stakeholders.ofcom.org.uk/market-data-research/market-data/communications-market-reports/cmr15/.

———. (n.d.). *List of L-DTPS award decisions*. Available at: http://licensing.ofcom.org.uk/tv-broadcast-licences/local/award-decisions/.

Oldenburg, R. (1999). *The great good place: Cafes, coffee shops, bookstores, bars, hair salons, and other hangouts at the heart of a community*. New York: Marlowe.

Oliver and Ohlbaum Associates. (2009). *A macro-economic review of the UK local media sector: A report prepared for Ofcom*. Available at: http://stakeholders.ofcom.org.uk/broadcasting/reviews-investigations/public-service-broadcasting/.

O'Regan, T. (1993) *Australian television culture*. Sydney: Allen and Unwin.

Ouellette, L. (2002). *Viewers like you? How public TV failed the people.* New York: Columbia University Press.

Pattie, C., and R. Johnston. (2011). "How big is the big society?" *Parliamentary Affairs* 64 (3): 403–24.

Pedwell, T. (2012, July 19). "CRTC scraps cable fee that boosted local programming." *Financial Post*, FP5.

Peters, J. D. (1999). *Speaking into the air: A history of the idea of communication.* Chicago: University of Chicago Press.

Pew Project for Excellence in Journalism (2011). *How people learn about their local community.* Retrieved from http://pewresearch.org/pubs/2105/local-news-television-internet-radio-newspapers.

Pickard, V. (2013). Social democracy or corporate libertarianism? Conflicting media policy narratives in response to market failure. *Communication Theory* 23(4): 336–55.

———. (2014). *America's battle for media democracy: The triumph of corporate libertarianism and the future of media reform.* Cambridge, U.K.: Cambridge University Press.

———. (2015). "The return of the nervous liberals: Market fundamentalism, policy failure, and recurring journalism crises." *Communication Review* 18 (2): 82–97.

Potschka, C. (2012). *Towards a market in broadcasting: Communications policy in the UK and Germany.* New York: Palgrave Macmillan.

Powell, A. (2012). "Wi-Fi Publics: Defining community and technology at Montreal's Ile Sans Fils." In A. Clement, M. Gurstein, G. Longford, M. Moll, and L.R. Shade, eds., *Connecting Canadians: Investigations in Community Informatics,* pp. 202–17. Edmonton: Athabasca University Press.

Powell, A., and L. R. Shade. (2012). "Community and municipal wi-fi initiatives in Canada." In A. Clement, M. Gurstein, G. Longford, M. Moll, and L.R. Shade, eds., *Connecting Canadians: Investigations in Community Informatics,* pp. 183–201. Edmonton: Athabasca University Press.

Powell, D. (2007). *Critical regionalism: Connecting politics and culture in the American landscape.* Chapel Hill: University of North Carolina Press.

Pulsipher, A. (1971/2007). "The properties and relevancy of merit goods." In W. Ver Eecke, ed., *An anthology regarding merit goods: The unfinished ethical revolution in economic theory,* pp. 152–74. West Lafayette, Ind.: Purdue University Press.

Putnam, R. D. (2000). *Bowling alone: The collapse and revival of American community.* New York: Simon and Schuster.

Raboy, M. (1990). *Missed opportunities: The story of Canada's broadcasting policy.* Montreal: McGill-Queen's University Press.

———. (2006). "Making media: Creating the conditions for communication in the public good." *Canadian Journal of Communication* 31: 289–306.

Raboy, M., and D. Taras. (2004, March). "The politics of neglect of Canadian broadcasting policy." *Policy Options,* 63–68.

Raboy, M., and J. Shtern. (2010a). Introduction. In M. Raboy and J. Shtern, eds., *Media Divides: Communication rights and the right to communicate in Canada,* pp. 3–25. Vancouver: University of British Columbia Press.

———. (2010b). "Histories, contexts, and controversies." In M. Raboy and J. Shtern, eds., *Media Divides: Communication rights and the right to communicate in Canada*, pp. 26–40. Vancouver: University of British Columbia Press.

Radcliffe, D. (2012). *Here and now: UK hyperlocal media today.* Nesta. Available at: http://www.nesta.org.uk/areas_of_work/creative_economy/destination_local/assets/features/here_and_now_uk_hyperlocal_media_today.

———. (2015). *Where are we now? UK hyperlocal media and community journalism in 2015.* Nesta. Available at: https://www.communityjournalism.co.uk/wp-content/uploads/2015/09/C4CJ-Report-for-Screen.pdf.

Radway, J. (1989). "Ethnography among elites: Comparing discourses of power." *Journal of Communication Inquiry* 13 (3): 3–11.

Reihnard, J. C., and S. M. Ortiz. (2005). "Communication law and policy: The state of research and theory." *Journal of Communication* 55 (3): 594–631.

Rennie, E. (2006). *Community media: A global introduction.* Lanham, Md.: Rowman & Littlefield.

Reynolds, J. (2014, September 15). "'Very unlikely' all local TV stations will succeed, says Ofcom." *The Guardian.* Available at: http://www.theguardian.com/media/2014/sep/15/unlikely-local-tv-stations-succeed-ofcom-london-live?CMP=share_btn_tw.

Roberts, J. (2014, November 21). "Streaming TV site Aereo files for bankruptcy, will reorganize." *Gigaom.com.* Available at: https://gigaom.com/2014/11/21/streaming-tv-service-aereo-files-for-chapter-11-will-reorganize/.

Robertson, R. (1995). "Glocalisation: Time-space and heterogeneity-homogeneity." In M. Featherstone, S. Lash, and R. Robertson, eds., *Global Modernities*, pp. 25–44. London: Sage.

———. (2006a, November 27). "TV networks want new rules." *Globe and Mail*, B1.

———. (2008a, January 26). "Networks press CRTC for piece of cable pie." *Globe and Mail*, B7.

———. (2008b, April 7). "CRTC battle over TV cable fees pits Rogers against networks." *Globe and Mail*, B1.

———. (2009a, November 14). "The battle over local TV." *Globe and Mail*, B1.

———. (2009b, February 26). "CTV closes two stations, raising fears for local TV." *Globe and Mail*, A1.

———. (2009c, February 13). "CRTC to ease burden on cash-strapped stations." *Globe and Mail*, B4.

———. (2009d, November 14). "The battle over local TV." *Globe and Mail*, B1.

Rodriguez, C. (2001). *Fissures in the mediascape: An international study of citizens' media.* Cresskill, N.J.: Hampton Press.

Rogers Cable Communications (2010). *Broadcasting notice of consultation CRTC 2009-661: Review of community television policy framework: Submission of Rogers Cable Communications Inc.* Available at: www.crtc.gc.ca.

Rogowsky, M. (2014, June 26). "Myth busting the Aereo decision." *Forbes.* Available at: http://www.forbes.com/sites/markrogowsky/2014/06/26/myth-busting-the-aereo-decision-no-the-supreme-court-didnt-kill-it-nor-did-they-kill-dropbox/.

Sabbagh, D. (2009, July 16). "Tories plan 80 city-based TV stations for local news." *Times* (London), 47.
Salant, J. (2003, August 21). "FCC will study how TV, radio serve regions." *Philadelphia Inquirer*, C02.
Sandel, M. J. (1990). "The political theory of the procedural republic." In R. Reich, ed., *The power of public ideas*, pp. 109–22. Cambridge. Mass.: Harvard University Press.
Sandvig, C. (2004). "An initial assessment of cooperative action in Wi-Fi networking." *Telecommunications Policy* 28 (7–8): 579–602.
Sasktel (2010). *Submission of SaskTel to broadcasting notice of consultation CRTC 2009-661: Review of community television policy framework*. Available at: www.crtc.gc.ca.
Scannell, P. (2014). *Television and the meaning of live*. Cambridge, U.K.: Polity.
Scannell, P., and D. Cardiff. (1991). *A social history of British broadcasting, 1922–1939: Serving the Nation*. Oxford, U.K.: Blackwell.
Schragger, R. C. (2001). "The limits of localism." *Michigan Law Review* 100: 371–472.
Schudson, M. (2007). "Citizens, consumers, and the good society." *ANNALS of the American Academy of Political and Social Science* 611: 236–49.
Schudson, M. (1999). "Introduction: All politics is local, some local politics is personal." *Communication Review* 3: 213–15.
Scolari, C. A. (2012). "Media ecology: Exploring the metaphor to expand the theory." *Communication Theory* 22: 204–25.
Shade, L. R., and M. Lithgow. (2010). "The cultures of democracy: How ownership and public participation shape Canada's media system." In L. Shade, ed., *Mediascapes: New Patterns in Canadian Communication*, 3rd ed., pp. 200–20. Toronto: Nelson Education.
Shecter, B. (2008, January 26). "TV giants team up on 'fees for carriage.'" *National Post*, FP6.
Sender, K. (2004). *Business, not politics: The making of the gay market*. New York: Columbia University Press.
Shaw. (2010). *Comments of Shaw. Re: Broadcasting notice of consultation 2009-661—Review of community television policy framework*. Available at: www.crtc.gc.ca.
Shott, N. (2010). *Commercially viable local television in the UK: A Review by Nicholas Shott for The Secretary of State for Culture, Olympics, Media and Sport*. Available at: http://www.culture.gov.uk/publications/7655.aspx.
Shuman, M. (1998). *Going local*. New York: Free Press.
Siklos, R. (2006, June 11). "Coming soon (maybe): Even more TV channels." *New York Times*, sec. 3, p.3.
Silverman, D., and D. Tobenkin. (2001). "The FCC's main studio rule: Achieving little for localism at a great cost to broadcasters." *Federal Communications Law Journal* 53 (3), 469–507.
Singleton, L. A., and S. Rockwell. (2003). "Silent voices: Analyzing the FCC 'media voices' criteria limiting local radio-television cross-ownership." *Communication Law & Policy* 8 (4): 385–403.

Smallwood, A.M.K., and S. J. Moon. (2011). "Predictors of localism in public television scheduling in the United States." *Journal of Broadcasting & Electronic Media* 55 (1): 36–53.

Small Market Independent Television Stations Coalition (SMITS). (2014). *Written comments of the Small Market Independent Television Stations ("SMITS") Coalition pursuant to The CRTC's Formal "Talk TV" Process, Broadcasting Notice of Consultation CRTC 2014-190.* Available at: https://services.crtc.gc.ca/Pub/ListeInterventionList/Documents.aspx?ID=218711&en=2014-190&dt=i&lang=e&S=C&PA=b&PT=nc&PST=a.

Smythe, D. (1981). *Dependency road: Communications, capitalism, consciousness and Canada.* Norwood, N.J.: Ablex Publishing.

Soja, E. W. (1989). *Postmodern geographies: The reassertion of space in critical social theory.* London: Verso.

Solent Television (2011). *Response to Ofcom's local TV licensing consultation.* Available at: http://licensing.ofcom.org.uk/tv-broadcast-licences/local/.

Sreberny-Mohammadi, A. (1992). "The global and the local in international communications." In J. Curran and M. Gurevitch, eds., *Mass Media and Society,* pp. 109–23. London: Arnold.

St. Andrews Community Television (2010). *Submission of St. Andrews Community Television to broadcasting notice of consultation CRTC 2009-661: Review of community television policy framework.* Available at: www.crtc.gc.ca.

Starr, P. (2011). "Goodbye to the age of newspapers (hello to a new era of corruption): Why American politics and society are about to be changed for the worse." In R. McChesney and V. Pickard, eds., *Will the last reporter please turn out the lights: The collapse of journalism and what can be done to fix it,* pp. 3–17. New York: New Press.

Stavitsky, A. G. (1994). "The changing conception of localism in U.S. public radio." *Journal of Broadcasting & Electronic Media* 38 (1): 19–33.

Stearns, J. (2011, June 9). "The three worst ideas in the FCC's Future of Media report" [Blogport]. *Free Press.* Available at: http://www.freepress.net/blog/11/06/09/three-worst-ideas-fcc%E2%80%99s-future-media-report.

Steinberg, J. (2003, August 21). "Facing criticism, F.C.C. is thinking local." *New York Times,* 1.

Stephens, N. P. (2014). "Toward a more substantive media ecology: Postman's metaphor versus posthuman futures." *International Journal of Communication* 8: 2027–45.

Stiglitz, J. (1989). "Markets, market failures, and development." *American Economic Review* 79 (2): 197–203.

Strategic Inc. (2014). *Small market realities: An analysis of the changing revenue landscape for independent television operators in small markets.* Available at: https://services.crtc.gc.ca/Pub/ListeInterventionList/Documents.aspx?ID=218711&en=2014-190&dt=i&lang=e&S=C&PA=b&PT=nc&PST=a.

Straubhaar, J. (2008). "Global, hybrid, or multiple: Cultural identities in the age of satellite TV and the internet." *Nordicom Review* 2: 11–29. Available at: http://www.nordicom.gu.se/?portal=publ&main=info_publ2.php&ex=269&m=.

Streeter, T. (1996). *Selling the air: A Critique of the policy of commercial broadcasting in the United States*. Chicago: University of Chicago Press.

———. (2013). "Policy, politics, and discourse." *Communication, Culture & Critique* 6 (4): 488–501.

Supreme Court of the United States (SCOTUS). (2014). *American Broadcasting Cos., Inc., et al. v. Aereo, Inc., FKA Bamboom Labs, Inc.* Available at: http://www.supremecourt.gov/opinions/13pdf/13-461_l537.pdf.

Sweney, M. (2013, January 28). "Canis Media wins contract to run local TV broadcast spectrum." *The Guardian*. Retrieved from: http://www.guardian.co.uk/media/2013/jan/28/canis-media-broadcast-spectrum.

Tam, H. (2011, March–May). "The big con: Reframing the state/society debate." *Public Policy Research*, 30–40.

Tarde, G. (1901/1989). *L'Opinion et al foule*. Paris: Presses Universitaires de France.

Taylor, G. (2013). *Shut off: The Canadian digital television transition*. Montreal: McGill-Queens University Press.

Texas. (2005). Util. Code Ann 66.003. Public Utility Regulatory Act. Available at http://www.statutes.legis.state.tx.us/Docs/UT/htm/UT.66.htm.

Tillson, T. (2007, April 16). "Lost in the spin." *Playback*, 21.

Timescape Productions. (2009). *Community television policies and practices around the world*. Retrieved from http://www.vcn.bc.ca/cmes/1pages/Community-Television-Around-the-World.htm.

Tinic, S. (2005). *On location: Canada's television industry in a global market*. Toronto: University of Toronto Press.

Tönnies, F. (1887/1957). *Community and society*. C. Loomis, ed. and trans. East Lansing: Michigan State University Press.

Toronto Star. (2005, April 12). "Feds' media stance is good news for moguls." D07.

Triplett, W. (2007, December 5). "Senators block FCC vote." *Daily Variety*, 4.

Turkle, S. (2011). *Alone together: why we expect more from technology and less from each other*. New York: Basic Books.

United Kingdom. (2003). *The Communications Act of 2003: Elizabeth II. Chapter 21*. Available at: http://www.legislation.gov.uk/ukpga/2003/21/contents.

———. (2004). *Community radio order. No. 1944*. Available at: http://www.legislation.gov.uk/uksi/2004/1944/contents/made.

———. (2008). *Early day motion 1013: Local public service television*. Available at: www.parliament.uk.

———. (2010a). *Future for local and regional media*. House of Commons: Culture, Media and Sport Committee. Available at: http://www.publications.parliament.uk/pa/cm200910/cmselect/cmcumeds/43/4302.htm.

———. (2011a). *The localism act 2011*. 2011 c.20. Available at: http://www.legislation.gov.uk.

———. (2011b). *The media ownership (radio and cross media) order 2011*. No. 1503. Available at: http://www.legislation.gov.uk/uksi/2011/1503/contents/made.

———. (2012). *The local digital television programme services order 2012: 2012 No. 292.* Available at: http://www.legislation.gov.uk/ukdsi/2012/9780111518212/contents.

United Nations. (2013). *The universal declaration of human rights.* Available at: http://www.un.org/en/documents/udhr/index.shtml.

United States (US). (1934). *Communications act of 1934,* 47 U.S.C. 151. Available at: http://www.fcc.gov/Reports/1934new.pdf.

———. (1976). *Copyright act,* 17 U.S.C. §101–810.

———. (1984a). *Cable communications policy act of 1984,* House Report No. 98-934. In U.S.C.C.A.A, 5, 4655-4753.

———. (1984b). *Cable communications policy act of 1984.* U.S. Code, vol. 47, §531–59. Available at: http://www.law.cornell.edu/uscode/17/.

———. (1992). *Cable television consumer protection and competition act.* Pub. L. No. 102-385, 106 Stat 1460 (47 U.S.C. §521–609).

———. (1996). *Telecommunications act of 1996.* Pub. LA. No. 104–104, 110 Stat. 56.

van Dijk, T. (1993). "Principles of critical discourse analysis." *Discourse Society* 4 (2): 249–83.

Variety. (2011, June 10). "FCC: Local news blues." *Variety,* 4.

Ver Eecke, W. (1998). "The concept of a 'merit good'": The ethical dimension in economic theory and the history of economic thought or the transformation of economics into socio-economics." *Journal of Socio-Economics* 27 (1): 133–54.

———. (Ed.) (2007a). *An anthology regarding merit goods: The unfinished ethical revolution in economic theory.* West Lafayette, Ind.: Purdue University Press.

———. (2007b). Introduction. In W. Ver Eecke, ed., *An anthology regarding merit goods: The unfinished ethical revolution in economic theory,* pp.1–18. West Lafayette, Ind.: Purdue University Press.

Vermont. (2005). Cable Television Systems. *Vt. Stat. Ann.* tit 30, chpt. 13, §501.

———. (2007). "Rules and general orders of the Vermont Public Service Board: 8.000 Cable Television." Available at: http://www.state.vt.us/psb/rules/rules.stm.

Videon Cable 11. (1975). *Access: Winnipeg's public access television newsletter.* Winnipeg: Videon Cable 11.

Vlessing, E. (2008, November 10). Broadcasters mixed on CRTC rulings. *Playback,* 6.

Waldman, S. (2011). *The information needs of communities: the changing media landscape in a broadband age.* FCC. At: www.fcc.gov/infoneedsreport.

Wallace, A. (2005). *Newspapers and the making of modern America: A history.* Westport, Conn.: Greenwood Press.

Watson, L., and L. Howell. (2011). Response to Ofcom's local TV licensing consultation. Available at: http://licensing.ofcom.org.uk/tv-broadcast-licences/local/.

Weber I (2003). "Localizing the global: Successful strategies for selling television programmes to China." *Gazette* 65 (3): 273–90.

Westwood, A. (2011). "Localism, social capital and the 'big society'." *Local Economy* 26 (8): 690–701.

White House. (2015, January 13). Fact sheet: Broadband that works: Promoting competition and local choice in next-generation connectivity. Available at: https://www.whitehouse.gov/the-press-office/2015/01/13/fact-sheet-broadband-works-promoting-competition-local-choice-next-gener.

Wildavsky, A. (1987/2007). "Opportunity costs as merit wants." In W. Ver Eecke, ed., *An anthology regarding merit goods: The unfinished ethical revolution in economic theory*, pp .84–113. West Lafayette, Ind.: Purdue University Press.

Wilken, R. (2011). *Teletechnologies, place, and community*. New York: Routledge.

Wilken, H., S. Ball-Rokeach, M. Matsaganis, and P. H. Cheong. (2007). "Comparing the communication ecologies of geo-ethnic communities: How people stay on top of their community." *Electronic Journal of Communication* 17 (1–2). Available at: http://www.cios.org/EJCPUBLIC/017/1/01711.HTML.

Williams, R. (1973). *The country and the city*. London: Chatto and Windus.

———. (1985). *Keywords: A vocabulary of culture and society*. Oxford, U.K.: Oxford University Press.

Williams, K. (2010). *Read all about it! A history of the British newspaper*. London: Routledge.

Wilson, R., and W. Dissanayake. (1996). "Introduction: Tracking the global/local." In R. Wilson and W. Dissanayake, eds., *Global-Local: Cultural Production and the Transnational Imaginary*, pp. 21–45. Durham, N.C.: Duke University Press.

Index

Access: Winnipeg's Public Access Television Newsletter, 82
Access Radio, 103
Adelstein, Jonathan, 98–99, 130–31, 136
Aereo, 184–85
Agyeman, J., 30
Aird Report, 12–13
Aldridge, M., 171
Ali, Christopher, 205
Alkon, A. H., 30
Alliance des producteurs francophones du Canada, 145
Alliance for Communications Democracy (ACD), 116
Alliance for Community Media (ACM), 95, 116, 170
ambiguity of local media, 176–77
American Broadcasting Company v. Aereo, 184–85
American Community Television (ACT), 96, 116
Andel, Norbert, 193
Anderson, C., 9
Annenberg School for Communication and Journalism, 121
AOL, 183
Appadurai, A., 168
Association of Free Community Papers, 61
Association of Public Television Stations, 213n6
Astra, 158
/A\ television network, 3

AT&T, 84, 95, 99–101, 199

Babe, R., 193
Ball-Rokeach, S. J., 38
Bell Aliant, 92
Bell Canada Enterprises (BCE), 14, 92, 146
Bell Media, 212n4
Belo Corporation, 115, 116
Big Centre TV, 185
Big Society project, 14–15, 153–54, 211n6
Birmingham, England vs. Birmingham, Alabama, 153–54, 185
"Blue Book." See *Public Service Responsibilities' of Broadcasting Licensees, Report on* ("Blue Book")
Bowling Alone, 44
Braman, S., 20, 33
Brennan Center, 135, 179
Briggs, Asa, 128, 167
British Broadcasting Corporation (BBC), 12, 15–16, 23, 74, 149, 188; BBCi project, 151–52; DCMS and, 157; history of 15–16; local media ecology and, 112, 113–14; partnership with ITV, 80; radio, 79; regional news, 76; regions associated with, 17; technologies of the local and, 113
broadband, municipal, 198–201, 215n1
Broadcast Distribution Undertakings (BDUs): community television and, 81, 86, 89, 92, 94; Local Programming Improvement Fund and, 139–49; policies of localism and, 63, 66–68, 70–74

248 · INDEX

broadcast localism, NPRM regarding, 137–39
Broadcasting Act of 1932 (Canada), 13, 122
Broadcast Localism Initiative, 62
Brozana, A., 35–36, 37, 178
Buchanan, C., 12
Bush, George W., 58
Buy Fresh, Buy Local campaign, 30–32, 41, 107

Cable Act of 1984 (United States), 94–95, 97, 99–100
"Cable Song, The," 3, 4, 26–27
Calabrese, A., 47
Canada: Broadcast Distribution Undertakings (BDUs), 63, 66–68, 70–74, 81, 86, 89, 92, 94, 139–49; community versus local programming in, 91–94; cultural sovereignty in, 121–26; deregulation and community television in, 82–84, 85–94; diluted policies and discursive agendas in, 88–91; Lincoln Report, 108, 122–26, 177, 179–80; localism in, 11–14; Local Programming Improvement Fund, 139–49, 174–75, 189; policymaking in, 62–74; Small Market Local Programming Fund, 189. *See also* Canadian Radio-Television and Telecommunications Commission (CRTC)
Canadian Association of Broadcasters (CAB), 140
Canadian Association of Community Television Users and Stations (CACTUS), 86, 90, 92–93
Canadian Broadcasting Act of 1991, 211n1
Canadian Broadcasting Corporation (CBC), 13, 123–25, 145–46, 188
Canadian Radio Broadcasting Commission (CRBC), 13
Canadian Radio-Television and Telecommunications Commission (CRTC), 4, 5, 7–8, 14, 19, 23, 187; ambiguity of local media and, 177; community television and, 84, 85–94; cultural sovereignty and, 122–26; "Let's Talk TV" campaign, 184; Local Programming Improvement Fund and, 139–49
Canis Media, 59
CanWest Global, 142, 144, 145–46
capitalism, 34–35, 40, 45–46, 203
Carpentier, N., 42–43, 46–47, 82

Carroll, Dave, 3, 4, 26–27
Casey, E., 38
Castells, Manuel, 6, 20, 34–35, 37, 39
Center for Digital Democracy, 130
CFCM-TV, 142–43
Challenge for Change, 85
Channel M, 102
Channel Seven, 102
Channel 9, 102
Charland, M., 12
CHCH-TV, 71, 72, 145, 146, 147
CHEK-TV, 145, 147
Chester, Jeff, 130
Chicago Tribune, 56
citizen participation, 7–8, 162
City Broadcasting, 158
City TV, 185
Clapman, Arthur Roy, 109
Clear Channel, 138, 188
Coca-Cola Inc., 42
Collins, R., 38–39
Comcast, 84, 95, 116; Internet service, 199; PEG and, 99–101; regulatory issues and lobbying by, 188
communication rights (CR) and right to communicate (R2C), 202
Communications Act of 1934 (United States), 9, 97, 211n1
Communications Act of 2003 (United Kingdom), 17, 155, 211n1
Communications Policy Research Network (CPRN), 109, 121, 187
community, local as, 39–41
Community Access Media Fund, 93
community media, 82–85, 106
community radio, 103–5
Community Radio Order of 2004 (United Kingdom), 104, 178, 181
community television, 82–85; in Canada, 82–84, 85–94; as PEG, 94–105, 200–201; in the United Kingdom, 101–5; in the United States, 200–201
community wi-fi, 200–201
Comux UK, 59
content quotas, 13–14
Cooper, Mark, 136–37, 139
Copps, Michael, 53, 99, 120, 136, 186, 198; opposition to deregulation, 58–59, 130, 131; on regulation and community media coming together, 100–101

Copps, Sheila, 125
copyright infringement, 184–85, 215n1
corporate libertarianism, 54
Cox Broadcasting, 138
crisis of localism, 128–29
critical, local as, 45–48
critical discourse analysis (CDA), 23–24
critical geography, 32
"Critical Information Needs of the American Public," 120–21
critical localism, 47
critical regionalism, 24, 25–26, 46, 47–48, 88, 168–69, 201; moments of, 177–80
CTV television network, 3, 142, 143, 145, 188; CTVglobemedia, 67, 68, 70, 142, 143, 212n4
Curtin, M., 9, 47
C21 Vox, 102

Daily Show, The, 183
Davies, Gavyn, 194, 195
de Certeau, M., 43
default localism, 25, 80–81, 172–74
democracy, 7–8; localism ecosystems and, 108; public goods and, 54–55, 189–94
Department for Culture Media and Sport (DCMS), 23, 111; Big Society and, 152–54; *Digital Britain* report, 151–57; framework for local television, 155–57, 214n9; local television licenses and, 159–63; regulation of local television and, 157–59; *Shott Report* and, 154–55
deregulation. *See* regulation
designated market areas (DMAs), 41–42, 61–62, 135–36; default localism and, 172–73, 174
Des Moines Register, 8
de Tocqueville, Alexis, 20
Dewey, John, 20, 35, 37, 172
Digital Britain, 111, 151–57
Digital Local, 149–51, 176
digital localism, 78–80
Dirlik, A., 45, 47
Diversity of Voices, 88, 91
Dorgan, Byron, 130, 135
Downie, L., Jr., 189
Dropbox, 185
Dunbar-Hester, C., 18, 125, 131
Duncan, Elizabeth, 148
Dunsmore, Dorthi, 82

Eastern Daily Press, 15
ecological conception of place, 45
ecosystems, localism, 126–27; in Canada, 121–26; defined, 109–10; information needs and, 107–9; in the United Kingdom, 111–14; in the United States, 114–21
Emporia Gazette, 8
Enders Analysis, 158
Escobar, A., 180
Essential Research, 79
"Ethnography among elite," 207
Evening Post, 15
Evening Standard, 162, 175

Facebook, 31, 35, 41
Fairness Doctrine, 120, 213n8
Fear Factor, 57
Federal Communications Commission (FCC), 5, 9–11, 19, 23, 54, 187; community television and, 96–100; "Critical Information Needs of the American Public," 120–21; default localism and, 172–73; deregulation and, 56–62; DMAs and, 135–36; *Information Needs of Communities,* 108, 115–17; on information needs of communities, 115–17; Local Franchising Authorities and, 95, 97–99; localism ecosystems and, 107–8; Localism in Broadcasting Initiative, 129–34; Main Studio Rule, 10, 137–38; municipal broadband and, 198–201, 215n1; 2010 Notice of Inquiry and, 59–60; ownership and, 55–63; *Report on Broadcast Localism and Notice of Proposed Rulemaking* (NPRM), 137–39; 1996 Telecommunications Act and, 56
Federalist Papers, 38
Federal Radio Act of 1927 (United States), 9
fee-for-carriage (FFC), 4, 54, 89, 139, 141; in Canada, 62–74
Ferrier, Michelle, 35
fetish, local as, 44–45
First Broadcasting, 158
Fox Network, 116, 188
Frampton, Kenneth, 45–46
franchising and ownership rules, NPRM regarding, 59–62
Franklin, B., 15, 23
Frau-Meigs, D., 113
Freedman, Des, 23, 186–87, 194, 195
Free Press, 60, 117

250 · INDEX

Friedland, Lewis, 35, 88, 109–10, 172, 201
Friesen, G., 125
Frulla, 126
Frye, Northrop, 29, 197
Fuentes-Bautista, M., 100
Future Foundation, 38
"Future of Media and Information Needs of Communities in a Digital Age, The," 115

Geertz, C., 24
gemeinshaft, 6, 37–38, 41
geographic media, 111–12
Geographic Interleaved (GI) spectrum, 154–55
geography, critical, 32
gesellschaft, 6, 38, 41
Giddens, A., 39
globalism, 19, 44–45
Global television network, 3, 188; Canwest and, 67, 68–69, 73, 142, 144, 145–46
Globe and Mail, 12, 14, 142, 148, 212n4
glocalization, 42–43
Goldstein, Kevin, 147
Goodman, Ellen, 115, 192
Google, 116
Graham, Andrew, 194, 195
Graham, Billy, 57
Great Community, 35, 37
Great Recession, 119
Greenwich Cablevision, 101
Guardian, The, 154–55, 162

Habermas, Jürgen, 35
Hall, S., 43
Hallin, D., 22
Hamilton, Alexander, 38
Harvey, David, 119, 203–4
Head, John G., 193
Head, S., 191
Herzog, Christian, 205
Hess, K., 181
Hewlett, Steve, 154–55
Hewson, C., 19, 101–2
Hilmes, M., 22
Horwitz, R., 10
Howley, K., 20, 84
Hunt, Jeremy, 7, 107, 152–54, 162, 175
hyperlocal media, 105, 183

Independent Broadcasting Authority (IBA), 16

Independently Funded News Consortia (IFNC), 113, 151–53, 163
Independent Television Commission (ITC), 16–17, 211n3
Information Needs of Communities, The (Waldman Report), 108, 115–17
Informing Communities: Sustaining Democracy in the Digital Age, 115
infrastructure and localism, 197–98
Innis, Harold, 213n3
Instagram, 41
Institute for Local Television, 158
International Covenant on Civil and Political Rights, 202
International Covenant on Economic, Social and Cultural Rights, 202
international news, 126
internet service providers (ISPs), 198–201, 215n1
Inverness Community Media, 158
Ion Media, 138
ITV television network, 54, 74–80; communities of place and, 171; local media ecology and, 112–13; negotiations with regulators, 175, 188; regional affiliates, 16–17, 149; regional news commitments, 151–52

Jefferson, Thomas, 8, 38
Jim Pattison Group, 145
Jin, D. Y., 43
Joseph, M., 34, 40, 42, 93, 173
journalism, 188, 194; citizen, 162; as a public good, 55
Just, N., 205

Kaleidoscope TV, 185
Kent Messenger, 15
Kings Cross Environment, 84
Kirkpatrick, B., 10, 39–40
Knight Commission, 35, 114–15
Koch, J., 192
Kraidy, M. M., 44–45

Lacroix, Hubert T., 148
Lamarre, Suzanne, 148
Last Week Tonight, 183
Lebedev, Alexander, 162
Lebedev, Evgeny, 162
Lefebvre, Henri, 40, 203–4
Lentz, R., 24
"Let'sTalkTV," 184

Lewisboro Community Television, 170
libertarianism, corporate, 54
Lincoln, Clifford, 108, 122
Lincoln Report (*Our Cultural Sovereignty: The Second Century of Canadian Broadcasting*), 108, 122–26, 177, 179–80
Lin Media, 115
Lippman, Walter, 195
Lithgow, Michael, 90
local: as community, 39–41; as critical, 45–48; as fetish, 44–45; as market, 41–43; as place, 37–39, 90–91; as practice, 33–37; as resistive, 43–44; right to be, 201–4; technologies of the, 113–14
Local and Regional Media in the United Kingdom, 108, 111
Local Community Radio Act of 2005 (United States), 170
Local Digital Television Programme Service (L-DTPS), 28, 162, 172, 214n9, framework for, 155–57; licenses, 159–63; regulation of, 157–59
local food movement, 30–32, 39, 41, 107
Local Franchising Authorities (LFAs), 95, 97–99
localism, 7, 167–70, 180–82; in Canada, 11–14; crisis of, 128–29; critical, 47; default, 25, 80–81, 172–74; defined, 5, 6–18; digital, 78–80; ecosystems (*see* ecosystems, localism); infrastructure and, 197–98; local food movement and, 30–32; "Local TV Matters" campaign and, 3–6; method and methodology in researching, 23–24, 205–9; neoliberalism and the market for, 163; paradox of media, 53–54; place of place and, 18–21; policies of place and, 21–22; political economy of, 24–26, 174–75; recent changes in media and, 183–86; regulatory agencies and, 4–5, 8; right to the city and, 202–4; spatial and social dimensions of, 19–21; in the United Kingdom, 14–18; in the United States, 8–11; value(s) of, 194–95
Localism Act of 2011 (United Kingdom), 15, 39, 211n2
Localism in Broadcasting Initiative, 120, 129–34
local media: ambiguity of, 176–77; as place media, 170–72; policy frameworks, 186–89
local news: Canada's cultural sovereignty and, 121–26; changing consumption patterns and, 185–86; corporate libertarianism and, 54; CRTC commitments to, 63–75, 89; decline of, 28; determining what counts as, 5; digital news sites and, 31, 34–35, 84; diversity of, 69, 105; ideology and, 27; ITV and, 76–80, 151; media localism and, 7, 36, 170, 172–74; newspapers providing, 8–9, 12, 15; NPRM and, 60–62; as public good, 54–55, 60, 189–94; reflecting information needs, 107–9, 198; regulation of, 6, 156, 157–59, 188–89; United Kingdom's "Buy local, live local, go local," 111–14; United States' information needs of communities and, 114–21; United States' Localism in Broadcasting Initiative and, 120, 129–34; as vital for democracy, 4, 8, 68–71
local ownership, 42, 59–60, 131–32
Local Programming Improvement Fund (LPIF), 139–49, 174–75, 189
Local TV Matters campaign, 3–6
London Live, 162, 185
Lott, Trent, 135
low power television (LPTV), 86, 214n3; defined, 212n3
Lowrey, W., 35–36, 37, 178

Mackay, J. B., 35–36, 37, 178
Maddin, Guy, 82
Madison, James, 38
Main Studio Rule, 10, 137–38
Mancini, P., 22
market, local as, 41–43
market failures, 54–55, 190, 192
Martin, Kevin, 134, 136
Marxism, 34, 44, 45, 168, 212n1, 214–15n1
Massey, D., 39, 45
Matei, S., 38
McDowell, Robert, 120
McLuhan, Marshall, 213n3
media: community, 82–85, 106; ecology, 213n3; political economy of localism in, 24–26, 174–75; as public good, 54–55, 189–94; recent changes in, 183–86; types of geographic, 111–12. *See also* localism
media, local: ambiguity of, 176–77; as place, 170–72; policy frameworks, 186–89
media ecology, 107, 213n3
Menzies, Peter, 141, 145
merit goods, 190–94, 204, 215nn5–6
Microsoft, 116

Midlands Asian TV, 102
Miller, Maria, 162
Miller, P., 53
moments of critical regionalism, 177–80
MonTV, 102
Morin, Michel, 94, 141, 146
Morison, Ora, 148
Moscow, Idaho, 30, 107
Moscow-Pullman Daily News, 107
multichannel video programming distributors (MVPDs), 56, 61, 215n3; dispute with Local Franchising Authorities, 95, 97–99
municipal broadband, 198–201, 215n1
Murdoch, Peter, 142
Murphy, D., 15
Musgrave, Richard A., 190, 191, 194–95, 215n5–6
Multiplex Operator (MuxCo), 155–58, 175

Nancy, Jean-Luc, 44, 106
Napoli, P., 20–21
National Association of Broadcasters (NAB), 58, 130, 138, 188; Future of Media hearing and, 115–16; media ownership and, 60–61
National Association of Telecommunications Officers and Advisors (NATOA), 97, 116
National Film Board (Canada), 85
National news, 12, 14–15, 126, 147
nationalism, 12
Native Public Media, 117
NBC, 138, 188
Nelson, R., 194
neoliberalism, 35, 40, 56–59, 167–68; ecosystems of localism and, 119; market for localism and, 163
Netflix, 183
New America Foundation (NAF), 110, 117, 200
news, international, 126
news, local: Canada's cultural sovereignty and, 121–26; changing consumption patterns and, 185–86; corporate libertarianism and, 54; CRTC commitments to, 63–75, 89; decline of, 28; determining what counts as, 5; digital news sites and, 31, 34–35, 84; diversity of, 69, 105; ideology and, 27; ITV and, 76–80, 151; media localism and, 7, 36, 170, 172–74; newspapers providing, 8–9, 12, 15; NPRM and, 60–62; as public good, 54–55, 60, 189–94; reflecting information needs, 107–9, 198; regulation of, 6, 156, 157–59, 188–89; United Kingdom's "Buy local, live local, go local," 111–14; United States' information needs of communities and, 114–21; United States' Localism in Broadcasting Initiative and, 120, 129–34; as vital for democracy, 4, 8, 68–71
news, national, 12, 14–15, 126, 147
newspapers, local: in Canada, 12; in the United Kingdom, 15; in the United States, 8–9
New World Information and Communication Order (NWICO), 202
New York Times, 8, 58
Nielsen, Rasmus Kleis, 188
Nielsen Company, 61–62, 174
Nigg, H., 101
North Atlantic triangle, 38–39, 201
Northern Echo, 15
Northern Visions Television (NvTv), 102–3, 162
Notice of Inquiry (NOI), 59, 132–33

Office of Communications (Ofcom), 5, 19, 23, 33, 74–80, 102, 175, 187; ambiguity of local media and, 176–77; community radio and, 104; creation of, 211n3; Department for Culture Media and Sport (DCMS) *Digital Britain* report and, 151–57; *Digital Local,* 149–51, 176; framework for local television, 155–57; on geographic media, 111–12; on local and regional media ecology, 107–8, 109, 111–13; Public Service Broadcasting and, 17–18, 74–80l Public Service on public versus private in local media, 114; regulation of local television, 157–59. *See also* United Kingdom
Oldenburg, Ray, 44
On Screen Manitoba, 145
O'Regan, T., 12
Ottawa Citizen, 12
Our Cultural Sovereignty: The Second Century of Canadian Broadcasting (Lincoln Report), 121–26 ownership, local, 42, 59–60, 131–32

paradox of media localism, 53–54
Patch network, 183
Pentefountas, Tom, 91
Perry, Roger, 152–53
Pickard, Victor, 54, 186, 188

Pits 'n Pots, 35, 85
place: local as, 37–39, 90–91; media, 170–72; of place, 18–21; policies of, 21–22; space of, 6, 37, 38; and space of media localism, 167–70
Playback, 126
Poirier, Louise, 148–49
policy and policymaking, 30–32; in Canada, 62–74, 86–94; community television, 86–94; defined, 31; moments of critical regionalism and, 177–80; neoliberalism and, 56–59; of place, 21–22; political economy of localism and, 24–26, 174–75; public *vs.* merit goods and, 54–55, 189–94; in the United Kingdom, 74–80; in the United States, 56–62
political economy of localism, 24–26, 174–75
political systems, Western, 38–39
Postman, Neil, 213n3
Powell, Alison, 200
Powell, D., 46, 47, 181
Powell, Michael, 129–30, 134
practice, local as, 33–37
preference distortion problem, 191–92
programming, local, 18–19, 57–58
Prometheus Project, 60
protectionism, 12
Public, Educational, and Governmental access television (PEG). *See* community television
public access television. *See* community television
public goods, 54–55, 189–94
Public Service Broadcasters (PSB), 17–18, 74–80
Public Service Responsibilities' of Broadcasting Licensees, Report on ("Blue Book"), 10, 129, 213n1
Pulsipher, Allan, 190, 193
Puppis, M., 205
Putnam, Robert, 35, 44

Qiu, J. L., 38
Quebecor, 188

Raboy, Marc, 13, 14, 125–26, 129
Radcliffe, Damian, 102
radio: community, 103–5; ownership rules, 56
Radio Authority (United Kingdom), 103, 211n3
Radio Television Digital News Association (RTDNA), 115

regionalism, 11; critical, 24, 25–26, 46, 47–48, 88, 168–69, 177–80, 201; Public Service Broadcasting and, 76–78
regulation, 4–5, 8, 11; ambiguity of local media and, 176–77; Canadian community television, 85–94; content quotas, 13–14; default localism and, 25, 80–81, 172–74; defined, 31; deregulation and, 35, 56–59, 155–56; local media policy framework, 186–89; local programming, 19–20; media as merit good and, 190–94; regulatory capture, 35; response to challenges of media localism in the United States, 129–39; United Kingdom local television, 157–59; United States community television, 94–100
Reith, John, 16
Rennie, E., 39
Report on Broadcast Localism and Notice of Proposed Rulemaking (NPRM), 137–39
Report on Chain Broadcasting, 10
Report on Public Service Responsibilities' of Broadcasting Licensees, 10, 129, 213n1
resistive, local as, 43–44
Restrictive Service Licenses (RSLs), 17, 101–3
right to be local, 201–4
right to the city, 202–4
Robertson, Grant, 142
Rogers Cable Communications, 92, 188

Sandel, M. J., 30
Sandvig, Christian, 200
Saskatoon StarPhoenix, 168
SaskTel, 92
Schudson, Michael, 183, 189, 195
Seattle P-I, 35
Shared Services Agreements, 60
Shaw, 92, 188
Shott, Nicholas, 154–55
Shuman, M., 42
SixTV, 102
Small Market Local Programming Fund, 189
social dimension of localism, 19–21
Solent TV, 102
space of flows, 34–35, 38, 39
space of place, 6, 37, 38
spatial dimension of localism, 19–21, 167–70
Spry, Graham, 12–13
St. Andrews Community Television, 92
Stanley, C. O., 167
Statement on Licensing Local Television (United Kingdom), 158

Streeter, T., 24
"Studying up," 207–8
Sustainable Independent and Important News, 111

Taras, D., 125–26
Taylor, G., 23
Telecommunications Act of 1996 (United States), 9, 56, 60, 95, 199
teletechnologies, 6, 38
Television Act of 1954 (United Kingdom), 16
Television Deregulation Order of 1984 (United States), 11
territorial turfs, 35
Thistle TV, 102
Timescape Productions, 102
Times of London, 102, 155
Time Warner Cable, 95, 116, 199
Tinic, Serra, 46
Tönnies, F., 6, 37, 41
Toronto Star, 12
translocalism, 46–47
2003 Media Ownership Report and Order (R&O), 58–59

United Airlines, 4
United Kingdom, the: BBCi project, 151–52; Big Society project, 14–15, 153–54, 211n6; community radio in, 103–5; community television in, 101–3; Department for Culture Media and Sport (DCMS), 23, 28, 111, 151–63. 214n9; *Digital Britain* report, 111, 151–57; *Digital Local* report, 149–51; ecosystems of localism in, 111–14; framework for local television, 155–57; Geographic Interleaved (GI) spectrum, 154–55; hyperlocal media in, 105; Independently Funded News Consortia (IFNC), 113, 151–52, 163; Jeremy Hunt and, 7, 107, 152–54, 162, 175; Local Digital Television Programme Service (L-DTPS), 28, 162, 172, 155–63, 214n9; local television licenses in, 159–63, localism in, 14–18; London Live, 162, 185; Northern Visions Television (NvTv), 102–3, 162; policymaking in, 74–80; regulation of local television in, 157–59; Restrictive Service Licenses (RSLs) in, 17, 101–3; Shott Report, 154–55; technologies of the local in, 113–14. *See also* British Broadcasting Corporation (BBC); ITV television network; Office of Communications (Ofcom)
United States: *American Broadcasting Company v. Aereo*, 184–85; AT&T in, 95, 99–101; Comcast in, 95, 99–101; community television in, 94–101; designated market areas, 41–42, 61–62, 135–36, 172–73, 174; information needs of communities in, 114–21; localism in, 8–11; Localism in Broadcasting Initiative, 129–30; municipal broadband in, 198–201; policymaking in, 56–62; regulatory response to crisis of localism in, 129–39; Waldman Report, 109, 117–19, 188, 193–94. *See also* Federal Communications Commission (FCC)
Universal Declaration of Human Rights, 202
Universal Service Fund, 189
user-generated content (UGC), 162

value for service. *See* fee-for-carriage (FFC)
Ver Eecke, Wilfred, 193
Verizon, 95
VPW (Videon, Public Access, West of the Red River), 82
V television network, 3

Wade, G., 101
Waldman, Steven, 117
Waldman Report (*The Information Needs of Communities*), 109, 117–19, 188, 193–94
Waller, L., 181
Walt Disney Company, 116
Weber, I., 43
Westwood, A., 20
WGN-TV, 56
wi-fi, community, 200–201
Wilken, H., 4, 6, 19–20, 27, 38
Williams, Bruce, 211n6
Williams, R., 20, 37, 41, 172
Winnipeg on Demand, 89
Wireless Telegraphy Act of 2006 (United Kingdom), 155
Wire Report, 120

York TV, 102
YouTube, 31, 153, 185

CHRISTOPHER ALI is an assistant professor in the Department of Media Studies at the University of Virginia. He is a coauthor of *Echoes of Gabriel Tarde: What We Know Better or Different 100 Years Later*.

THE HISTORY OF COMMUNICATION

Selling Free Enterprise: The Business Assault on Labor and Liberalism,
   1945–60   *Elizabeth A. Fones-Wolf*
Last Rights: Revisiting *Four Theories of the Press*   *Edited by John C. Nerone*
"We Called Each Other Comrade": Charles H. Kerr & Company,
   Radical Publishers   *Allen Ruff*
WCFL, Chicago's Voice of Labor, 1926–78   *Nathan Godfried*
Taking the Risk Out of Democracy: Corporate Propaganda versus Freedom
   and Liberty   *Alex Carey; edited by Andrew Lohrey*
Media, Market, and Democracy in China: Between the Party Line and the
   Bottom Line   *Yuezhi Zhao*
Print Culture in a Diverse America   *Edited by James P. Danky and Wayne A. Wiegand*
The Newspaper Indian: Native American Identity in the Press, 1820–90
   John M. Coward
E. W. Scripps and the Business of Newspapers   *Gerald J. Baldasty*
Picturing the Past: Media, History, and Photography   *Edited by Bonnie Brennen
   and Hanno Hardt*
Rich Media, Poor Democracy: Communication Politics in Dubious Times
   Robert W. McChesney
Silencing the Opposition: Antinuclear Movements and the Media in the
   Cold War   *Andrew Rojecki*
Citizen Critics: Literary Public Spheres   *Rosa A. Eberly*
Communities of Journalism: A History of American Newspapers and
   Their Readers   *David Paul Nord*
From Yahweh to Yahoo!: The Religious Roots of the Secular Press   *Doug Underwood*
The Struggle for Control of Global Communication: The Formative Century   *Jill Hills*
Fanatics and Fire-eaters: Newspapers and the Coming of the Civil War
   Lorman A. Ratner and Dwight L. Teeter Jr.
Media Power in Central America   *Rick Rockwell and Noreene Janus*
The Consumer Trap: Big Business Marketing in American Life   *Michael Dawson*
How Free Can the Press Be?   *Randall P. Bezanson*
Cultural Politics and the Mass Media: Alaska Native Voices   *Patrick J. Daley
   and Beverly A. James*
Journalism in the Movies   *Matthew C. Ehrlich*
Democracy, Inc.: The Press and Law in the Corporate Rationalization of the
   Public Sphere   *David S. Allen*
Investigated Reporting: Muckrakers, Regulators, and the Struggle over
   Television Documentary   *Chad Raphael*
Women Making News: Gender and the Women's Periodical Press in Britain
   Michelle Tusan
Advertising on Trial: Consumer Activism and Corporate Public Relations
   in the 1930s   *Inger L. Stole*
Speech Rights in America: The First Amendment, Democracy, and the Media
   Laura Stein

Freedom from Advertising: E. W. Scripps's Chicago Experiment   *Duane C. S. Stoltzfus*
Waves of Opposition: The Struggle for Democratic Radio, 1933–58
  Elizabeth Fones-Wolf
Prologue to a Farce: Democracy and Communication in America   *Mark Lloyd*
Outside the Box: Corporate Media, Globalization, and the UPS Strike   *Deepa Kumar*
The Scripps Newspapers Go to War, 1914–1918   *Dale Zacher*
Telecommunications and Empire   *Jill Hills*
Everything Was Better in America: Print Culture in the Great Depression
  David Welky
Normative Theories of the Media   *Clifford G. Christians, Theodore L. Glasser,*
  Denis McQuail, Kaarle Nordenstreng, and Robert A. White
Radio's Hidden Voice: The Origins of Public Broadcasting in the United States
  Hugh Richard Slotten
Muting Israeli Democracy: How Media and Cultural Policy Undermine
  Free Expression   *Amit M. Schejter*
Key Concepts in Critical Cultural Studies   *Edited by Linda Steiner*
  and Clifford Christians
Refiguring Mass Communication: A History   *Peter Simonson*
Radio Utopia: Postwar Audio Documentary in the Public Interest   *Matthew C. Ehrlich*
Chronicling Trauma: Journalists and Writers on Violence and Loss   *Doug Underwood*
Saving the World: A Brief History of Communication for Development and
  Social Change   *Emile G. McAnany*
The Rise and Fall of Early American Magazine Culture   *Jared Gardner*
Equal Time: Television and the Civil Rights Movement   *Aniko Bodroghkozy*
Advertising at War: Business, Consumers, and Government in the 1940s
  Inger L. Stole
Media Capital: Architecture and Communications in New York City   *Aurora Wallace*
Chasing Newsroom Diversity: From Jim Crow to Affirmative Action
  Gwyneth Mellinger
C. Francis Jenkins, Pioneer of Film and Television   *Donald G. Godfrey*
Digital Rebellion: The Birth of the Cyber Left   *Todd Wolfson*
Heroes and Scoundrels: The Image of the Journalist in Popular Culture
  Matthew C. Ehrlich and Joe Saltzman
The Real Cyber War: The Political Economy of Internet Freedom   *Shawn M. Powers*
  and Michael Jablonski
The Polish Hearst: *Ameryka-Echo* and the Public Role of the Immigrant Press
  Anna D. Jaroszyńska-Kirchmann
Acid Hype: American News Media and the Psychedelic Experience   *Stephen Siff*
Making the News Popular: Mobilizing U.S. News Audiences   *Anthony M. Nadler*
Indians Illustrated: The Image of Native Americans in the Pictorial Press
  John M. Coward
Mister Pulitzer and the Spider: Modern News from Realism to the Digital
  Kevin G. Barnhurst
Media Localism: The Policies of Place   *Christopher Ali*

The University of Illinois Press
is a founding member of the
Association of American University Presses.

_____

University of Illinois Press
1325 South Oak Street
Champaign, IL 61820-6903
www.press.uillinois.edu